The Essentials of
CORPORATE COMMUNICATIONS *and* PUBLIC RELATIONS

The Business Literacy for HR Professionals Series

The Business Literacy for HR Professionals Series educates human resource professionals in the principles, practices, and processes of business and management. Developed in conjunction with the Society for Human Resource Management, these books provide a comprehensive overview of the concepts, skills, and tools HR professionals need to be influential partners in developing and executing organizational strategy. Drawing on rich content from Harvard Business School Publishing and the Society for Human Resource Management, each volume is closely reviewed by a content expert as well as by senior HR professionals. Whether you are aspiring to the executive level in your organization or already are in a leadership position, these authoritative books provide the basic business knowledge you need to play a strategic role.

Other books in the series:

The Essentials of Finance and Budgeting
The Essentials of Managing Change and Transition
The Essentials of Negotiation
The Essentials of Power, Influence, and Persuasion

BUSINESS LITERACY FOR HR PROFESSIONALS

The Essentials of
CORPORATE
COMMUNICATIONS
and PUBLIC
RELATIONS

Harvard Business School Press
Boston, Massachusetts

and

the Society for Human Resource Management
Alexandria, Virginia

Copyright 2006 Harvard Business School Publishing Corporation
and the Society for Human Resource Management
All rights reserved
Printed in the United States of America

09 08 07 06 05   5 4 3 2 1

Library of Congress Cataloging-in-Publication Data

The essentials of corporate communications and public relations.
p. cm. — (Business literacy for HR professionals) (The business literacy
for HR professionals series)
Includes bibliographical references and index.
ISBN 1-59139-819-3
1. Communication in management. 2. Communication in personnel management.
3. Public relations. I. Society for Human Resource Management (U.S.) II. Series:
Harvard business literacy for HR professionals series.
HF5549.5.C6E87 2006
658.4'5—dc22
                                        2006007136

The paper used in this publication meets the minimum requirements of
the American National Standard for Information Sciences—Permanence of Paper
for Printed Library Materials, ANSI Z39.48—1992.

Contents

Introduction

- Your organization is making a change to its health insurance that will impact employees through a premium increase and coverage changes that may be perceived negatively.

- Your company is merging with another organization, which will result in a variety of changes throughout the organization in terms of reporting structure, corporate image, policy revisions, and so on—and layoffs are anticipated.

- A disgruntled former employee is sending threatening letters to the supervisor who made the termination decision.

- A senior official at your organization writes a letter to the editor expressing a personal opinion that is contrary to the organization's position on an issue. The senior official's workplace was included in the printed version of the letter.

- You discover that an incorrect version of the corporate logo is being used on forms in a particular department.

- Your organization's advertising campaign is criticized by a public interest group.

- The media have identified a group of consumers who are unhappy with a decision your organization has made. They're requesting interviews with key executives.

Each of these situations impacts *corporate communication*—the process by which organizations communicate with their various stakeholders, including employees. Corporate communication is a far-reaching function that has impacts throughout the organization as well as with various stakeholder groups outside the organization. It is a function that crosses the boundaries between other communication functions, including public relations, marketing, shareholder relations, and customer relations.

It is also a function that is becoming much more widely recognized as having a significant impact on an organization's ability to recruit and retain qualified workers *and* to have a healthy bottom line. And it significantly affects the human resource management process within an organization.

In 2004, Harris Interactive released the results of an online survey conducted for Towers Perrin. The survey—of one thousand working Americans—represented a typical cross section of the "average worker" in U.S.-based organizations with at least one thousand employees. The sample cut across a broad range of industries and included a statistically valid range of ages, education levels, genders, and incomes.

The survey, perhaps not surprisingly, revealed that American workers were increasingly cynical and suspicious of information they received from their own organizations. Just over half (51 percent) of the respondents believed that their company generally told employees the truth, while almost a fifth (19 percent) disagreed. At the same time, 51 percent believed their companies tried too hard to "spin" the truth. The survey also showed that employees believed their companies communicated more honestly with shareholders (60 percent) and customers (58 percent) than with workers.

The degree to which employees believed corporate communication varied by age and length of tenure with the organization. Two-thirds of workers under thirty-five believed their companies were forthright in their communications, while only 44 percent of those fifty or older agreed with this statement. Tenure also affected the degree to which employees believed corporate communication. Fifty-nine percent of employees with less than five years of service with their companies believed their organizations were entirely open and honest in employee communications, while less than half (48 percent) of those with more than five years of service believed the validity of corporate communication to employees. With age, experience, and familiarity, apparently, comes distrust!

Why are employees so cynical? Let's look back at a few of the examples used at the beginning of this section:

- Your organization is making a change to its health insurance that will impact employees through a premium increase and coverage changes that may be perceived negatively.

How have these decisions been communicated in the past? To what extent do employees believe that benefits have been "taken away" or that their total compensation packages have diminished over time?

- Your company is merging with another organization, which will result in a variety of changes throughout the organization in terms of reporting structure, corporate image, policy revisions, and so on—and layoffs are anticipated.

How have employees learned of these changes? Directly from leadership or through the corporate grapevine? Are the messages they read or see in the media (messages no doubt shared by the company's PR staff) consistent with internal messages? Are the messages they may receive as shareholders of your organization (messages no doubt created by shareholder communication staff) consistent with HR messages?

- A senior official at your organization writes a letter to the editor expressing a personal opinion that is contrary to the organization's position on an issue. The senior official's workplace was included in the printed version of the letter.

Which message should employees "believe"—the corporate message they've seen internally or the opinion of this organizational leader? If there is a disconnect, how might that impact employees' level of trust with the organization?

- The media have identified a group of consumers who are unhappy with a decision your organization has made. They're requesting interviews with key executives.

How is your organization responding to this criticism? Are your actions in this instance consistent with your espoused mission, vision, and values?

There are multiple opportunities each and every day for employee trust to be eroded. A key impact on the erosion of trust is communication. Without question, HR plays a significant role in ensuring that communication with employees is timely, accurate, honest—and consistent with other organizational messages. This consistency, unfortunately, is often where the process breaks down.

HR professionals have an opportunity, and a responsibility, to take a more active and strategic role in corporate communication to help ensure that the messages received internally by employees are consistent and aligned with the messages received by those same employees through external media.

How can this occur? Through alignment of the HR function with other critical communication functions within the organization—functions that have collectively come to be called "corporate communication." Whether HR is formally a part of the corporate communication structure or not, there are opportunities to better coordinate and align their efforts with those of other communication colleagues.

How to Use This Book

This book takes a look at the corporate communication function in all its incarnations, specifically addressing the role that human resource professionals can and should play in ensuring that corporate messages are shared consistently, accurately, and honestly with employees.

Chapter 1 provides an overview of corporate communication in organizations and how it is organized and coordinated with HR. The term *corporate communication* is defined, and the various functions of communication are discussed. You'll learn how HR and corporate communication functions interact within organizations, and you'll discover the essential skills that strong HR communicators must have.

Chapter 2 offers a look at communication fundamentals: understanding audiences, selecting the appropriate source, creating appropriate messages, selecting appropriate channels, and the importance of timing. The components of corporate identity are described, and the impact of communication on influencing various target audiences is discussed. This chapter also provides guidance on selecting target audiences and identifying key messages to meet their specific needs, the characteristics of successful spokespeople, and how to strategically develop and coordinate messages through various channels.

Chapter 3 looks at the process of developing an integrated corporate communication strategy; how to develop goals, objectives, and action plans; and the importance of monitoring and measuring success. You'll learn the value of research in identifying communication focus and a process for developing, implementing, and measuring communication impacts. In addition, this chapter looks at a comprehensive tool—the communication audit—and its value for organizational use.

Chapter 4 offers insights on what and how to measure in terms of communication results and impacts. The chapter begins with a discussion of outcome and process measures, emphasizing the value of focusing on outcome over process. Common research methods and their advantages and disadvantages are discussed in addition to specific techniques for improving the effectiveness of measurement efforts.

Chapter 5 reviews the various audiences—internal and external—that the corporate communicator needs to be aware of, their individual needs, and tips on effective communication tactics. Specific audiences include customers and consumers, the news media, investors, governmental bodies and agencies, and the community at large. While HR is often most focused on the employee audience, there is a role for HR to play in communicating with each of these constituencies. Opportunities and specific tactics are explored.

Chapter 6 looks specifically at the employee audience, the challenges of effective employee communication, and the process for developing an effective internal communication strategy. Special opportunities in employee communication are also considered. Employee communication is viewed as part of a broad process that requires leadership support and commitment. This chapter discusses the critical role of frontline managers, how to encourage two-way communication, and specific steps to take in the development of an effective internal communication strategy. Strategies, techniques, and tips are offered for effective employee communication designed to achieve measurable results.

Chapter 7 discusses issues management and crisis communication—the difference between the two, the role of HR, and tips and guidelines for effectively handling issues and crisis communication. You'll learn how crises result in issues and how communication can be used effectively to address these issues. Different types of crises are explored, along with suggestions for anticipating and responding to each. Finally, you'll be provided with specific tips on working with and responding to the media.

Chapter 8 provides a step-by-step process for the development of communication plans. The different types of communication plans and how they can be used most appropriately are discussed, along with benefits for each. A specific eight-step process outlines how to develop communication plans. In addition, the chapter recommends a way to respond to internal requests for communication tactics, with techniques for taking a more strategic approach.

Chapters 9 and 10 discuss the various tools and tactics available to the corporate communicator and how to select from among these tools to have maximum impact. Chapter 9 offers several key questions to ask when formulating a communication strategy that can be helpful in selecting the appropriate tools. Tools in three categories—verbal, written, and electronic—are discussed, with specific pros and cons offered for each.

Chapter 10 expands on the use of individual communication tools, providing guidance on how to select the most appropriate tool for specific situations according to the communication objective and the audience. The importance of communicating multiple times in multiple ways is discussed. In addition, this chapter includes a specific discussion on the value and use of the intranet to strengthen HR communication.

Chapter 11 discusses various HR communication challenges and offers tips for dealing with each, including the areas of compensation and benefits, health plan benefits, employees in off-site locations, downsizing or restructuring, and budget cuts.

Chapter 12 takes a look ahead and offers advice for HR professionals for developing and enhancing competencies that will ensure a "seat at the table."

The appendixes supplement the chapters, offering examples, worksheets, and planning tools to aid in the communication process.

Although the materials in this book won't make you an expert on corporate communication, they do provide authoritative, *essential* advice you can use to get going and to stay on track.

The content in this book is based on books, articles, and online products of the Society for Human Resource Management (SHRM) and Harvard Business School Publishing (HBSP). SHRM resources include numerous white papers and surveys from SHRM's Web site, articles from *HR Magazine,* and books published or copublished by SHRM. Harvard Business School Publishing resources include a wide variety of books and articles on communication and communication-related issues.

For additional resources, visit the SHRM Web site at www.SHRM .org and the HBSP Web site at www.harvardbusinessonline.org.

The Essentials of
CORPORATE
COMMUNICATIONS
and PUBLIC
RELATIONS

CHAPTER ONE

Corporate Communication and the HR Professional

The HR Professional's Role in the Communication Function

Key Topics Covered in This Chapter

- *A definition of corporate communication*
- *Communication functions and their interactions*
- *HR and corporate communication structure and relationships*
- *Essential skills for HR communicators*

CONSIDER A YOUNG married couple. Newly wed, they have many new and challenging experiences and decisions facing them. One of the key areas of challenge, they're told, is "communication." They must communicate openly and honestly with each other to avoid misunderstanding that may lead to dissension that could damage the relationship and ultimately the marriage. But hard as they work, communication problems occur. Perhaps the two have been discussing the purchase of a new vehicle. He understands that a decision has been made to move forward with that purchase. She, on the other hand, believes the decision has yet to be made. And of course, there are also outside influences impacting the quality of their communication and the outcomes of their interactions—friends, family, coworkers, and so on.

As their family grows, the issues become more complex. Consider a family of four—two parents and two children. Instead of two people interacting with each other, you now have four individuals and, of course, all those individuals outside the family relationship whose inputs and opinions affect the quality of communication within the family. Sam's friends don't agree with the curfew of the household. Chris's boss feels a business trip is more important than attending a child's hockey game. Pat saw nothing wrong in sharing some personal family information with a friend—the family disagreed.

Each of these family members also interacts within other communication environments—work, school, social organizations. Each environment is affected by communication challenges. While few family or social interactions are formally "managed," the same is no longer true within a work or business environment.

What Is Corporate Communication?

Today there is a widespread recognition that effective communication within an organization has a significant impact on the prosperity of that business. That recognition is bolstered by research. Watson Wyatt, an HR consulting firm, conducted a landmark research study in 2003 —the *Communication ROI Study*—that focused on the relationship between an organization's internal communication strategy and practices and its shareholder returns. Their findings indicated that:

- A significant improvement in communication effectiveness is associated with a 29.5 percent increase in market value.

- Companies with the highest levels of effective communication experienced a 26 percent total return to shareholders from 1998 to 2002, compared to a −15 percent return experienced by firms that communicate least effectively.

- Organizations that communicate effectively were more likely to report employee turnover rates below or significantly below those of their industry peers.

Communicate effectively, say the study authors, and businesses can drive performance by:

- Building a strong foundation of formal communication structure and processes, which rely on employee feedback and use technology to connect with employees effectively

- Dealing directly with the strategic issues of change, continuous improvement, and business strategy integration and alignment

- Creating real employee behavioral change by driving change in managers' and supervisors' behavior and by developing a line of sight between employees and customers

Their conclusion: "Communication is no longer a 'soft' function. It drives business performance and is a key contributor to organizational success."[1] Watson Wyatt wasn't the first firm to recognize the value of managing communication within the corporate environment to achieve greater results—just the first to quantify the impact of that formal management.

In his introduction to the second edition of the book *Corporate Communication,* Paul Argenti, a professor of management and corporate communication at the Tuck School of Business at Dartmouth (and formerly an instructor at the Columbia and Harvard Business Schools), refers to corporate communication as "a new field of study," resulting from the realization that this functional area of management has equal footing with the more traditionally recognized functions of finance, marketing, and production.[2]

At some point—Argenti says in the 1990s—the field of what is now called "corporate communication" emerged as a means of harnessing and coordinating all the various communication elements in an organization so that messages could be managed and consistency could be ensured.

Today, corporate communication encompasses a variety of functions, all involving relationships between various groups in much the same way that a family's communications challenges emerge from the various relationships that impact that family. For instance, consider the term *public relations.* What is today most commonly called the corporate communication department has been in the past more often referred to as public relations or public affairs. Today, the public relations function is generally considered as one of the elements of corporate communication.

The American Marketing Association defines *public relations* as "that form of communication management that seeks to make use of publicity and other non-paid forms of promotion and information to influence the feelings, opinions, or beliefs about the company, its products or services, or about the value of the product or service or the activities of the organization to buyers, prospects, or other stakeholders."[3]

Other elements of corporate communication also center around relationships with various groups of individuals:

- Public relations

- Community relations

- Media relations

- Shareholder relations

- Employee relations

Advertising or marketing communications are less frequently considered part of the corporate communication function, although a strong argument could be made that this should, indeed, be the case. After all, if an organization's advertisements are not delivering messages consistent with internal communication, shareholder communication, or communication with key local constituencies, there will be critical disconnects that can undermine the efforts of each of these functions.

"Organizations that successfully brand their customer service grasp that advertising is designed as much for employees as it is for customers," say Barlow and Stewart in *Branded Customer Service: The New Competitive Edge.* "The brand and the story communicated in advertising highlight staff spirit, attitude and values. Unfortunately, this opportunity is frequently lost, especially when advertising is used primarily to promote specific products or offerings. Even worse, sometimes advertising undermines the branded customer service proposition."[4]

An organization is supremely concerned with its ability to *influence various constituencies through communication.* It is in every organization's best interests to ensure that its important constituencies—or stakeholders—hold certain beliefs or feelings about the organization. Organizations want employees to believe that the organization is a great place to work. They want customers to believe that the organization is a great place to buy products or services. They want shareholders to believe that the organization represents a sound financial investment. They want communities to believe that the organization is a good corporate citizen. And they want the general public to believe that the organization is honest, reliable, and responsible.

The influence of these individual relations can be challenging enough. Consider, though, the complexity that ensues from the interactions *between* constituencies:

- Disgruntled employees share their frustration about the company with their relatives, friends, and neighbors, negatively impacting this group of stakeholders and their impressions of the organization as a corporate citizen.

- Employees who believe the organization they work for is doing well hear reports on television about impending layoffs or declining stock value.

- Dissatisfied customers lodge complaints with consumer advocacy groups about the quality of the organization's products or services. And during this time of public outcry, the organization's advertising campaign continues to tout the "high quality" of the organization's products and services.

It is the management of these overlapping communication impacts that is the purview of the corporate communication function. Organizations must communicate with "one voice." This can't occur if human resources is delivering one message, the advertising department another, media relations another, investor relations another, and so on.

Another critical function of corporate communication is protecting the organization's "image" or managing its "identity." In everyday parlance, that often means serving in the role of "logo police"—a role that many corporate communicators eschew. Why? Because all too often their peers—even high-level management peers—consider such "policing" to be petty, inconsequential, or downright "silly." What difference does it make if an old version of the corporate logo appears on some internal document currently being circulated? So what if the logo is "re-created" in a design program by some product manager's administrative aide and sent to a vendor for use in a trade show ad?

"Most managers who have not participated in developing an identity program tend to underestimate its value," says Argenti in *Cor-*

porate Communication. "Particularly those on the financial side of the operation often think, for example, that such a process is silly and trivial. Some of this hesitation emerges from a lack of understanding of what corporate image and identity, as well as reputation, are all about and what they do for an organization. But such skeptics should understand that an inappropriate or outdated identity can be as damaging to a firm as a weak financial performance. People seek consistency, and if perceptions about a corporation fail to mesh with reality, constituents take their business elsewhere."[5]

"To become well regarded, companies must deserve it," writes Fombrun in Reputation: Realizing Value from the Corporate Image. "They must develop coherent images and a consistency of posture internally and externally. And that's true whether they present themselves to the world as reclusive introverts or as outgoing extroverts. Identity and self-presentation beget reputation."[6]

As Argenti points out in Corporate Communication, "Whether an organization is trying to develop a coherent image for itself through corporate advertising, to communicate effectively with employees about health benefits, to convince shareholders that the company is worth investing in, or to simply get customers to buy products, it pays to use a coherent communication strategy."[7]

The changing structure of communication within organizations became most prevalent in the 1990s. The Conference Board released a report in 1993 titled Managing Corporate Communication in a Competitive Climate and based on a survey of individuals from seven hundred of the largest U.S. corporations. The report stated that "the global competitive forces, technological advances and other changes that continue to alter the ways in which companies organize and manage in the 1990s require new levels of expertise in internal and external communication. In previous downturns, communications was often viewed by top management as a function that was 'nice to have' but expendable. In the current period of rapid change, communications is being harnessed as a 'strategic resource' in many major corporations."[8]

At the time of the study, eight out of ten respondents were working to align their communications planning with their firm's strategic goals and were crafting their own strategic plans. At least three-quarters were moving toward more cross-functional cooperation with peers in human resources, marketing, and government relations.

Today, ten years later, external environmental impacts on organizations continue—as does the need to ensure that HR and corporate communication are strategically aligned in their efforts to communicate with internal and external constituencies.

Why is corporate communication achieving greater recognition and heightened importance in organizations today? For a variety of reasons. Interestingly, Argenti pointed to these reasons in the second edition of his classic *Corporate Communication:*

- We live in a more sophisticated era in terms of communication.

- The general public is more sophisticated in its approach to organizations than before.

- Information comes to us in more beautiful packages than it did before.

- Organizations are more complex today.[9]

Further, as we all know, confidence in large organizations and their leaders has been eroding over the past few years, fueled by scandals that have shocked the public and put on display the foibles of leaders in such formerly respected organizations as WorldCom and Enron and public figures such as Martha Stewart and Dan Rather.

And, says Karen Horn, senior director of human resources for Cisco Systems, Inc., in San Jose, California, the "barriers to entry" to communicate have virtually disappeared. "Today almost anyone can communicate with anyone in any way they want so we, as communication professionals, have to recognize that our roles have fundamentally changed. The big shift is we're no longer the person who is simply 'the bearer of information.' Our jobs have become much more strategic. Today's communicators have to be far more sophisticated and masters of understanding the art of communication. It's a huge, huge change."[10]

The more complex environment that today's communicators operate in and the growing availability of multiple communication options and multiple sources of information both within and outside the organization make it ever more critical that communication is carefully coordinated. There are no tried-and-true models to follow, unfortunately. In fact, there is a great deal of variation in how internal communication is handled and in the relationships between the various communication functions.

Human Resources and Corporate Communication

The human resource function clearly plays an important role in communicating with employees. Regardless of the formal communication structure within an organization, it is impossible for HR to be uninvolved in corporate communication activities.

"Human Resources should be working with corporate communication to ensure that information coming from HR is being conveyed appropriately to internal and external audiences," says Leza Raffel, president of the Communication Solutions Group, Inc., in Jenkintown, Pennsylvania. "For example, if there is a new component of in-house training, which has been coordinated by HR, corporate communication should be briefed on it so that the benefits of this training can be conveyed in internal newsletters or the intranet, as well as in external publications and press releases. HR might not see the public relations angles on the initiatives they are involved with, but corporate communication should. Therefore, it's important that they work together."

An added challenge in any organization is the reality that communication functions may well exist outside the boundaries of HR and corporate communication. The marketing communication function, for example, may formally lie within the marketing division. The shareholder relations communication function may formally lie within the finance division.

To be effective, obviously, communication needs to be managed. But who is—and who should be—responsible for managing communication with employees? Human resources? After all, human resources is clearly the function within the organization that is most concerned with employee needs. Corporate communication? After all, corporate communication is the place where the *professional* communicators typically reside. Should the communication function be centralized or decentralized?

A more centralized function provides a much easier way for companies to gain consistency and control for all communication activities at the top of the organization, says Argenti in *Corporate Communication*. A decentralized function, on the other hand, gives individual business units an opportunity to adapt the function to their own needs rather than the needs of the organization as a whole. Obviously, the larger an organization becomes and the more business units or locations it has, the more difficult it becomes to operate the communication function in a totally centralized manner. Because of this challenge, Argenti goes on the say that "perhaps the best structure of all for large companies is some combination of a strong, centralized, functional area . . . plus a network of decentralized operatives helping to keep communications consistent throughout the organization while adapting the function to the special needs of the independent business unit." The bottom line, according to Argenti: "A strong, centralized function with direct connections to the chief executive officer is the best way for a company to ensure the success of its corporate communication function."[11]

But despite Argenti's scholarly perspective, reality is less clear or consistent. When it comes to communication, there is no single, agreed-upon structure—no "one size fits all" approach. A survey by the International Association of Business Communicators (IABC) of its members demonstrates the variability among job responsibilities for members of what is the most recognized association devoted to the practice of corporate communication (see figure 1-1). While corporate communication and public relations represent the most commonly mentioned functions, responsibility for employee and marketing communications is also relatively high at 18 and 17 percent, respectively.

Does it matter? "I've seen a whole spectrum of reporting relationships for internal communication," says Shirley Gilbert, director of employee communications at Xilinx, a complete programmable logic solutions company based in San Jose, California. "I frankly think the least preferred, for me, is reporting into a marketing and PR department. The concern there is that all the employee communica-

FIGURE 1-1

Members' job responsibilities

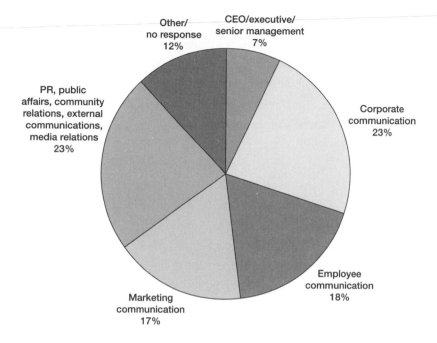

Source: International Association of Business Communicators (IABC.com). Used with permission.

tions can have a PR spin. For big companies I would say that corporate communication is on its own, but in smaller companies they often report to either PR or marketing or HR."

HR, says Diane Nix, vice president of corporate services for HP Financial Services (HPFS), "should be closely linked to the corporate communication function. In HPFS, communications is hard lined into the corporate development (marketing) function, but we are closely aligned. Internal communication contacts and their regional communicators are dotted line into my position." That dotted-line relationship, she says, should be "at a minimum."

HR and corporate communication, says Raffel, "should be on the same vertical, but interface regularly with each other." In other words, HR should not report to corporate communication, and vice versa. The two areas, Raffel feels, should be at the same level on the organizational structure. "They should remain separate, but there should be a regular exchange of information between parties, both at the strategic and tactical levels," she says.

Gilbert agrees. "It's my belief that communication and HR should be close partners," she says. "Whatever the organizational structure, I believe it's important for HR and communication to partner because HR has a big piece of seeing that the culture is alive and well, and communication should support all this with communication." Structure, says Gilbert, "really doesn't matter a whole lot.

"I've heard quite often that communicators dislike reporting to HR because HR folks are so guarded in what they say to employees," says Gilbert. At Xilinx, she says, that's not an issue. The communication function reports to HR at Xilinx, says Gilbert, "because our VP of HR, Peg Wynn, believes that it is very important to be very honest and open with employees. She's often more open than I would be—and that's the important part of the equation. Does your HR department know the right voice for employees? That voice needs to match the culture and values of your company, and we try very hard to do that in Xilinx."

John Clemons, currently vice president for communications at Raytheon Technical Services Company, LLC, in Reston, Virginia, has reported both through HR and through a separate communication function. "Quite honestly," he says, "I believe it works better and there is better alignment when the communication function reports directly to a senior communicator and is separate from the HR function."

Clemons says he has found that when communication reports through the HR function, "communication has a tendency to not be as pure because HR is introducing their own perspectives into the communications." It is difficult for the communication professional in this situation, he says, to "provide pure, unfettered, uncluttered communications."

On the other hand, says Joyce LaValle, senior vice president for human resources at Interface, Inc., a global carpet and textiles manufacturer with headquarters in Atlanta, Georgia, a reporting structure between HR and communication *can* work. Organizations in which employee communication reports through HR simply need to find ways to ensure a broader perspective and close alignment with other organizational communication functions, says LaValle. That's exactly what she has done. Recognizing the potential for the close alignment with the HR function to isolate the internal communication function (which also reports to her) from the rest of the organization, LaValle suggested an innovative approach to connecting with business units throughout the geographically dispersed organization: create a "virtual team" of individuals appointed in each business unit to work on the internal communications team.

"Traditionally," she says, "you have people who are responsible specifically for communicating to the company. But, here, we've pulled other people together who have jobs in marketing and we've added internal communication—and accountability—to their job descriptions."

Each business unit identified an employee to serve on the team. A weekly conference call keeps the group connected and results in critical sharing of information. The structure has increased organizational learning among the different business units and increased LaValle and her department's ability to respond effectively to communication needs.

Recognizing that your internal audience is not homogeneous and taking steps to understand and meet their diverse communication needs is critical to success, says LaValle. Drawing upon the resources, knowledge, and energy from communicators who are physically or organizationally in other areas can optimize the communication process. At Interface, says LaValle, that approach "has helped us be inclusive in our thinking."

Laura Luke is director of corporate communication at SRA International, Inc., an information technology services and solutions organization in Fairfax, Virginia. "At SRA," says Luke, "corporate communication resides in marketing and sales, employee communication resides in HR and investor relations resides in finance, reporting to the CFO." But, she adds, "while the three functions are all in different organizations, we all work together closely since our activities certainly overlap."

Luke says that in her interactions within the government contracting industry, she sees little consistency in the way these functions are structured. "I hear about some organizations combining the employee communication and corporate communication function, some combining the corporate communication and investor relations function, and others setting up in a similar fashion to SRA."

Francesca Karpel is manager of internal communications and community relations at Network Appliance, Inc., in Sunnyvale, California. In some ways, says Karpel, "it doesn't matter what the structure is as long as everyone works together. To be effective, it's not so important where you live as whether or not people respect what you have to say and listen to you." Karpel's background is in marketing, but she's currently in the HR organization at Network Appliance, and she feels her new home is a good fit. More important than where the function resides, she says, is "having access to the CEO. I would say you should have as short a line between you and the CEO as you can have."

Norman Crouse, author of *Motivation Is an Inside Job* and a partner in Personal Alternatives, LLC, a firm that provides consulting, coaching, and training services to a broad range of organizations, says, "Typically what I see is corporate communication focused on the external—customers, government, community—and HR focused on the internal communication with employees." This structure, though, he says, "often leads to the two having a very different look and feel—sometimes not even using the same logos, icons or color schemes.

"Many times," says Crouse, "the organization doesn't look at the HR communication function as part of the overall communication effort and, thus, it typically seems disjointed from the rest of the effort. In many cases, the HR staff's role gets diminished to some sort of internal newsletter or, even worse, an outsourced effort. In either case, they are usually not tied closely to strategy and objectives."

While their company's structures and their opinions on structure may vary, all these communicators agree on one thing: the functions must work together to ensure that communication is handled effectively at all levels and across all department and division lines. Regardless of the formal structure within an organization, opportunities exist to strengthen relationships, and HR can certainly play a role in this process.

At SRA, says Luke, working together across organizational boundaries to ensure consistent communication is a given. "One important project that HR and corporate communication work on together," says Luke, "is our nomination for the *Fortune* 100 Best Companies to Work For. HR has the lead, but corporate communication contributes much of the written material we submit and also plays a role in the writing and editing function."

Another joint project at SRA is Luke's review and approval of all employee communication materials that discuss contracts and clients "to make sure it meets disclosure guidelines, since SRA is a public company, and is consistent with all of our external communication on the same topic."

At HP Financial Services, Nix says, "we have one-hour meetings at a minimum every two weeks and work regularly on projects at other times. Communication is regularly working with HR on rolling out strategies, priorities, operating philosophy, as well as compensation communications. They are responsible for ensuring that colleague messages are aligned to our overall messages and strategies."

Gilbert worked with Hewlett-Packard (HP) for twenty years and reported to a corporate communication function, an HR function, and a quality function. "I usually found that I partnered with HR folks when I needed to, with business partners when I needed to." And, she adds, don't forget PR. The communication department should also work to forge close relationships with people in the PR function, says Gilbert. "We have an extremely close relationship—we meet every two weeks, discuss what products are coming out externally and what we need to do internally to tell employees about those products. We're all very used to the matrixed organization, and we partner with the folks we need to depending on the communication."

Ultimately, despite the boxes and the lines—dotted or otherwise—on the org chart, relationships matter. "The important thing," says Gilbert, "is that communication has some kind of seat at the executive table. At Xilinx, I have a close affiliation with the CEO and it doesn't really matter where I report—I know I'll continue that close alliance."

Another key, says Kathryn Yates, head of Watson Wyatt's global communication practice, regardless of the formal structure, is that messages be coordinated and consistent. "No matter where the function sits," says Yates, "the alignment and consistency are very important because it's so easy to lose credibility and it's very difficult to gain it back. If you have one set of messages going out of corporate communication and a separate and somewhat unrelated set of messages going out of HR, people will feel a lack of leadership or they'll imply a certain mismanagement to those disparate messages. For me one of the roles that HR plays is to make sure that they're playing nicely with their functional neighbors—it's so interrelated."

Francesca Karpel's experience generating awareness of her organization's recognition as one of the *Fortune* 100 Best Companies to Work For demonstrates effective collaboration between internal and external communications. See "Collaborating to Get the Word Out."

Collaborating to Get the Word Out

Francesca Karpel is manager of internal communications and community relations at Network Appliance, Inc., in Sunnyvale, California. Karpel is within the HR structure at Network Appliance, but, she says, "we work closely with our MARCOM (marketing communications) group and we share the belief that branding—whether it's advertising, collateral, or whatever—should have the same look and feel internally as it does externally."

For example, she tells of a campaign developed in 2004 to support the Total Customer Experience initiative, originally directed at an internal audience. Karpel and her team worked with the MARCOM group "to get images and to refine the language." It was a win-win effort, she says. "I'm able to use this wonderful internal resource and, as they're building brand, we can build into it what we're going to do from an internal perspective. So it's very synergistic and I know what's going on with the external messaging, so I can share that with people internally." This teamwork happens on a regular basis, she says, and enhances the value of the communication function organization-wide, ensuring consistency of messages and images both internally and externally.

At Network Appliance, says Karpel, "we are all about being effective. How can we leverage what we do one place in another place." For example, she says, when Network Appliance learned it was going to be part of the *Fortune* 100 Best Companies to Work For list for the third year, "we were thinking about how could we really make a statement to our employees that would say you're really the ones who make this organization phenomenal—it's because of your hard work, and your living our corporate values that drives success and builds a model company."

Karpel's team talked to the PR team about what they might do to recognize that employee contribution in a meaningful way. "At one point," she says, "the senior director of PR said, jokingly, 'I don't really want a little toy; what would matter to me would be a day off.'" His words resonated with one of Karpel's staff members, particularly since Network Appliance ranked number twenty-four on the list—a nice connection to twenty-four hours in a day.

What if, she suggested, we gave everybody an extra day off, a floating holiday to use when they wanted to, as a way of celebrating Network Appliance's position in the list. She looked at the financial implications and went to talk with the CFO and the CEO, who liked the idea; it was announced soon after by the CEO at a meeting.

While the idea, says Karpel, "was formally proposed by HR, the genesis of the idea came from the marketing department. The ability to have those types of interactions—the type of interactions that lead to communication synergy—doesn't happen without strong and respectful relationships."

The optimal structure, says Karpel, depends on the organization and its needs. "I don't think there's just one way you can structure organizations any more than there's one way you can structure a Web page." Ultimately, she says, regardless of where communication lies in the formal structure, it's the relationships that really matter.

Assessment Tool: Gauge Your Knowledge of Corporate Communication

To gauge your current understanding of the concepts in this book, take the following multiple-choice test. Then review the answer key that follows, which points you to particular chapters for more information on specific aspects of communication and the HR professional's role.

1. Which of the following is generally *not* considered to be part of "corporate communication":

   a. Employee communication

   b. Public relations

   c. Investor relations

   d. Marketing

2. The most important consideration in selecting an appropriate spokesperson to represent an organization is:

   a. Position within the organization

   b. Ability and experience in communicating with the media

   c. Direct knowledge of issue to be addressed

   d. Availability to meet reporter's deadlines

3. HR can strengthen its role in communication planning by:

   a. Assuming responsibility for coordinating the development of any communication plan that impacts employee audiences

   b. Promoting an organization structure that has a direct-line reporting relationship between HR and corporate communication

   c. Partnering with corporate communication staff to meet shared goals

d. Becoming involved in the hiring process for corporate communication staff

4. A measurement result that states, "75 percent of employees read the employee newsletter," is:

a. An outcome measure that indicates communication impact

b. A process measure that does not adequately measure impact

c. A good way to demonstrate the effectiveness of the employee newsletter

d. An unrealistic expectation

5. HR has a role to play in communicating with all the following external audiences *except:*

a. Employees

b. Investors

c. Customers

d. HR has a role to play in communicating with all these audiences

6. HR and corporate communication may fail to work effectively together if:

a. The two areas report to different areas of the organization.

b. There is not a process—formal or informal—established for communicating, planning, and collaborating on a regular basis.

c. The HR manager does not have a background in communication.

d. The corporate communication manager does not have a background in HR.

continued

7. Which of the following is not one of the four types of crises an organization should be prepared to respond to:

    a. Personnel

    b. Bizarre

    c. Sudden

    d. Smoldering

8. Communication plans should include goals that are:

    a. Measurable, short- and long-term, balanced

    b. Specific, cross-departmental, time-framed

    c. Measurable, realistic, long-term

    d. Specific, time-framed, measurable

9. The *best* tool for communicating with employees is:

    a. It depends

    b. Direct, face-to-face communication

    c. Employee newsletters

    d. The intranet

10. All of the following should influence the selection of communication tools *except:*

    a. Goals

    b. Culture

    c. Demographics

    d. Organizational structure

11. When communicating during difficult or challenging situations, an important point to remember is:

    a. The CEO should approve all communication plan elements.

    b. The communication need doesn't end when the crisis is over.

   c. HR should review all documents before their release.

   d. Employees should receive information on a "need to know" basis only.

12. In the future, HR professionals will need to:

   a. Focus on strategic issues to ensure involvement in important organizational issues

   b. Identify outcome-based measures of success

   c. Maintain well-developed interpersonal and communication skills

   d. All of the above

Answers and chapter references:

1. d—chapter 1

2. c—chapter 2

3. c—chapter 3

4. b—chapter 4

5. d—chapter 5

6. b—chapter 6

7. a—chapter 7

8. d—chapter 8

9. a—chapter 9

10. d—chapter 10

11. b—chapter 11

12. d—chapter 12

Summing Up

- Effective communication drives business performance and is a key contributor to organizational success.

- Corporate communication can encompass a number of relationships between key organizational constituencies: public relations, community relations, media relations, shareholder relations, and employee relations.

- The communication function within organizations exists to influence various constituencies through these relationships.

- There is a great deal of variation in how internal communication is handled and the relationships between various communication functions.

- Despite the organizational variation, however, one point remains consistent across all organizations: the primary function of corporate communication is to protect and enhance the reputation of the organization through communication with its various publics.

Leveraging Chapter Insights: Critical Questions

- In what ways does your job relate to each of the elements of corporate communication? What specific actions might you take to better leverage your ability to impact these areas positively?

- How does the HR department at your organization influence various internal constituencies through communication? How could these activities be improved or strengthened?

- Is the corporate communication function in your organization centralized or decentralized? Do you believe the current structure is effective? Why or why not?

CHAPTER TWO

Communication Fundamentals

The Basics of Corporate Communication

Key Topics Covered in This Chapter

- *Basic communication models*

- *The components of corporate identity*

- *Communication and influence*

- *Target audiences and "WIIFM"*

- *Selecting the appropriate spokesperson*

- *Messages, channels, and timing*

A RISTOTLE WAS a Greek philosopher known for his skill at rhetoric, or the use of language for persuasion. Aristotle's *The Art of Rhetoric* defined the three critical elements of any speech: the speaker, the subject, and the audience. A simple model but clearly still the basis for *any* communication. One might add: the *right* speaker (e.g., the source or spokesperson most likely to exert influence over the audience), the *right* subject (e.g., content or key messages), and the *right* audience (e.g., those most likely to be positively influenced or impacted by the message).

We're all familiar with the traditional communication model that includes a "sender" and a "receiver" of a message. That model is *deceptively* simple. What underlies this simple model is the presumption that the sender of the message is the *appropriate* sender—the source with the maximum amount of credibility to influence the receiver—and that the receiver of the message is the appropriate receiver—the individual or group most likely to be positively impacted by the message. In addition, if those bits of complexity weren't enough to cast doubt on the apparent simplicity of the model, a lot can go wrong in between—the sender may use language that is unfamiliar or confusing to the receiver, there may be "background noise" or distractions interfering with the delivery or receipt of the message, the receiver may be predisposed to distrust the sender or the information itself. The receiver may not be the appropriate audience for the message. In short, the process is not simple! It becomes even more complex when the number of senders and receivers of messages increases, as it does in any organization.

In *Reputation: Realizing Value from the Corporate Image,* Charles J. Fombrun provides a slightly more complex model depicting the relationship between a company's identity and its name, image, and reputation, as shown in figure 2-1.[1]

Corporate identity, says Fombrun, "describes the set of values and principles employees and managers associate with a company. Whether widely shared or not, a corporate identity captures the commonly understood features that employees themselves use to characterize how a company approaches the work it does, the products it makes, and the customers and investors it serves. Corporate identity derives from a company's experiences since its founding, its cumulative record of successes and failures. It describes the features of the company that appear to be central and enduring to employees. On a day-to-day basis, corporate identity appears in the managerial practices managers employ in their dealings internally with employees and externally with other constituents."

FIGURE 2-1

The relationship between a company's identity and its name, image, and reputation

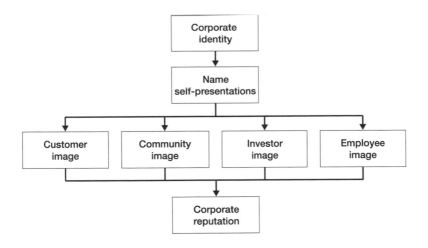

Source: Charles J. Fombrun, *Reputation: Realizing Value from the Corporate Image* (Boston: Harvard Business School Press, 1996). Used with permission.

Fombrun's model suggests that an organization's corporate identity is directed in part by the things it says about itself—its "self-presentations." Its logo. Its mission. Its communication materials. Those self-presentations, in turn, are influenced by a number of things, including the image that customers, community, investors, and employees have of the organization. While those images can be influenced by the organization's communications—its self-presentations—they are also influenced, often to a greater degree, by the things the organization and its staff members do and the experiences that members of these various "publics" have with the organization and those staff members. Those experiences, along with the organization's self-presentations, result in corporate reputation.

It is that reputation that the corporate communication function is charged with influencing—and protecting. Considering again that simple model of sender and receiver and the complexities that are created when the number of senders and receivers is multiplied exponentially gives you an idea of the complexity of the communication function within any organization.

Understanding Audiences

It's impossible to communicate effectively without a solid understanding of the audience you will be communicating with. That seems like such an obvious and simple statement, yet the reality is that far too often organizations send messages to various audiences *without* that solid understanding.

The simple truth is, the more you know about the audience you're attempting to reach (and, ultimately, influence), the greater your likelihood of achieving your objectives. Again, think of this type of interaction on a personal level. Suppose it's Friday night and you'd like to go out to eat at an expensive restaurant. You need to communicate this desire to a significant other or a good friend. What is the process that you quite naturally go through? You'd consider the ways in which your desire would be most meaningful to the person you're attempting to influence. You'd anticipate possible objections (too expensive,

I'm too tired, etc.), and you'd come up with possible responses to those objections.

Consider another example: you'd like to attend a professional conference in some attractive resort location and need to convince your boss that he should allow you to attend. What process would you go through? You'd consider everything you know about your boss—how he has responded to similar requests in the past, the things that are important to him (the value of gaining knowledge through training and networking, the importance of being able to demonstrate some tangible ROI, potential concerns about time away from the office, etc.). As you considered ways to approach your boss, you would develop messages that bolstered the positive feelings your boss might have (e.g., "Lifelong learning is very important") and countered potential objections he might have (e.g., "I can't afford to have you out of the office that that many days"). The more you knew about your boss and his beliefs and opinions, the better able you would be to craft messages that would lead to a positive response.

Children learn this ability to persuade at a very early age, and it's all based on their intimate knowledge of the individual they're attempting to influence—most commonly their mother or father. Throughout our lives, we quite naturally use these same techniques in our interpersonal interactions—and obviously some of us are more successful than others.

This process of understanding an audience and its frame of reference, and anticipating and being prepared to respond to potential objections, is what takes place—or what *should* take place—in organizations when the company wishes to communicate with any given audience. Communication is *always* about influence. Even if the communication is intended simply to inform, that information is being provided with a purpose: to influence the existing beliefs or understanding of an audience, and to impact, and often change, their opinions or beliefs on some topic.

It is *all* about influence. Recognizing and accepting that fundamental principle as a communicator can help you more strategically develop and communicate messages that have their intended impact.

The communication process, at its most basic, is quite simple:

1. What is your intended result or objective?

2. Who are you attempting to influence?

3. What are their current attitudes, interests, and opinions?

4. What messages would be effective to impact those attitudes, interests, and opinions in a way that would achieve your intended results?

Quite clearly, the more you know about your target audience, the more successful you will be. The first step is identifying the target audience or audiences. Who do you need to communicate with? Can your message be sent to a very large, heterogeneous group, or does that large group need to be broken down into smaller constituencies?

For example, suppose you need to communicate with your workforce about a change in health care benefits. If you are working with a small organization and the change will impact everyone in the same way, you might consider the entire workforce your audience. On the other hand, if you are working with a much larger organization and the impact of the changes will be different for different groups within the organization, you may need to divide the workforce into smaller segments according to these impacts. In both cases, you may also decide that you wish to segment managers from the general employee audience to provide them with specific information on how to respond to employee questions and address employee concerns.

In any communication situation, you will be faced with decisions related to the audience you need to communicate with and will need to consider the value of breaking a large audience into smaller segments. The more you break the audience down, of course, the more resources—time and money—will be needed to convey your messages. There is always a trade-off to be made between effort and outcome. Finding that balance is one of the first challenges you will face as a communicator. There are no right or wrong answers, simply shades of gray along a continuum that extends from too little communication to a group too broadly defined (resulting in ineffective communication that does not accomplish its objectives) to too much communication to too many individual segments (resulting in wasted time, effort, and expense).

Once you have determined the appropriate audience (or audiences) for your message, the next step is determining how this target audience will be most effectively impacted or influenced. In the field of advertising, an acronym is used to help advertisers focus on the needs and interests of their target audience: WIIFM, or What's in it for me? Whether or not we would like to believe differently, we are all inherently driven by self-interest. We do things because we think we will benefit in some way. We don't do things because we want to avoid perceived negative consequences. All audiences have these same basic human reactions to the messages they receive. The initial response, however subconscious, is always "What's in it for me?"

The challenge for the corporate communicator lies in the reality that most audiences represent a wide array of attitudes, interests, and opinions. One size does not fit all. The objective, then, becomes selecting an approach that will have the maximum impact with the maximum number of people.

The more you know, the more effective you can be. Of course, you need to make decisions about how much time and effort to place on gathering information about your target audience according to your communication objectives. For example, the time and effort you expend will be very different if your objective is simply to let employees know that a new parking lot will be opening up for employee use than if your objective is to let employees know about an impending merger and how that merger will affect them.

Some things you will know about your target audience through experience. If you're a communicator within the HR structure, you may have many years of experience within your organization communicating with specific employee segments, responding to questions, and coming to understand very well the attitudes, opinions, and interests of staff members.

Some things you will need to find out about your target audience through research (see chapter 4). The decision of whether research needs to be done to provide more information about an audience will again depend on the message that needs to be conveyed, its intended impact, and the likelihood that the message could generate a negative response of some kind that could potentially damage the organization and its goals.

Understanding your target audience will not only help you to craft messages that will have the desired effect, but will also provide you with insights about the best ways in which to convey those messages. If you need to communicate with a group of nurses who spend most of their time with patients, a message on the hospital intranet is not likely to reach your intended audience. If, on the other hand, you need to communicate with members of an IS department who work at computers daily, the intranet might be the perfect communication tool.

A thorough understanding of your audience will help you make more informed, and consequently more effective, decisions about:

1. The significance of the message and the amount of time and effort to expend on conveying the message

2. The target audiences that will be impacted and what approaches or messages will have the most impact for each target audience

3. The communication tools that will be most likely to reach and influence the target audience

4. The frequency and reach of the messages—how often the message should be shared, in how many vehicles, and to how many individuals

5. The order in which messages should be shared (e.g., managers generally need to receive messages before their employees)

These considerations all become elements of a communication plan (see chapter 8)—a blueprint that helps direct the efforts of the corporate communicator and other communication partners within the organization.

Selecting the Appropriate Source

Another important aspect of any communication effort is the *source* of the message—the sender. Much thought goes into selecting the appropriate spokesperson according to the message to be conveyed and the audience to be reached. For example, if your organization has just been the target of a computer hacker, and the personal infor-

mation of customers has been put at risk, who is the best spokesperson to participate in a media interview to convey this information to
the public? Your corporate communication director? The head of
IT? Your CEO? Your customer service director?

There are a number of issues to consider when selecting a spokesperson, says Larry Smith of the Institute for Crisis Management, who
adds, "I don't believe that 'one size fits all' really works." Instead, he
says, when the Institute for Crisis Management works with an organization, it generally defines several broad categories of crises that
need to be prepared for (legal or ethical issues, death or incapacity of a
corporate leader, natural disaster, etc.) and, for each type, identifies the
most appropriate person to put "out front." For example:

- Legal issue—corporate attorney

- Death of an executive—another high-level executive

- Natural disaster—operations manager

"You're looking for somebody who has credibility, who has the
knowledge of the issue, whatever it may be, and who has the time—
because being a spokesperson is a big job," says Smith.[2]

Benjamin Rudolph is marketing manager at Parallels, Inc., in
Herndon, Virginia. He was formerly communications manager at
Jinfonet Software in Rockville, Maryland. He has operated a D.C.-
based communication consultancy and has also served as director of
corporate communication for Aptagen, a gene synthesis and molec-
ular evolution biotechnology company. In all these positions, says
Rudolph, "I have always created communication programs that
specifically target the audience we're after, which could be potential
clients, potential partners, techies, investors or the media. A huge
part of that is putting the right person in the spotlight as the company's spokesperson."

Without a doubt, says Rudolph, the first step in selecting a spokesperson is a "deep understanding of who you're speaking to. Once
that's established, it's really just a matching game. Find someone from
Column A that matches Column B."

Scott Sobel agrees that the correct choice of a spokesperson for
each communication situation is critical. Sobel is vice president of

Levick Strategic Communications, LLC, in Washington, D.C., a crisis communication and media relations firm. He has counseled *Fortune* 50 companies, banks testifying before Congress, and celebrities like Rosie O'Donnell. Choosing the right spokesperson, says Sobel, is important for a variety of reasons. "In the end, it's going to be a self-fulfilling prophecy of failure," he says. "If you choose the right person for politics and the wrong person for communication, they possibly will not do well, they'll get the wrong message across, they'll alienate people or fail to persuade people, they'll look bad, and they'll be unhappy with you for choosing them."

When selecting a source, says Sobel, you should consider various aspects of that source's background—both professional and personal—including presentation style, familiarity with subjects they would be speaking about, and their history of performance as a source. "For instance, if you have somebody you want to speak for an organization relative to a crisis situation, you want to know not only are they qualified to know all the details or at least bring together the various sources relative to the crisis, but you want to know whether they're even-tempered, whether they've had a good or bad history speaking under these kinds of conditions before, whether they've been media trained or counseled, and whether they have any personal issues with what has happened."

All spokespeople are not created equal, Sobel points out—and not all are appropriate for all situations. "Sometimes the right spokesperson for one kind of corporation situation and somebody who has done well is absolutely the wrong kind of spokesperson for something else."

An important consideration in your selection should be whether the individual you're considering has been counseled, message trained, or media trained. "The assumption is that if there's a very high-level person running your organization, they must certainly be well spoken and able to convince people," says Sobel. "However, that's not always the case. They may have some very, very strong talents and capabilities, but dealing with the media, for instance, may not be one of them for a variety of reasons."

Who to use? Generally, the person who has the most knowledge or expertise and credibility about a particular issue. That isn't always the CEO—in fact, frequently it's not. "We recommend as strongly as we possibly can that most times the CEO or president of the company should not be the ongoing spokesperson when that organization is in trouble," says Smith. Why? "We argue that if the CEO is the spokesperson and the CEO misspeaks, there isn't anybody left to step in and fix it." Smith tells of a situation that underscores the CEO's role in a crisis. See "The Appropriate Use of CEO as Spokesperson During a Crisis."

The Appropriate Use of CEO as Spokesperson During a Crisis

A plane crash. Many people killed. The CEO of the airline is put on a plane and flown to the nearest airport and then taken to wherever the media center is. The CEO appears before the press very briefly, identifies himself, expresses his personal and his company's sorrow and grief for the victims and their families, pledges his personal and his airline's cooperation with the investigating authorities, turns around and introduces the ongoing spokesperson, and if there are survivors, excuses himself because he's on the way to the hospital to be with the victims' families. In more recent years when there have been no survivors, he excuses himself because he's on his way to the command center to participate in managing this operation. He turns and walks out. There is no Q&A.

There is another person within organizations who should generally *not* serve in the spokesperson role, says Larry Smith of the Institute for Crisis Management: the head of corporate communication. The role of corporate communication, says Smith, is to help manage the media and the message and to prepare the spokesperson or spokespeople. "They're going to be the source for all of the background information reporters need, but probably in most organizations they should not be the ongoing

continued

spokesperson because that is a role and a responsibility that takes so much time and is under so much pressure."

While there are organizations that turn to "corporate communication spokespeople" to convey messages to the media, Sobel agrees that's not always the best strategy. "Under the most sensitive 'bet the farm' situations, especially if you're dealing with consumer or regulatory issues," says Sobel, "audiences want to hear from a top person what the state of affairs happens to be. Generally—generally—that's a wise tactic to consider."

And even if the issue isn't sensitive, conveying a message through a technical or issue-specific expert is generally preferable to using corporate communication staff as the communication conduit. For most general media interactions or presentations—internal or external—you should select a spokesperson who:

- Is closest to the issue in terms of having information and knowledge that will lend credibility to their statements

- Is able to communicate clearly, professionally, and appropriately with the specific audience

"What you're looking for is somebody who is calm and methodical," says Smith. "Somebody who will not rise to the level of excitement that the press may throw at them, but who will bring that level of heat down. Somebody who can be calm and deliberate—human, show a little empathy."

Never—*never*—settle for "the best of the worst." In other words, there is never a good reason to put an ineffective spokesperson on the front lines for your organization. "You can't afford to be stuck with a spokesperson who's really bad," says Smith.

HR executives can play a key role in the selection of spokespeople because of their knowledge of the employee population, including the organization's leaders. "HR folks should try to use as much influence as they can because they may know better than anybody else in an organization the strength and weaknesses of a lot of the top people in the company," says Smith.

Nonmedia Situations

The selection of spokespeople doesn't only occur when the media call! There are a variety of situations for which you'll need to select someone to go before one, a dozen, or several hundred individuals to deliver a message—the announcement of a merger to a group of affected employees, the announcement of an organizational change to a group of management staff, the delivery of a presentation to an association or a trade group, and so on.

The skills needed to be effective in these different situations will vary. "Some people have the ability to talk to hundreds, if not thousands of people in a meeting," says Sobel, "some have the ability to go on camera or talk to a reporter, and some have the ability to speak well to a small group but may not relate well to a large group, or vice versa."

A good communication professional, with a "thick skin," he says, "can be honest about those individual capabilities and help in choosing who the best spokesperson should be during what circumstance."

A Structured Process

It pays to be proactive whether dealing with internal or external audiences. Having a process in place to help you quickly and appropriately select the right spokesperson for an event or an interview can save you time and boost effectiveness—and credibility for your organization.

Rudolph has developed a structured process that helps him quickly and efficiently select the right spokesperson for the right venue. He uses "skill cards" for each member of his management team so that, at a glance, he can match skills and expertise with upcoming engagements, media interviews, or presentations. The skill cards include information such as:

- Basic biographical facts—name, age, short summary of corporate history, and résumé

- Specific areas of expertise or knowledge

- Presentation or speaking ability

- Past interviews they've done

Assert Your Role!

Finally, don't back down in your quest to match the right spokesperson with the right venue. Communication professionals, says Sobel, "need to take themselves out of the politics of the moment and try to be objective in their choices." An example of not being objective, he says, would be "a knee-jerk reaction to picking the head of a department or a CEO or a C-level person to be a spokesperson because, politically, you think that's the correct thing to do, as opposed to using all the other valid criteria to make the correct choice."

Good communication operatives, says Sobel, are just like good attorneys, "who are, to a degree, fearless and will speak what they know to be right or at least what they believe to be right regardless of whether that news will be taken well or not. You have to have thick skin to be a good communication person."

Creating Appropriate Messages

Your messages will be driven from two directions: the messages that some internal constituency wishes to convey and the characteristics of your target audience.

It can be very helpful when you are working with message "owners" to start, as Stephen Covey would say, "with the end in mind." What is the intended outcome? For example, suppose the head of a particular business unit wants to share information about the introduction of a new product with employees. What are the communication objectives?

- To inform employees in production of an impending increase or change in workload?

- To inform the sales team of the benefits of the new product and how it relates to existing products so they can most effectively sell the new item to their customers?

- To inform employees at large so they can serve as "ambassadors" in the community, spreading the word about the product to friends and relatives?

Each of these objectives will result in different messages.

Your goal as a communicator is to convey a clear, simple, concise, and consistent message to all audiences. In short, to get your point across!

In *Branded Customer Service,* Janelle Barlow and Paul Stewart offer some helpful guidelines for message creation:

1. Communicate from your audience's point of view.

2. Connect with the heart as well as the head.

3. Focus on communication outcomes, not quantity of inputs.[3]

Your identification of target audiences should include an analysis of the expected impact of your communication on those audiences. For instance, the impact of a merger announcement may be shock and legitimate concern about "what's going to happen to my job?" The impact of an announcement of the introduction of a new employee benefit will be much different.

The following is a helpful process to use in the development of key messages:

1. Try to put a "face" on your audience. If your audience is employees, for example, picture a specific employee that you wish to impact with your messages.

2. What is your target audience's "current state"? What does your target audience currently believe, think, or feel about the issue?

3. What is the "leave behind" for the audience you are targeting? What beliefs, feelings, or emotions do you want the audience to have after hearing your message?

4. What is the "gap" between where your audience is today and where you would like them to be (e.g., what level of influence do you need to exert to change their beliefs, feelings, or emotions)?

5. What questions or objections do you anticipate from your audience in response to your messages?

6. What are the key "proof points" to support your leave-behind message? What evidence can you provide—data, facts, statistics—both to support your key messages and to be responsive to perceived questions, challenges, or objections?

For example, HR may be introducing a Health Savings Account (HSA) as an option for employees, replacing the traditional health care coverage. A first step is considering the target audience for the message—in this case, the group of employees most likely to consider this change a "takeaway"—those that have a high level of health care need or those who have concerns about their ability to pay for health care coverage costs.

The current state of awareness or understanding of HSAs is likely to be very low and the anxiety high. Your goal would be to reduce this anxiety by providing information that addresses employee concerns and helps employees wade through what might be, for many, a complex issue. Questions or objections might relate to fear of increasing costs, lack of trust in the organization that this is an option that is "good for" employees, or simply resistance to change in benefit structure. Important proof points might include examples of how various segments of employees might be impacted, data from the plan administrator, and so on. Key messages would focus on closing the gap between employees' current state of awareness or understanding and where you would like them to be.

Selecting Appropriate Channels

The appropriate channel for your message will be driven by both the content of the message and the audience you wish to speak to.

For example, if your organization is involved in a building expansion that will have an impact on the surrounding community, one obvious audience will be your immediate "neighbors." The appropriate channels for communication will be determined by the number and makeup of that neighborhood population. Are your neighbors other businesses? Residents? A combination of both? What types of businesses? What types of residents? What are their schedules? Their habits—professional and personal?

A small, relatively homogeneous group could lend itself to direct, personal contact either by phone, door to door, or in small information meeting settings. A larger group might prompt the need for community meetings, a newsletter or mailing to the community, or some combination of the two.

The content of the message will also drive the channel used. A straightforward, noncontroversial message can be handled in a more impersonal way—through a mailing or newsletter, for example. A more sensitive message that may generate a negative response or a debate would lend itself more to a forum that allows for two-way discussion.

Chapter 9 provides a discussion of various communication tools or channels, their advantages and disadvantages, and tips for effective use.

The needs, preferences, and habits of your audience will direct your selection of communication channels. Employees who work at desks and have ready access to computers would be an audience that could be reached conveniently and effectively through e-mail or a corporate intranet, for instance. Nursing staff who spend most of their time working with patients and not in an office environment would not be reached as effectively through these means.

Communication channels should not be selected or used in isolation. Communication professionals often use the phrase "eight times/eight ways" to convey the importance of using multiple channels, multiple times to have the maximum impact on an audience. So, for example, in communicating a benefit change to an employee group, you might use a combination of tools including an all-hands meeting, face-to-face discussions with managers, flyers, handouts, articles in the staff newsletter, items on the intranet, a mailing to employee homes, and so on. Repetition is a good thing when it comes to communication. When staff start saying, "Oh, I heard about that already," you know that your messages may be *just beginning* to really hit home.

Planning Appropriate Timing

At an all-hands meeting, the CEO announces to staff that the company is shifting from an HMO to an HSA plan for medical coverage. Managers haven't yet been informed of this change or how it will impact their staff. Bad timing.

The company newsletter includes an article about a product innovation. The product is still in the planning stages, and the director of R&D is very concerned about the impact of local competition on who gets to market first. Bad timing.

When, and the order in which, you communicate messages is another important consideration. Determining the best timing and order depends, again, on your target audiences and the content of your message. Ensuring that messages are delivered in the proper order—and with consistency of content—is critical and can have a decided impact on your organization's credibility with all impacted audiences. "Today we have a lot more ink than we used to have so it's much more important when we roll something out internally and externally that what we say externally really, really synchs with what we said internally," says Francesca Karpel of Network Appliance, Inc.

Network Appliance, says Karpel, has been involved in a number of acquisitions, and she has worked very closely with both the public relations and investor relations groups to ensure "if something is material that we've made sure the public notice is made first, because we want to follow the law, but that within minutes we have information up on the web—a video message from our CEO making the announcement—or an e-mail message. We work really closely together. That's just one of my fundamental beliefs about employee communication—employees should learn about changes in the business from within the business and not in the news."

It can be helpful to literally draw a timeline to indicate the audiences you need to address and the point at which each needs to be communicated with. Showing these audiences visually along a continuum can help you easily identify areas of potential conflict (e.g., a newsletter article to all staff that precedes notice to management or a public announcement that needs to be quickly followed by an internal notification of staff).

The bottom line—regardless of the issue, the spokesperson, or the audience—is persuasion. The goal of *any* communication is to persuade an audience, whether that persuasion is as simple as sharing a bit of information (and persuading the audience that the piece of information is important enough to remember) or as complex as influencing the opinion of an entrenched constituency (e.g., a political campaign).

Summing Up

- Communication is a complex process that becomes more complex as the numbers of senders and receivers increase.

- The experiences of various publics, combined with the messages that an organization sends about itself, result in its corporate reputation.

- It's impossible to communicate effectively without a thorough understanding of the audience you will be communicating with.

- Communication involves understanding an audience and its needs, and anticipating and being prepared to respond to potential objections.

- The selection of an appropriate spokesperson involves a variety of considerations, including role or expertise, presentation style, and past history.

- The communicator's goal is to convey a clear, simple, concise, and consistent message to all audiences.

- The appropriate channel is driven by the content of the message and the audience you wish to speak to—multiple channels used in combination are most effective.

Leveraging Chapter Insights: Critical Questions

- How does your current role at your organization impact your organization's corporate identity? What opportunities exist to increase your positive impact? Are there ways in which you might negatively impact your organization's reputation?

- What are some of the specific internal audiences in your organization that you communicate with? What are the differences between these audiences? How might your communication approaches and messages differ among these audiences?

- Think of a specific communication challenge that your HR department is currently facing. Considering the various audiences within your organization, how might the acronym WIIFM come into play in planning communications for these audiences?

- Who are your corporate spokespeople? How are they selected? Is there a situation in which you might be called upon to serve as a corporate spokesperson? How would you prepare to serve in this role?

CHAPTER THREE

Developing an Integrated Corporate Communication Strategy

A Strategic Approach to Corporate Communication

Key Topics Covered in This Chapter

- *The importance of an integrated communication strategy*
- *How to build your corporate communication strategy: research, goals and objectives, action plans, budget, measurement*
- *The communication audit*
- *Integrating corporate communication and HR strategies*

If you don't know where you're going, any route will get you there.

FAR TOO OFTEN, organizations do not have a formal, written communication plan that clearly outlines "where they're going" in terms of communication strategy. An integrated communication plan will be tied to the organization's overall mission, vision, values, and objectives and will clearly support these objectives through communication with a variety of critical audiences.

One of these critical audiences is, of course, internal, and it is this key piece of the overall strategy that demands a high level of input from the HR function in both the development and the implementation of the plan.

As Argenti points out in *Corporate Communication,* "the first variable of an effective corporate communication strategy relates to the organization itself. The three subsets of an organization strategy include (1) determining what the *objectives* are for the particular communication, (2) deciding what *resources* are available for achieving those objectives, and (3) diagnosing the organization's *image credibility* in terms of this task."

In addition, says Argenti, the organization should identify and analyze its constituencies: Who are they? What are their attitudes toward the organization? What do they know about the organization and the messages it wishes to convey?[1]

Finally, communication strategy must focus on delivering messages appropriately, which includes both deciding on the appropriate communication challenge and carefully structuring the messages to be delivered. Throughout this process, the communication function must be focused on and aligned with the organization's overall mission and vision.

A company's reputation, suggests Fombrun in his book *Reputation,* "derives from the more or less healthy relationships it establishes with seven audiences:

- Customers

- Investors

- Employees

- Competitors

- The local community

- Government

- The public at large"[2]

In its direct responsibility for the important corporate audience of employees, HR has a critical role to play in the deployment of the organization's corporate communication strategy. HR has an obvious impact on customers, employees, and the local community. It arguably has an impact on the public at large.

- Customers—hiring employees who have the knowledge, skills, and abilities (KSAs) to serve customers effectively.

- Employees—attracting and retaining high-quality staff.

- Local community—through an impact on employee relations and satisfaction with the organization, ensuring that positive word of mouth ensues.

- The public at large—in HR's interactions with employees, both prospective and current, there are related impacts with the public in general. A company's reputation for being a "good place to work" is spread through word of mouth as well as media coverage in both tangible and intangible ways.

Clearly, the scope of the corporate communication function is wide and pervasive.

To manage *all* these various constituencies, Fombrun suggests the creation of a new executive role within organizations—the role of "chief reputation officer," or CRO. In essence, that is the role that the communication function plays within any organization. In proposing this position, Fombrun quotes PR consultant Alan Towers, who says, "The CRO's tactical responsibilities would include oversight of pricing, advertising, quality, environmental compliance, investor relations, public affairs, corporate contributions and employee, customer and media relations. Rather than literally do each of these jobs, the CRO would act as a corporate guide, working with specialists in each area to help them see the reputation consequences of their decisions."[3]

While the role of CRO has yet to take the world by storm, there is a role to be played by corporate communication professionals throughout the organization in ensuring that all communication efforts are coordinated and driven from organizational strategy and objectives.

The Importance of an Integrated Communication Strategy

- Why should we have a strategic internal communication plan? What is it and what does it or doesn't it do?

- What's the matter with the one we have now? (The assumption being that you *have* one now)

- Says who? Who says we need a new plan?

- How much will it cost? (Time and dollars)

- How does this affect me? What are you going to ask me to do? What are you going to tell me I *can't* do anymore?

- If I have to do something, what's in it for me? (WIIFM)

- If there's a "master plan," what if there are changes and additional things that need to be communicated? How does it impact other more project- or initiative-based communications?

The preceding represent actual questions from a manager at an organization whose corporate communication director brought up the need for an integrated corporate communication strategy for the organization. They're legitimate—if somewhat uninformed—questions, and they are quite likely to represent the response that corporate communication and HR managers can anticipate from leaders within *their* organizations.

Why do we need a strategic plan for communicating? "From my vantage point," says John Clemons, vice president for communications at Raytheon Technical Services Company, "it's very important to have a corporate communication strategy because what my research has shown is that CEOs and presidents of companies tend to fail when they cannot execute on their strategies." The ability to successfully flow down their strategies, goals, and objectives to the people who have to implement them, says Clemons, is critical. "If staff is not in synch with the road map, that's where you have a problem. The bottom line is that a communication strategy is critical to the success of a business."

The process of developing a plan, says Clemons, "is very formulaic." The essentials, he says, involve "doing the research, looking at the landscape—what's happening in the business, what are the goals and objectives, the mission of the organization or the business or the agency, who is the leadership team, what are you trying to achieve, what does the marketplace look like, what are your core competencies? Then develop communication goals and objectives that support this research you've put together."[4]

Benjamin Rudolph, formerly communications manager at Jinfonet Software, agrees that overall strategy is critical. When Rudolph first came to Jinfonet, he sat down with key players within the organization—the CEO, COO, marketing director, and sales reps who had a long period of tenure with the organization and talked about the organization, its products, its key messages, and so on.

Rudolph points out that communication in all its forms throughout the organization has an impact on the brand. Because of that it needs to be, if not controlled, at least carefully coordinated, he says. "A big part of what I do and what I've done both here and elsewhere," he says, "is tightly monitor what's going into the company information-wise and what's going out of the company information-wise." That involves advertising, speaking, letters, marketing collateral, phone calls—everything. While at Jinfonet, Rudolph and the marketing director oversaw all corporate communication, even down to the letters written by sales reps.

Jinfonet made sure that employees understood the organization's communication philosophy and culture during their first days with the organization. "When new people came to the company," says Rudolph, "as part of their new hire manual they also got a corporate communication packet that explained how their job functioned, what they were going to be doing, and the general rules on communicating inside and outside the company."

Whether the impetus for an integrated corporate communication plan is coming through a corporate communication structure, an HR structure, a marketing structure, or some combination thereof, the key is to ensure that all the appropriate players are involved in the process—that they are "at the table" sharing their insights, perspectives, and impacts on every point where communication occurs with the organization's various constituencies.

How to Build Your Corporate Communication Strategy

As Clemons suggests, the process for creating a strategic corporate communication plan is fairly formulaic. Certain key elements must be included, and certain basic steps must be followed. For example:

- The communication plan must flow from the organization's mission, vision, and values (MVV).

- The communication plan must tie to and support the organization's strategic plan. One important point that can help alleviate many of the fears of leaders in your organization is this: "The

communication plan doesn't *drive* the organization's strategy—
it *derives from* the organization's strategy," says Clemons.

- Each element or objective of the strategic plan should be tied
  to key internal audiences that need to be influenced in some
  manner.

- Influence should be tied to outcomes. What will the "end
  state" look like for each of the audiences you've identified?

- Key messages that are likely to impact the desired end state
  should be identified.

- Tactics to deliver the key messages (e.g., intranet, town hall
  meetings) should be identified. What has worked in the past?
  What hasn't worked in the past?

- A budget should be established according to the identified
  tactics. How can you use the vehicles you've identified most
  effectively within budget parameters to achieve your desired
  outcomes?

- Methods of measurement should be identified and results
  tracked with modifications made to the plan as appropriate.

This is basically the same approach that you will see in chapter 8
when we discuss communication plans for individual initiatives. Of
course, when you are considering an overall communication strategy, the process is much more complex.

Karen Horn is senior director of human resources at Cisco Systems in San Jose, California. She joined Cisco Systems in 2000 from
GE Capital, where she was the global leader of organizational communication and diversity for its twenty-eight global businesses in
forty-four countries. She has also held management positions at a
core GE industrial business, a regional medical center, and Bristol-
Myers Squibb. In 2004 Horn received the IABC Chairman's Award
in recognition of the creation of an online communication-planning
tool, My Communication (MyComm). Communication, stresses
Horn, is a "process"—not a tactic. It's not an article in a newsletter or
a posting on the intranet. It's not a town hall meeting. To be effective,

corporate communicators need to view their activities not as isolated events, but as integrated activities all designed to support the overall organization's mission, vision, values, and strategy.

A thorough understanding of those key elements—your organization's mission, vision, values, and strategy—is a good starting point for the development of a corporate communication strategy. The vision and mission of your organization provide a framework for your communications—the personality of the organization. For example, in October 2002 Microsoft changed its mission statement from "To empower people through great software—any time, any place, and on any device," to "To enable people and businesses throughout the world to realize their full potential." Consider the implications of this change on the communication strategy. If the communication strategy is not aligned with the mission and vision of the organization, how likely is it that the people "on the front lines" will be aligned with that strategy?

In addition to the mission and vision, your organization's values will provide an indication of the tone or theme of your communication. Your organization's strategy will give you direction for your communications and an indication of the type of outcomes you should strive to achieve.

It is important for communicators to thoroughly evaluate the organization's strategic plan and current progress toward meeting plan objectives. Consider these questions: What do staff need to know about these objectives to perform their jobs most effectively? What messages need to be conveyed to all stakeholders (internal and external) to support these objectives?

While corporate communication and HR professionals can and should play a role in helping the organizations they work for review, revisit, and even revise the corporate mission, vision, values, and strategy, the starting point for the development of a corporate communication strategy is not challenging the status quo—but using these inputs as the foundation for your plan.

Following a formal process in the development of a communication plan can help to ensure success. See "Building a Communication Strategy."

Building a Communication Strategy

When a major integrated health care system in the Midwest began its search for a director of corporate communications, it was with one imminent need in mind: the development of a formal communication strategy. Once hired, the director started the process by speaking to communications and HR professionals at ten of the country's best-practice organizations about their internal communication efforts. Interviews with executives at such companies as FedEx, 3M, and Eastman Kodak uncovered many consistent points:

- Communication starts at the top, with values "real" and "lived" by senior management.

- Multiple messages must be communicated in a wide variety of vehicles.

- Communication is a process, not an event or a tool.

- Managers and supervisors play a critical role in the communication process.

- There is no single "right" answer to the communication challenge.

As a result of these interviews, the next steps involved:

1. Gaining commitment from senior leadership. In this case, that piece was easy because the charge had come initially from senior management. In other organizations, this may not be the case.

2. Conducting individual and group interviews with various internal audiences. The CEO believed that he needed to be more open with financial information, wanted to push harder at two-way communication, and wanted to be more visible. Vice presidents indicated that the organization had a history of not sharing information and needed to do a better

continued

job of answering "why." Managers said that information did not get down to their level, and they needed more information so they could better serve employee needs. Employees believed that upper management needed to be more visible and that there should be more consistency between words and deeds. Through these interviews and guided by senior leaders, communication outcomes were established.

3. Identifying gaps between current and desired communication outcomes. A critical step here was identifying key communication issues that could be measured over time—for example, how well do employees understand the organization's chief issues and goals, and how well do they feel those are being communicated?

4. Developing an action plan designed to "close the gaps." The plan included eight objectives designed to help meet the organization's goals. Tactics were developed for each of the objectives, with accountability assigned to "owners" (administrative vice presidents) and "partners" (key departments), with ongoing support provided by corporate communication.

A difficulty at this stage was making sense of all the information gathered. The key was to find common points and consistencies. It was also important to maintain a focus on "really need to know" information—information required to do a better job—rather than "want to know" or "nice to know." Management commitment was crucial to making the whole plan work. They—not the communication department—needed to own the plan and its desired outcomes

Baseline research was used to put a "stake in the ground," and results were measured over time. First-year results indicated statistically significant improvement in each of the objectives identified, but work remains to be done. An ongoing challenge will be updating and modifying the plan to meet changing needs both within and outside the organization.

Research

Research is an important step in developing a corporate communication strategy. Part of the background research, says Clemons, should involve interviews and meetings with top functional and business leaders within the organization to "find out what their hot buttons are, what their issues are, what they think of communications, and what they think you should be doing."

Getting that involvement, up front, he says, can help ensure buy-in and support of the plan once it's developed. "Make sure you walk around and share the plan with the key leaders in your business," he advises, "and also that in that plan there is some element of what they shared with you when you initially went to them. If they see some of their comments and opinions reflected in the plan, there's a greater likelihood that you'll receive buy-in."

Background research should also involve a review of any previously developed plans and the activities and results associated with those plans, a review of existing communication materials and a review of any surveys or research that has been done—internally or externally—to indicate the effectiveness of various efforts. In addition, there is a wide variety of internal information—reports and data—that can be helpful to you in your process, most notably the organization's strategic plan and progress toward meeting the goals and objectives identified in the plan.

The research you do will also help you identify challenges or barriers that you might face, Clemons points out. Will low morale cause employees to avoid the road show meetings? Are you lacking the technical capacity to do global Webcasts? Are you missing editorial talent required to produce an electronic newsletter? "You have to figure out what the challenges are and how you're going to address them," says Clemons. "That also needs to be part of the plan."

When you are conducting background research to develop or support the communication strategy, it can be extremely helpful to:

- Interview key leaders. Ask leaders to identify the pros and cons of current communication initiatives and offer suggestions for improvement. What do they believe the top three key messages should be for each of your top three internal and external constituencies?

- Identify and involve appropriate internal stakeholders—for example, IT, education, business unit leaders.

- Hold focus groups with staff. What do they view as the pros and cons of current communication efforts? Do they have the information they need to effectively do their jobs? What additional information do they need? What are their preferred sources of information?

- Review existing internal and external survey data. What are the current perceptions and beliefs held by internal and external audiences? Are these existing perceptions aligned with the organization's stated MVV and strategic objectives?

- Review past efforts—content, format, and effectiveness.

Develop Goals and Objectives

Your communication goals and objectives will be developed as a result of all the information you've compiled. After you have these goals and objectives, you have to decide, How am I going to make these things come to life? How am I going to put actions behind the goals and objectives?

Communication goals and objectives should be directly aligned with the strategic goals of the organization and the constituencies that need to be influenced and informed to meet those strategic goals. The following step-by-step process can be a helpful means of linking goals to audience and desired outcomes:

1. For each strategic goal or objective, what are the key audiences you must influence?

2. For each audience, what are the intended impacts (e.g., what do you want them to know, do, or believe)?

3. What does each audience currently know, do, or believe?

4. What's the gap?

5. What messages do you need to convey to most effectively narrow or close that gap?

6. What are the best methods (tactics) of delivering those messages to achieve maximum impact?

Develop Action Plans

The goals and objectives will be accomplished through specific actions that must be identified. From an internal standpoint, says Clemons, those actions could be anything from starting an employee newsletter to holding town hall meetings with employees, to doing domestic or global Webcasts, to developing a QA program that allows employees to ask questions of senior management anonymously, to road shows where the executives go out on a regular basis to meet with employees and management and share strategies, goals, and progress updates.

Externally, your tactics might involve contact with specific media outlets (press releases, news conferences, editorial briefings), coordination of messages with marketing or sales, mailings to key constituencies, and so on. As discussed previously, your action plans should be plotted against a timeline to clearly indicate the order of events and the target dates for each deliverable.

The need to partner with other members of the organization in maximizing the impact of your corporate communication plan quickly becomes obvious. As discussed earlier in this book, the corporate communication function does not neatly reside in any one functional area. A partnership between the formal communication function (if it exists within your organization), HR, and areas like investor relations, public relations, marketing, and sales can ensure that your strategy is deployed effectively.

Budget

You can spend a lot of money creating tactics to inform and influence your target audiences. But that money will be misspent if you don't first devote time and effort toward educating and influencing the key members of your organization who will have an impact on the consistency of the messages you convey.

A corporate communication strategy's strength lies in the development and deployment of key messages that are aligned with the organization's MVV and strategic plan. But creating those messages is not enough. They must be conveyed to key points throughout the organization so that *everyone* in a position to communicate with *any* key audience is aware of the content, theme, and tone of the messages you wish to convey. This is exactly what Rudolph has done at Jinfonet, and it's helped to ensure that messages are consistently conveyed and they support the organization's brand and position.

Beyond laying the groundwork to ensure consistency of messages both internally and externally, your identified tactics will generally require some out-of-pocket costs for either staff time or production to accomplish your communication objectives. "You have to determine what kind of budget you need to make all of this happen," says Clemons. "You need to lay it out that this global Webcast will cost this much, the e-newsletter will cost this much, to do a road show will cost this much, etc." Later, those costs can be compared against the achieved outcomes, serving as a tangible means of demonstrating the value of communication to the organization—and of helping to identify areas of opportunity or needing improvement.

Measurement

Once you have your plan outlined and your budget established, the final step is to develop a means of tying these efforts back to your goals and objectives. For example, if one of your goals is that employees receive accurate and timely information on the status of the annual corporate goals and objectives, and you do a number of road shows during the year at all your business locations, you can check that off the list, says Clemons. But, he adds, there's still more involved. You might have evaluation forms at the end of the meetings to show what people understood, to find out if the information helped them, to understand what additional questions they might have. "Then you have a barometer or gauge of how effective you've been in addressing the sharing of information about the corporate goals—it all has to tie back," he stresses. "In your strategic plan, if you're doing anything that does not support those goals or objectives, you're on the wrong track and you need to correct the plan and then keep moving forward to make sure you're back on track."

Chapter 4 provides more detailed information on how to measure communication efforts.

The Communication Audit

A communication audit can be a good way to analyze existing communication strategies and tactics and identify gaps and opportunities. It can be the starting point for the development of an overall strategic communication plan.

In *Communication Research, Measurement and Evaluation: A Practical Guide for Communicators,* Louis C. Williams Jr., ABC, APR, suggests a number of environmental factors that might prompt the need for a communication audit:

- Installation of a new CEO or management team

- New or changing market conditions

- New regulatory restrictions

- Recent mergers or acquisitions

- Organizational restructuring

- New or increased competition

- Poor public image

- Threats to management's authority or credibility

- Major expansion plans[5]

An audit can also be an appropriate starting point for the development of a strategic communication plan in an organization that doesn't have one, or in a situation where a new communication leader is brought into an organization with the specific purpose of making "improvements."

Watson Wyatt's "Steps for Conducting Communication Audits" (see appendix G) offers helpful steps for both a core audit and a comprehensive audit.

A communication audit is not a simple undertaking. It involves more than a "survey" or review of communication materials, and frequently requires the assistance of an outside consultant to help guide you through the process. The process itself involves a number of activities that might include individual interviews with senior management, focus groups, surveys, literature review (print, electronic, etc.), analysis, and recommendations. (More detail on these types of activities is provided in chapter 4.)

An example of an audit survey, provided by Talon Communications Group, that could be used as a starting point with an internal audience is included in appendix H.

Integrating Corporate Communication and HR Strategies

If you follow the process outlined earlier, HR will be integrally involved with the development of the corporate communication strategy, and HR strategies and objectives will be clearly linked because the organization's strategic plan served as a driver for the communication plan. So, for example, if an objective of the organization's strategic plan is to decrease turnover, you will have identified communication strategies to support this objective.

"The HR piece is really critical," says Clemons, "because the HR team or the HR executive has a sense of what morale is like, they have a sense of what the culture is like, and that needs to be included as part of your research when you're putting together a strategic plan. HR knows what some of the hot buttons are and have their fingers on the pulse of what's happening with employees." The issues that HR identifies may become, he says, part of the challenges you may face. "You need to work hand in hand to address these issues in your plan. It's a partnership," he says.

Summing Up

- HR has a key role to play in ensuring the successful deployment of an organization's communication plan through its relationships with employees and the employment community.

- Corporate communication activities need to be coordinated and driven from organizational strategy and objectives.

- The vision and mission of the organization should provide a framework for communications.

- A sound plan involves thorough background research, development of objectives and goals, identification of messages specific to various target audiences, action plans, and an indication of the budget that will be allocated to achieve objectives.

- The final step in a strong communication plan is measurement—the communication audit is a good way to analyze overall communication effectiveness.

Leveraging Chapter Insights: Critical Questions

- HR has an obvious impact on the employee audience. But there are other important audiences that HR may also influence, including customers, competitors, and the community at large. In what ways might your HR department increase its ability to positively impact these groups?

- Does your organization have an integrated communication strategy? Who is involved in developing that strategy? How is the effectiveness of the strategy measured? If no such strategy exists, what role might you play in aiding in its development?

- Consider the various communication efforts that take place in your HR department. How is the effectiveness of these efforts measured? What processes might you put in place to better measure results achieved?

Communication Research, Measurement, and Evaluation

The Use of Research in the Communication Process

Key Topics Covered in This Chapter

- *Outcome versus process measures*

- *The value of measurement*

- *Weighing cost against value*

- *A process for determining whether your communication efforts are working*

- *Common research methods and their advantages and disadvantages*

- *Improving the effectiveness of your measurement efforts*

NOT EVERYTHING that can be counted counts, and not everything that counts can be counted." That quote is attributed to Albert Einstein, a scientist who certainly understood the importance of facts and data. Yet, obviously, he also understood that when it comes to research and measurement, there are infinite possibilities and many decisions to be made about the importance of measurement according to the value of the information obtained.

Many things *can* and should be measured. For example, what percentage of employees is currently satisfied with their compensation plan? How does that level of satisfaction compare with that of other organizations? Can that satisfaction be impacted through communication?

Or you're considering eliminating classified ads to announce job openings and moving toward online applications only. What impact will this have on the level and quality of applications received?

When you are measuring the impact of your communication efforts, it's important to focus on outcome—not process—measures. For example, does it really matter how many employees visited the HR department home page? Or are you really most interested in knowing how many employees used online benefit enrollment following this year's communication campaign? Does it matter how many news releases were mailed to various media outlets? Or are you more concerned with the *outcome* of sending those releases?

Numbers of Web hits, numbers of press releases generated, numbers of press conferences, numbers of town hall meetings, and so on are all *process* measures, or measures of "things being done." They are not that meaningful aside from providing an indication of the effort expended by your organization and its staff members. What matters is the effectiveness of those efforts—or the outcomes.

Angela Sinickas has been measuring the effectiveness of communication since 1981 and is the president of Sinickas Communications, Inc., an international consulting firm dedicated to helping corporations achieve business results through focused diagnostics and practical solutions. The challenge for some HR professionals, says Sinickas, is that they tend to not make the connection between the actions they took and the results that were achieved. They don't build the "chain of evidence." "There's a big hole in the middle between the activity that HR did and the outcome achieved," she says.[1]

Kathryn Yates, head of Watson Wyatt's global communication practice, agrees and says that Watson Wyatt's research on employee communication has shown that many companies "only measure the effectiveness of communication through soft measures—awareness and understanding." There's nothing wrong with these measures, she says, but they're not enough. "When you measure awareness that's a nice measure and it's good to have, but it's not really measuring an outcome."[2]

The practice of measuring communication effectiveness is very common among organizations globally, according to various studies. See "Who's Measuring?"

Who's Measuring?

More than one thousand communicators in twenty-five countries responded to an online global survey on communication measurement conducted by Benchpoint, with the help of Donald K. Wright, professor of communication at the University of Alabama. Of those responding, nearly 70 percent indicated that they measure the effectiveness of what they do; 61 percent indicated that measurement was an important element of their PR

continued

process. Even those who weren't currently measuring the impact of their activities indicated that they were planning to do so in the future—77 percent!

Still, even those who are taking steps to measure their efforts are often more focused on outputs than outcomes, particularly when it comes to external measurement. The most used tools included media evaluation, internal reviews, and benchmarking. Focus groups and opinion surveys—which could provide insights into outcomes—were used less often than advertising value equivalents (AVEs).

Internal communicators, though, tended to be more outcome focused. Employee feedback was listed as the most used criterion for success, followed by "desired outcome." Employee surveys were indicated as the most used and effective tool. Interestingly, 31 percent of internal communicators indicated that they correlated their results with HR data—24 percent correlated results with marketing data.

All survey participants felt positive about the benefits of measurement and believed that it was possible to calculate ROI on communication—88 percent said they would be interested in the development of an ROI tool.

What keeps communicators from measuring? Not surprisingly, the top responses were time and money.

SOURCE: Richard Gaunt, "A Global Agenda: The World Gets Serious About Communication Measurement," *Communication World,* January–February 2005, 32–37. Used with permission.

The Value of Measurement

In God we trust, everyone else should bring data!
—ATTRIBUTED TO W. EDWARDS DEMING[3]

Karen Horn, senior director of human resources at Cisco Systems in San Jose, California, says, "The role of communication within organizations has evolved to a need to change behavior. We've gone from a 'tell' to a 'we need you to do something different' perspective. As companies try to work smarter with fewer people that means, in effect, I really need to have you doing the right stuff—there's not the space anymore for people to be doing things that aren't aligned with the business function. We have a real reason to get you engaged."

HR staff can add a significant contribution to their organizations if they can become more adept at meaningful measurement. "Leadership is trying to show, or trying to find, the payback for everything that they're doing," says Sinickas, "especially in staff functions like HR, finance, IT and communication. If *we* don't come up with effectiveness measures that show ROI, *they'll* come up with the wrong measures for us!"

Of course, as Einstein wisely suggested, not everything that can be measured, should be measured. There are costs involved and savvy communication practitioners will learn to weigh the value of the information desired against the cost of obtaining that information. It pays to think wisely—and practically—about the options available to you (see the section at the end of this chapter, "Research Isn't Always the Answer").

In *Communication Research, Measurement and Evaluation: A Practical Guide for Communicators,* Louis C. Williams Jr., ABC, APR, suggests some guidelines to help determine the value of conducting research:

1. How important is this program or project to you and your organization? Is success vital to survival? Will it move your organization to a new plateau, put money in the till, improve market share, increase productivity, or frame an issue impeding organizational progress? If the answers to these questions are affirmative, then more money should be committed, rather than less.

2. Will you need to benchmark results so that you can show improvements over time? If the answer is yes, then research is imperative and spending money becomes more valuable.

3. Is the research in line with the cost of the program or project? A rule of thumb is that research should be budgeted at about 10 percent of the total cost of the project.

4. Are you trying to measure too much? One of the truisms of research is that the more complicated or larger the program, the

more research will cost and the less likely you are to be happy with the results. Try to measure small pieces which will keep your budget smaller. The same principle holds for audience size—the larger the audience, the more you will be likely to spend.

5. Will access to the information provider be easily available? It's a given in research that the closer you can get to your research subject, the better the results. The best information comes from a one-on-one interview. The problem with this approach is cost. It is the single most expensive way to gather information.[4]

What Can Be Measured—What *Should* Be Measured

HR professionals, suggests Sinickas, already have a "leg up" on their non-HR communication colleagues. "Much of what HR does has dollars attached to it," says Sinickas. "If we're trying to reduce accidents at the company, that would reduce the number of lost work days, it would reduce health care claims, it would reduce workers' compensation claims, so there are dollars attached to something like that. It's very easy to find a return on the communication because that money is already being captured and counted. Some of the other things that corporate communication does are a little harder because there might not already be somebody else capturing the dollars involved."

Measurement shouldn't be overwhelming. It's just a matter of looking at things a little differently, says Sinickas. For example, instead of launching a campaign at every site in your organization, do a pilot study. Pick a couple of locations or a random sample of your entire audience, and try the campaign with just that group. Then check to see whether the decisions or behaviors that occur are different for that group than for the group you didn't communicate with.

For example, Sinickas tells of an HR colleague who completely changed safety communication in three of the seven branches at her company, reducing accidents to the extent that the insurance premium went down $1 million the next year. To do that, says Sinickas, her colleague had to say, "I want to show the worth of what I'm going to do." She talked to the safety manager and said, "Do whatever you do normally for safety at half of our sites; all I ask is that you do the same thing everywhere." Then, she took the other half of the sites—one small, one medium-sized, and one large—and modified the communication efforts. She was able to demonstrate a significant financial difference in the results at the sites where communication was modified.

The key to meaningful measurement, Sinickas stresses, is demonstrating impact through a chain of events that starts with communication and ends with some measurable change in behavior. Suppose, she says, you do an activity that has an impact on knowledge. The knowledge has an impact on behavior. The behavior is known to have a financial value. That represents a "chain of evidence." But, she adds, "You have to prove that every link in that chain had a financial impact. You can't just say, 'We communicated five-year vesting and retention went up.' There's a big gap in the middle—you have to make the connection."

HR staff, says Sinickas, have an advantage when it comes to measuring impact, because they are often focused on dollars: "It's always part of their objective to reduce the rate of health care costs, or to reduce accidents or to improve retention—it's just built into the kind of goals that HR has." Communication professionals, on the other hand, Sinickas says, don't always deal with money. "So, if they can work together they can both positively impact ROI."

An important first step is to ensure that research objectives are clear. See "Clarifying Research Objectives."

Clarifying Research Objectives

At the outset of any measurement effort, it's important to clarify your research objectives. In *Communication Research, Measurement and Evaluation,* Williams offers a series of questions that can help you clarify your research objectives and identify the appropriate approach:

• What do I need to know?

• Why do I need to know it?

continued

- What will I do with the information when I find it?

- Who is my audience?

- Do I know what I need to know about them?

- How do I best reach them?

- What is my budget?

- Qualitative or quantitative—or both?

- How do I write the questionnaire?

- How do I administer in the most cost-effective/efficient way?

- How do I tally my results?

- Do I have enough information?

- Do I need causative support?

- How do I best report to management? What results, established benchmarks, and recommendations for moving forward should I present?

- What's the best way to report back to my respondents?

- How do I monitor progress?

- When do I repeat my research?[a]

Can an organization ever be certain that its communication efforts are having an impact? More importantly, can an organization ever be sure its communication efforts are having the *right* impact? The answer to both questions is yes, by developing methods to measure those impacts.

Too often, human resource and employee communication experts lament that "the impact of our communication with employees is difficult—perhaps impossible—to measure. There are too many variables involved. The results are too qualitative."

[a]Louis C. Williams Jr., *Communication Research, Measurement and Evaluation: A Practical Guide for Communicators* (San Francisco: IABC, 2003), 41. Adapted with permission.

Unfortunately, not only does this approach fail to yield information that could be used to improve employee communication, it also adds to an organizational perception that HR is a "soft science." The truth of the matter is that effective employee communication can have a profound impact on an organization and its success.

Most organizations do not measure the effectiveness of their communication programs. Even among the high-performing companies in the Watson Wyatt study, only 29 percent had an ongoing communication program evaluation in place. Of those that did do a formal evaluation, the most common measurement used was the communication audit (66 percent).

Measuring communication impacts is often viewed as an overwhelming and unrewarding endeavor. The human resource or communication professional may feel "intuitively" that the organization's employee newsletter, for example, has a positive impact, but how can that positive impact be demonstrated in a quantitative way?

At its most basic level "measuring" the impact of employee communication could involve nothing more complex than following up a conversation with an employee by asking, "Do you read the employee newsletter?" But measurement doesn't end there. The impact of communication goes beyond usage data. In this case, the next step might be for the communicator to determine how the employee applies the information gleaned from the newsletter in performing her job duties. The question isn't whether the organization is communicating with employees— communication, formal and informal, occurs all the time. The question is whether the things being communicated are having a positive impact on the organization.

How do you know if your communication efforts are working? The process itself is straightforward.

1. Determine, specifically, what it is that you want to impact through improved communication. You can't measure

continued

effectiveness if you don't know what it is you're trying to achieve. For example, perhaps your organization has embarked upon a new organizational direction. Your communication goal might be to ensure that all employees are familiar with the organization's core goals. You want employees to have this awareness so they can direct their own individual performance toward helping the organization meet these goals.

2. Develop a baseline. Where are you now? In this example, you would determine the percentage of employees who are currently aware of the core goals. A simple employee survey could provide you with this information.

3. Develop interventions—communicate! You know what you need to communicate, and you know the current level of awareness of the issue you need to communicate. The next logical step is to develop specific tactics for sharing this information with employees. A good way to do this is through the use of a communication plan—a written document that identifies the audiences you are attempting to reach, the tools that will be used to reach them, a timeline for communication deliverables, and an estimated budget. (More about communication planning is covered in chapter 8.)

4. Do a follow-up measurement. Once the plan has been implemented, a follow-up measurement will determine the impact your communication has had. In this case, do a higher percentage of employees know the organization's core goals following the implementation of the communication plan? Does more work need to be done?

This example was a relatively simple one. Obviously, communication issues are often much more complex. In spite of this complexity, though, it is possible to develop measurement tools that will yield useful information to support the continued use of specific tactics or provide valuable feedback on how to modify those tools so they are more effective.

Common Research Methods

A number of tools can be used to gather information about the effectiveness of your communication efforts, from informal feedback to full-blown communication audits. The tool you choose will depend on the issue you are measuring, the time frame you are dealing with, your budget, and your organization (its size, culture, etc.).

Informal feedback may be as simple as a one-on-one discussion between you and an employee. It might involve a discussion session with a group of employees. Or you might choose to hold a series of focus groups to gather input.

Surveys are a more formal way to gather information and are used when quantitative results are important. Surveys, too, can range from the simple to the more complex. Simple surveys can be developed and used to gauge the effectiveness of various communication efforts—from town hall meetings to "lunch with the CEO."

Focus on questions that provide you with actionable information. For example, a town hall questionnaire might include questions like these:

- Do you feel your time was well spent at this meeting?

- Did you learn information that will help you in your job?

The time, effort, and expense you put into developing measurement tools should be directly related to the importance of the information being conveyed. A simple, do-it-yourself tool would be appropriate for measuring employee response to "lunch with the CEO." A more formal instrument would be more appropriate for measuring the impact of communication related to an organizational merger or restructuring.

In the Internet world, the acronym HITS is often said to stand for "how idiots track success." Simply measuring how many times an Internet page is accessed does not provide information that is actionable or useful. The same theory applies when measuring corporate communication efforts. Knowing that X percent of employees read your internal newsletter is really rather meaningless information. For it to be meaningful, you would need to use this information in conjunction with other data by asking, for example, How do employees *use* the information they receive?

What the "right things" to measure are will vary by company. At a basic level, however, your communication efforts should be designed to further the goals and objectives of the organization. For example:

- Your company is anticipating a major change in health care coverage that it feels will be viewed negatively by employees. A communication plan is put in place to educate employees about the change, why it is happening, and what the change will mean to them. Measuring the percentage of employees aware of the change is not the most meaningful measure. Measuring the percentage of employees who respond favorably to the change might be.

- Your organization is developing a new product for the consumer marketplace. Employees are viewed as important ambassadors for the organization and its products, and a plan is put into place to familiarize all employees with the new product. Measuring the number of employees who know about the product launch is not the most meaningful measure. Measuring the number of employees who respond positively to the new product and who indicate they will share this information with friends and family might be.

The best time to begin thinking of how you will measure the impact of your communication efforts is during communication planning. Start with the end result you hope to achieve. Then work backward from that point to develop the most appropriate tactics to achieve the desired result. Build measurement into the plan so you can determine how effective your communication efforts were.

Typically, when people think "research" they think "survey." While surveys can be useful, you should also consider other methods that are easier, cost less, and are less intrusive to the target audience. Table 4-1, from Williams's *Communication Research, Measurement and Evaluation,* provides a good overview of the advantages and disadvantages of various research methodologies.

TABLE 4-1

Advantages and disadvantages of research methodologies

Methodology	Advantages	Disadvantages
One-on-one interviews	Allows observation, probing, deep, very personal	Location issues, usually not projectable
Focus group	Allows probes, observation, personal	Not projectable, location issues, time to assemble group
Telephone	Allows some probing, interviews somewhat personal, direct, may be projectable (in quantity)	Can't get as deep, time limited, not as personal
Mail	Allows more contacts, orderly, controlled, projectable	Impersonal, slow, postage costs, lower response levels, mostly closed responses and forced choice
Group distribution	Somewhat personal, conveys importance of questionnaire to job for higher response rate	Geography is a factor, as is cost of time off to complete questionnaire
E-mail/ Web site	Fast, much less expensive, easy to tabulate	Must have computer capability, hard to control who responds, must get respondent's attention
Intercepts (personal, one-on-one interviews)	Personal, may allow probing	High turn-down rate, not projectable

Source: Louis C. Williams Jr., *Communication Research, Measurement and Evaluation: A Practical Guide for Communicators* (San Francisco: IABC, 2003). Used with permission.

How can you improve the effectiveness of your measurement efforts? Here are a number of tips and suggestions to get you started:

- **Start with clear objectives.** Before you conduct any research, know what you want to know—and what you will do with the information after the research is completed. Don't ask questions just for the sake of asking. Make sure your research is focused and actionable. And don't just repeat the same research year after year because it's part of your ongoing practices. The work environment changes rapidly, and your research needs to reflect those changes.

- **Choose an appropriate sample.** While you may decide to survey an entire population group (e.g., an employee segment) simply to create a feeling of inclusion, generally you will be selecting a valid sample of an entire population.

- **Choose an appropriate time.** Timing can be a very important factor when you're conducting a survey. For example, you should avoid holidays. You probably wouldn't want to survey employees about job satisfaction during a major corporate downsizing or restructuring (unless, of course, you were attempting to determine how well you were maintaining historical satisfaction levels during this difficult time). The point is, make sure you give consideration to the timing of your research in light of other intervening events.

- **Don't ask what you already know.** For example, if you know that your company's managers are not providing performance evaluations in a timely manner, don't ask employees whether their performance evaluations are conducted in a timely manner. If you have quantifiable data or other sources of information about issues or attitudes, don't waste your—and your employees'—time with a survey.

- **Test your survey before distributing it.** It's easy to overlook the obvious when you're developing a survey. Before rolling out any survey instrument, test the tool on a segment of the overall group—ten to twelve samples should give you a good idea of whether the survey was easy to understand and follow, whether questions were meaningful, and whether you inadvertently missed a key point.

- **Ensure anonymity when appropriate.** Employees, particularly, may be hesitant to respond to surveys unless they're assured that their individual responses will be confidential.

- **Don't ask if you don't want to know.** If you ask employees whether they would be interested in receiving an annual, year-end, cash bonus, and 85 percent say yes, will you be prepared to put such a plan into action? Be cautious about establishing expectations among employees that you won't be able to meet. If you can't (or don't intend to) respond to a need or address a problem, don't ask whether the need or problem exists.

- **Use multiple methods to gather information.** Surveys can be done in a variety of ways—interviews, focus groups, telephone, pen and paper, online. Not all individuals respond equally well to all methods. Consider using multiple methods to meet the needs of all audiences.

- **Consider automating your surveys.** Intranet-based surveys not only provide convenience for those being surveyed but can simplify the analysis process as well. And online surveying can be a good way to do quick "pulse checks."

- **Use benchmarks to measure results.** If 65 percent of your employees say they are highly satisfied with your benefit plan communication, what does this mean? Is this a high percentage or a low percentage? You can't tell unless you have a way to compare your results with results from other comparable studies.

Certain information can help you maximize the effectiveness of your communication research. See "Tips for Effective Communication Research."

Tips for Effective Communication Research

- When using a scale, use an even number of points to force respondents to make a judgment of favorable versus unfavorable. For instance, a 5-point scale allows respondents to select 3, a neutral number. A 4-point scale, on the other hand, forces respondents to choose either a favorable (3 or 4) or an unfavorable (1 or 2) score.

- Don't oversurvey.

continued

- Consider getting employee feedback *before* a communication campaign is initiated. Employees can provide valuable insights that may lead to modifications in messages or approach.

- Don't ignore the feedback you receive. If employees are telling you that they don't read the employee newsletter or they don't find your town hall sessions valuable, you need to act on that information. There are no sacred cows.

- Consider using outside resources when developing surveys or facilitating focus group sessions. Outside perspectives can lend objectivity.

- Beware of "nice to know" versus "need to know." Employees may be interested in birth announcements or birthdays, but will this information help them be more productive, loyal, or efficient?

- An important rule of surveying is, share the results of your survey efforts with respondents. They will be interested in the results and should be rewarded for their participation by learning what the results were.

Research Isn't Always the Answer

A seminar company considering the introduction of a new line of programs that would appeal to a certain profession in a particular state was pondering the appropriate next step. Offer the program, or research the target audience first? The advertising manager suggested doing some market research with the identified target audience before developing and promoting the program. The marketing manager said, "Let's just mail the brochure and see what happens." The advertising manager thought, What a frivolous waste of company resources! But was it?

Let's take a look at some estimated costs of both approaches (see table 4-2).

The cost of "just doing it" in this case, might be slightly higher. *However,* even if the research results indicated that the program seemed promising, you would *still* need to incur an additional $2,750 in expenses to actually promote the program, *and* the results would reveal only what people indicated that they *intended* to do. The actual results obtained from "just doing it" are obviously more meaningful and more accurate than the indication obtained through the survey. And even if the mailing proved to not yield results and the program were canceled, the slightly higher cost might be worth taking the risk of "just doing it."

Sometimes it truly can be wiser and more effective to "do it and see what happens." The key is weighing your options and making thoughtful decisions about when research is—and when it isn't—an appropriate use of resources.

TABLE 4-2

Estimated cost of approaches

Activity	Research	Just do it!
Develop research plan and tool	$75/hr. for 10 hours = $750	N/A
Develop program outline	N/A	$75/hr. for 10 hours = $750
Mail survey	$1,000	N/A
Mail program brochure	N/A	$1,000
Analyze survey response	$75/hr. for 10 hours = $750	N/A
Reserve room, secure speakers	N/A	$1,000
Totals	$2,500 (est.)	$2,750 (est.)

Summing Up

- When you're measuring the impact of your communication efforts, it's important to focus on outcome—not process—measures.

- Not everything that can be measured should be measured!

- Using the "chain of evidence" can help you substantiate communication impacts.

- The right things to measure will vary by company, but your communication efforts should be designed to further the goals and objectives of your organization.

- Considering practical implications and cost versus value can help you determine when—and how—to measure communication efforts most effectively.

Leveraging Chapter Insights: Critical Questions

- Make a list of the process and outcome measures currently used by your HR department. Do you have more process or more outcome measures? Which do you feel are most valuable? Why?

- If you could measure only one communication outcome, what would it be? Why?

- Suppose your organization is considering a change to its health care benefit plan. What research techniques would you use to determine employee preferences for enrollment? Why?

CHAPTER FIVE

Communicating with External Audiences

The Communication Needs and Requirements of Various External Audiences

Key Topics Covered in This Chapter

- *Communication needs of, and HR's role with, key external audiences:*
  - *Customers and consumers*
  - *The news media*
  - *Investors*
  - *Governmental bodies and officials*
  - *The community at large*

W HEN AN ORGANIZATION is communicating with internal (employee) audiences, the role of HR is obvious. But what about when communicating with external audiences? Is there a role for HR to play here as well? There certainly is, although that role may not be so readily apparent. Organizations will be concerned with a number of key external audiences, including customers and consumers, the news media, investors, governmental bodies and officials, the public at large, and the local community.

When you're considering interactions with each of these audiences, remember that they are not mutually exclusive. For example, members of the news media may also be your customers, and their messages certainly reach your customers. Investors may include members of your staff—your internal audience. The interdependencies of these audiences require careful attention to the consistency and timing of communication. Publicly held companies, for example, must follow stringent requirements about the timing of communications that may impact investment decisions—the announcement of a merger, for example. But even private or not-for-profit organizations need to consider the timing of their messages—making sure, for example, that key customers or community leaders are notified of important information before the public at large.

The communication planning process discussed in chapter 8 must take into consideration all these potential audiences and their unique traits and characteristics.

Customers and Consumers

Without customers, clients, or consumers, no business in any industry can prosper. It doesn't matter whether you're a for-profit or a not-for-profit, whether you sell widgets or provide consultative services, whether you're independently owned or publicly traded. Customers are a key stakeholder group and can make or break your business.

Mary Heimstead is a communication consultant with more than twenty-five years' experience in corporate communication and media relations. Customers and consumers, says Heimstead, "can ruin your corporate credibility if you don't tap into their needs quickly. Electric and gas utilities, for example, are regulated by state commissions that hold utilities to a certain standard for consumer complaints. A politically savvy neighborhood association that's suffered through a few long power outages will know how to work the system and the media to its advantage."[1]

As Heimstead points out, consumers can do significant harm to an organization—even when their claims are untrue. Consider the impact of the woman who said she found part of a human finger in her bowl while eating chili at a Wendy's restaurant in San Jose, California, on March 22, 2005. While the woman dropped a lawsuit threat after reports that she had a history of filing claims against other corporations, and was later arrested for attempted grand larceny, her claim resulted in a decline in sales at northern California franchises, causing layoffs and reduced hours, according to the company. Wendy's also incurred expenses in addressing the charge, including the hiring of private investigators, the establishment of a hotline for tips, and the creation of a $100,000 reward for information leading to the finger's original owner.

False claims aren't the only risks that companies face from consumers. The impact of the Internet on organizations' abilities to communicate with customers and consumers has been significant, leading to both positive and negative impacts.

One of the potential negative impacts is "cybersmear," a topic that John L. Hines and Michael H. Cramer covered in an *SHRM*

Legal Report in May–June 2003. The perpetrators of cybersmear, the authors say, are "very difficult to find because they use screen names, guest accounts, anonymizers and other devices to make tracking difficult." And, they add, "even if your company is able to hurdle technological obstacles to find the 'bad guy' or is able to convince a court to order disclosure, taking an aggressive approach may just compound the harm. For example, a corporation may find its cease and desist letter published in a chat room and all its 'threats' of legal action repeated word for word and held up to ridicule."[2]

What can you do? The authors note that a company's program to fight cybersmear should start with its HR department because prevention is the best defense. Most notably, in terms of impacting the customer market, they point out that HR can ensure that executives, managers, and supervisors are trained in the proper way to handle complaints.

In fact, HR serves a critical role even beyond this in terms of ensuring that all staff know the organization's expectations and requirements or standards for interacting with customers and consumers. How your organization communicates with customers—both through general communication materials and through one-on-one interactions—can have a significant effect, positive or negative.

While many organizations point to their customers as their "most important audience," this is not necessarily so! In fact, HR professionals might legitimately argue that *employees* are the most important audience. Without qualified and well-trained employees committed to strong customer service, all other efforts to satisfy customers will be futile.

Ensuring that employees have the knowledge, skill, and ability to effectively interact with and meet the needs of customers is undoubtedly a role for the HR department. HR has a direct impact in terms of hiring individuals with the appropriate knowledge, skills, and abilities (KSAs) to meet customer needs. But from a corporate communication standpoint, HR can also impact communication with customers by ensuring that every individual in the organization is familiar with the organization's customer service philosophy and that they understand how their positions—regardless of how far removed from the actual customer—have an impact on service. HR may also play a role in developing and/or delivering customer service training, which is focused on:

- A customer service philosophy based on the company's unique organizational objectives

- Service delivery expectations and policy guidelines

- Service recovery practices

Employees need to clearly understand the organization's expectations and their role in meeting those expectations. What are the policies and procedures they must follow? How much autonomy do they have in meeting customer needs? Answers to these questions must accurately reflect corporate reality. If employees are told in a training session that "the customer is always right," yet your organization has a thirty-day limit on returns, you are sending a mixed message. It is better to say that you will "meet customer needs within the confines of our generous return policy," or something to that effect.

Most organizations have some form of ongoing measurement of customer satisfaction. For employees serving specific customers or customer groups, this feedback can be directly tied to individual performance—and can be used as an input to the communication planning process. There are a number of ways to gather information on customer satisfaction, including direct observation, phantom shoppers, customer feedback cards and surveys, telephone surveys, and focus groups. Results can help drive improvements through the identification of gaps in current and desired performance and the implementation of communication tactics designed to reduce or eliminate those gaps.

HR has a role to play in helping organizations maintain positive customer relationships. See "How HR Can Help Maintain Positive Customer Relationships" for an outline of the steps HR practitioners can take to enhance their role in this area.

How HR Can Help Maintain Positive Customer Relationships

- Hire right. Select employees who share the organization's values and have the core competencies required to interact positively and effectively with customers.

- Establish and communicate service standards. Make sure employees know what is expected of them in terms of their interactions with customers. What behaviors will and will not be tolerated?

- Provide training focused on specific job or service requirements. General "customer service training" is not enough. Employees must understand specifically what is required of them in their positions and must be provided with the tools and resources needed to perform their jobs.

- Define success. Employees need to have clear expectations; they want to succeed, but they need to know what success "looks like" and how you will be judging their efforts. According to the objectives you identified, quantify as best you can measures of customer service success. Provide these measures to employees as the goals they will be charged with attaining.

- Communicate your expectations—be specific. Don't assume that employees know what you expect in terms of service. Be specific and make sure you "catch them early." A new employee's orientation is the time to communicate your service expectations.

- Provide the tools that employees need to serve your customers. Employees need tools, and need to know how to use those tools, to serve customers effectively. For example, if employees don't have access to e-mail, they may be hampered in communicating effectively with their customers.

- Let employees know their limits. Employees need to know your policies and practices for satisfying customers and responding to complaints. The more flexibility you offer and the more clearly you communicate these guidelines, the better your employees can meet customer needs. Customers benefit, too, when employees can resolve situations "on the spot" instead of having to "talk to my manager."

- Share failures—celebrate successes. Don't just focus on successes. Don't just point out failures. You need a good balance of both failure and success stories to build a strong service culture. Staff can learn from their own failures as well as the failures of others.

- Set a good example from the top down. Employees not only watch how their leaders interact with customers, they listen to what they *say* about customers. If management's attitude toward customers is disparaging, this sends a strong, negative message to employees.

The News Media

Few organizations would relish the thought of Mike Wallace or Michael Moore showing up on their doorstep. The relationship between business and the media is often guarded, sometimes contentious—their goals often at odds. Organizations want to convey a "positive face" to the public; media want to generate news. Reporters are not concerned about making your organization look good or about telling your story. Reporters are, unfortunately, often *most* interested in your company when something bad has happened—when a CEO is involved in a scandal, when an employee or a customer files a lawsuit, when there are rumors of layoffs.

You want to talk about the new product you're introducing. The media want to talk about the environmental damage done by your manufacturing process. You want to talk about the award your company just received. The media want to talk about recent reports of product defects. These divergent goals inevitably lead to conflict. But you can minimize these conflicts by proactively taking steps to build strong relationships with the media.

Your approach to working with the news media, like your approach to any other communication initiative, should be strategic—not tactical or reactive. "Companies waste plenty of time churning out news releases when they really should be focused on strategic plans and tactics that advance their objectives," says Heimstead, who has worked on both sides of the media—as a news reporter and city editor for a newspaper and as a media relations representative for a major utility company.

Having a media strategy involves aligning your media relations efforts with other organizational communication efforts. While the role of HR professionals in relationships with the news media is not as readily apparent as their role with customers, there are opportunities for HR staff to partner with their corporate communication colleagues.

"In addition to a media relations strategy that is responsive to the various calls for information and interviews," says Heimstead, "a smart HR department, for example, will partner with corporate communication to advance projects." For example, in the health care industry, the ability to recruit and retain nursing staff is critical. HR can partner with corporate communication to develop a media strategy that focuses on conveying messages about the working environment that position the organization as an "employer of choice." Or an organization with high turnover and a local perception that it's "not a good place to work" may benefit from a strategic initiative between HR and corporate communication that focuses on improving that image.

Creating "positive press," however, doesn't occur without a great deal of forethought, planning, and—most importantly—relationship building. A number of steps need to be taken:

- Identify the media market that is most critical to your organization. That could mean anything from a few local media outlets to hundreds of outlets, representing every form of media throughout the country—and even internationally.

- Make sure your media market mirrors your consumer market. In other words, view the media as a conduit between your organization and its key customer markets. If the primary market is local, the media market will be local. If the primary market represents a small niche in a particular industry, the media market might consist of a Web site or trade publication that reaches that audience.

- Prioritize. Develop a tiered list of media outlets, with the top tier representing those outlets most likely to cover your organization.

- Learn as much as you can about each of these media outlets, the type of information covered, the tone, the reporters, and so on. The more you know, the better you'll be able to target your own pitches to meet their needs—and the more comfortable you'll be in responding to their inquiries.

- Build relationships. You don't want your first interaction with the media to be when you're not prepared or when the coverage may be negative or critical. If you've developed a solid relationship with the media, you'll be in a much better position to respond to requests that may not show your organization in the best light. An established relationship of trust will serve you well.

- Anticipate issues and be prepared. If a national report comes out that stresses the value of flexible schedules for employees, and your organization has long offered flexible schedules, that's a story you can use to help promote your organization.

- Look for opportunities to tie your activities to national news. Think creatively and look for connections that may not be immediately obvious. Even the personal and professional interests of your staff members can provide opportunities for tie-ins. Anticipating issues also means addressing crises—see more about this in chapter 7.

- Focus your general messages on what you want the media— and, ultimately, your target audience—to know about you. By

developing and focusing on two to three key messages that
you'd like to communicate, you can be sure to include these
messages in each interview you do and each pitch you make.
For example, you might have key messages about your high
percentage of internal promotions, your community support
efforts, or, if you operate in a manufacturing environment, your
safety record. These key messages should relate to and reinforce
your organization's strategies. What messages do you want the
readers or viewers of your media coverage to take away? Those
are the points that you should stress. Regardless of the issue
you're responding to, your goal is to attempt to somehow include your key messages in your response. Often, at the end of
the interview, the reporter will say something like, "Do you
have anything else to add?" or "Are there any additional points
you would like to make?" That's your opportunity to say, "Yes.
I'd just like to emphasize that we feel our efforts are very
important to this community because . . ."

- Refer to your key messages often throughout an interview.
  While you can never anticipate with 100 percent accuracy
  what questions the reporter might ask you, you do know with
  100 percent certainty what *your* key messages are. Don't be
  afraid to repeat them. Keep in mind that interviews are made
  up of sound bites, and you can never know which comments
  the reporter will decide to use. If you make the same key points
  again and again, albeit in slightly different ways, you can be
  more confident that *your* messages will reach the audience.

- Choose spokespeople that represent you well. The best person
  to offer for any media interview is the person with the most
  knowledge of or expertise with the topic being covered—and
  the person closest to the story.

- Maintain control. Don't be intimidated by the media. They
  need you and your cooperation as much as you need their
  unbiased and professional handling of whatever issue you're
  being interviewed about. So while you should be aware of

media deadlines and attempt to honor them whenever possible, never feel pressured to respond to a media inquiry. Always take the time to make sure that you've gathered the background information and facts you need, that you've developed your key messages (the points you want to come out in the resulting story), and that the right spokesperson has been selected and adequately briefed and prepared.

- Take advantage of live interviews. Most spokespeople dread the live interview, never realizing that it is their best opportunity to ensure that the points they want to make are made—and received by the audience. What you say is received verbatim by the television or radio audience, which gives you a great deal of control over the messages you communicate. Take advantage of that opportunity by focusing on your key messages. If you study seasoned spokespeople, you'll see that they can respond to just about any reporter's question by "looping back" to one of their own messages with such statements as "I don't have any information about *that,* but what I *can* tell you is (insert key message)," or "We haven't found that to be true, *but* (key message)."

- Make the reporter's job easy. Provide background information and additional materials, especially if your message is complex and you're concerned about the reporter getting it right. The added benefit of providing background information is that because reporters are busy people, if you've provided good information that's well prepared and not too self-promotional, it's likely to be used.

- Know when to let a story die a natural death. When a negative story hits the news, especially when you feel some information has been left out or misstated, it can be tempting to strike back by writing a letter to the editor or running a paid ad with your side of the story. This is rarely a good strategy. Even the most scandalous stories will fade away if the flames aren't fanned by additional coverage. When you respond, you invite further response. The end result of a defensive response often is that the story drags out over several days, weeks, or months, reaching far more people and generating far more interest than the initial story might have generated. Sometimes it's just best to take it on the chin and move on.

Some simple tips can help HR professionals deal with the media positively. See "Dos and Don'ts of Dealing with the News Media."

Always remember that the media are not in control, says Larry L. Smith, president of the Institute for Crisis Management. You are. "If

Dos and Don'ts of Dealing with the News Media

- Don't offer information "off the record." There is no such thing. Everything you say or do is "on the record" and fair game for the reporter to use.

- Don't say "no comment." You should always be able to offer some sort of comment, even if it's something as generic as "We can't really offer an opinion about that" or "We haven't had an opportunity to review that study."

- Don't ask whether you can review the article, hear the specific sound bite that will be used, or view the TV segment before it's aired. That marks you as an amateur. But do feel free to say something like, "Please let me know if you have any additional questions once you start developing this piece, or if there are any facts you'd like to check."

- Do contact the reporter if an error is made. You have every right to follow up with a reporter if incorrect information has been used. Be polite and nonaccusatory. (But make sure you can distinguish between facts and perspectives.)

- Finally, understand that the media can't report your story if you're not willing to talk. Companies frequently refuse to share information with the media and then later lament that the media "got it wrong" or "didn't tell the whole story."

you abdicate the control, it will be a very unsatisfactory outcome for you." Smith recommends telling the media, up front, what the rules and expectations are. "You have to have people who know how to take control—how to be firm, but fair."

Smith preaches a "use and be used" philosophy. "It's moral, ethical, and legal. Reporters are looking for sources to get information for their stories. Everyone in an organization should be looking for reporters to tell their story." On any given day, every organization has some story to tell. Look for those opportunities to tell your story.

In dealing with the media, says Smith, "there are two unwritten rules. The reporter has to be fair and the spokesperson has to be honest. If you abide by those two unwritten rules, everybody is going to benefit. The story will probably not be exactly what the reporter was looking for, or exactly what you wanted it to be, but by and large most of the time the story will be beneficial to the organization that's putting it out there and will meet a need that the reporter has to fill time and space."

Larry Smith shares an example of crisis communication from the Columbine tragedy. See "Staying Calm During Columbine."

Staying Calm During Columbine

Larry Smith, president of the Institute for Crisis Management, says that during the Columbine shootings, Steve Davis, the Sheriff Department's public affairs officer, did an exceptional job of controlling what could have easily become a very out-of-control situation by taking charge and setting ground rules. Media from around the world descended on the community—Davis held them at bay. In a "calm and measured" voice, says Smith, Davis said, "I'll take your questions one at a time." Smith adds, "It didn't take long for those folks to figure out that if they reacted calmly and responsibly, he would answer their questions as best he could." Before that briefing was over, they were orderly, he had control—and the media were getting their questions

continued

answered. He excused himself and came back an hour later. The media had multiplied threefold. Again they were unruly. Again he restored control calmly and firmly. "As the evening progressed," says Smith, "the news conference became more orderly, Davis had more time to answer more questions. He had confidence in himself and he set the rules."

The media face that same control when reporting from Capitol Hill, says Smith, who spent time in Washington, D.C., as press secretary to then-Senator Dan Quayle. "There's a set-up time and a start time. You're either in at the start time or you don't go in. There are parts of the room you can move around in and parts of the room that you can't," Smith says.

The bottom line is, you can—and should—have rules for how you will and will not interact with the media. Be fair, but be firm.

Investors

Enron. The scandal that brought this corporation to its knees had perhaps the greatest impact on investor relations since the beginnings of the New York Stock Exchange in 1792. Enron wasn't alone. It was joined in scandal by several other notable companies, all challenged to defend questionable accounting practices and all contributors to the environment of mistrust that today's organizations and their CEOs find themselves in.

HR and communication professionals have a key role to play in helping to rebuild or maintain the trust that investors have in their organizations. A good place to start is with an understanding of Regulation Fair Disclosure (FD), the Sarbanes-Oxley Act (SOX), and the implications of these regulations on communication and disclosures.

Regulation FD was adopted on August 15, 2000, by the Securities and Exchange Commission (SEC) to address the selective disclosure of information by publicly traded companies and other issuers. Regulation FD provides that when an issuer discloses material nonpublic information to certain individuals or entities—generally, securities market professionals, such as stock analysts, or holders of the issuer's securities who may well trade on the basis of the information—the issuer must make public disclosure of that information.

The Sarbanes–Oxley Act of 2002 came about as a direct result of corporate scandals involving organizations like Enron, WorldCom, and Arthur Andersen. Effective in 2004, all publicly traded companies were required to submit an annual report of the effectiveness of their internal accounting controls to the SEC. The major provisions of SOX include criminal and civil penalties for noncompliance violations, certification of internal auditing by external auditors, and increased disclosure regarding all financial statements. Sarbanes–Oxley also established new accountability standards for corporate boards and auditors, and established a Public Company Accounting Oversight Board (PCAOB) under the SEC.

"If they haven't already," says Heimstead, "HR departments need to bone up on newer disclosure regulations to ensure they aren't speaking about material issues that need to be disclosed in a particular manner. HR departments also ought to be relying on consultants or in-house experts to work with the investor community. And HR ought to be cognizant of employee reactions when major events are disclosed to the investor community before or at the same time that they are disclosed to internal audiences."

In addition, Heimstead advises, "on an ongoing basis organizations should inform employees of strategies and rules that prevent prior disclosure. If your company is involved in mergers and acquisitions, you need to educate your workforce on these investor-related issues."

Concerns about the impacts of these regulations on communication between publicly traded companies and shareholders and analysts prompted the National Investor Relations Institute (NIRI) to conduct a survey of its members to determine whether there had been any negative impacts. According to a news release issued on June 11, 2003, there was "no evidence to suggest that companies are restricting the flow of information to key audiences in any significant way or shying away from traditional forums for shareholder and analyst communications. Participation rates of companies in one-on-one and small group analyst/investor meetings and in breakout sessions following presentations at analyst/investor conferences continue to track those preceding the adoption of Regulation FD and the enactment of Sarbanes-Oxley."[3]

Effective investor relations requires communication strategies that address both the investor and internal audiences. A 2003 survey of corporate investor relations officers (IROs) by MessageBank, LLC, a provider of conference calling services to the investor relations marketplace, found that corporate communication was providing "consistent information and real-time feedback to all levels of management in order to comply with governance and disclosure regulations." About 58 percent of respondents were communicating to employees about earnings following the quarterly call. "Clearly, IROs are increasingly focused on expanding communication efforts with what is often the largest shareholder base in a public company: the employees," said Steven Fink, executive vice president of MessageBank, in a news release issued by the company.[4]

The survey identified the following factors as being most critical in influencing and establishing a company's investment appeal: earnings growth, cash flow, sales or revenue growth, quality of senior management personnel, adherence to fair-disclosure and governance regulations, corporate strategy executive, and the company's long-term strategy. In addition, IROs were increasingly active in conducting and promoting formal communication with the investment community. Nearly all (94 percent of respondents) held live meetings with the investment community, 96 percent conducted one-on-one sessions, and 98 percent held quarterly conference calls. Additional findings included the following:

- The number of conference call attendees averaged 171 in 2002.

- Nearly all conference calls were Webcasts—94 percent broadcast live Webcasts of their conference calls (up from 67 percent in 2001).

- Webcasts were archived on corporate Web sites for at least fourteen days by most companies (88 percent) and remained posted for up to thirty days by 76 percent.

- The most common method of providing access to a playback of the call was via Web archive (79 percent), followed by a toll-free audio playback (65 percent).

- Companies typically provided the following information on their sites:

  - Quarterly earnings releases (99 percent)
  - Press releases other than earnings (95 percent)
  - Annual report (95 percent)
  - SEC filings such as the 10-K or 10-Q (92 percent)
  - Transfer agent information (87 percent)
  - Detailed information on products and services (77 percent)
  - Calendar of events (76 percent)
  - Archived audio conference calls (88 percent)
  - Biographies of senior management (72 percent)
  - Fact sheets or corporate profiles (68 percent)
  - Historical stock price information (68 percent)

Unfortunately, the nature of this information is often complex—unnecessarily so, say some. Mark Utting, a chartered financial analyst (CFA) and financial writer with experience writing management's discussion and analysis (MD&A) and annual reports, wrote an article titled "Readable MD&A" for IRontheNet.com in March 2003, in which he offered some helpful suggestions for the preparation of the MD&A that readily apply to *any* aspects of investor communication:

- Wazzup? Forget the boring business overview. Deliver all the company's key messages of performance, strategy, and financial position.

- What are you leveraging? Clearly discuss the factors that drive the company's financial results and share price.

- Where are you taking the company? Present the MD&A "through the eyes of management," focusing on long-term strategy and value creation.

- Given your strategy, how did you do? Provide an assessment of performance relative to management's expectations. Candor is a great way to build credibility.

- Can you pay your bills? Most investors don't care about accounting wizardry. They want to know what is likely to cost the company money and if you have the cash to pay for it.

- What keeps you awake at night? Management knows what they're concerned about, and what risks are most often discussed at board meetings.

- What happens next? How much further does the company plan to progress with its strategy in the coming year?

- Who's calling the shots? When reporting through the eyes of management, it helps to know whose eyes.[5]

At an SEC Financial Disclosure and Auditor Oversight Roundtable in 2002, Louis Thompson Jr., president and CEO of NIRI, said, "I would re-emphasize that the role of investor relations is to minimize investor risk by assuring that the company is providing information that is clear and understandable through means that achieve full and fair disclosure. The lower the perceived risk in investing in a company, the lower the company's cost of capital. There is a true bottom line benefit of full and fair disclosure."[6]

Governmental Bodies and Officials

Another important corporate audience is governmental bodies and officials. Every organization is governed to some degree. Some organizations—public utilities, health care organizations, and so on—are subject to significant governance. In addition, organizations often wish to influence governmental bodies and officials to generate support for laws and policies that may have a favorable impact on the organization.

Government relations departments developed in the 1960s and 1970s as companies struggled to find ways of maintaining positive relationships with regulators. Key strategies for doing this include distributing position papers, testifying before committees, lobbying regulators, and supporting the political campaigns of elected officials. By forming close ties with legislators and regulators, managers try to ingratiate themselves with powerful monitors and participate in shaping more favorable environments for their activities.[7]

What is government relations all about? The best way to illustrate is with an example. The Portland Business Alliance—the chamber of commerce for Portland, Oregon, states its government relations goal as follows: "To develop and advocate policies that contribute to an enhanced business climate for the downtown area, the greater metropolitan region, and the state of Oregon." Toward that end, it has a number of objectives that illustrate the types of activities that a government relations function might undertake:

- In partnership with other area and regional associations and governments, drive the development and launch of a Portland-Vancouver regional business planning process.

- Address issues of affordability for business in the Portland metropolitan area, by working with other civic organizations to implement reforms suggested by the City Budget Review, focusing on establishment of a City Budget Review Advisory Committee, continuing work to contain and drive down water and sewer costs, and advocating for review of the city/county business tax structure.

- Develop a report which establishes an information baseline for evaluating K-12 investments and performance, adopt a comprehensive statement of policy on K-12 education, define the manner in which the Alliance will be involved, and work with education partners on efforts to identify workforce training needs.

- Support regional efforts to draft land-use policies that reflect the needs of a strong economy, with a focus on Goal 5 policy-setting and identification of readily developable industrial lands and the city of Portland's River Renaissance program.

- Continue to support strong transportation policies and projects in the region, focusing on Portland Mall rehabilitation, implementation of a comprehensive regional transportation investment package, improvement of Columbia River bridge crossings, and implementation of regional and statewide freight mobility strategies.

- Support action in the 2005 Regular Legislative Session regarding health care cost containment legislation, providing adequate K-12 funding, and supporting area transportation projects.

- Work with city and county officials and other partners to decrease the level of criminal activity in downtown Portland.

- Assist the new Mayor of Portland in the transition in office and over the next year whenever possible.[8]

As with other communication efforts, the key to effectiveness with the government relations function lies in clearly tying communication efforts to the strategies and goals of the organization.

Much like a company's employees, governmental agencies and community officials like to be in the know, says Heimstead. "HR should be aware of the need to inform these groups whenever there are major announcements. Whenever possible," she adds, "these groups should be in the loop ahead of the news media because they will likely be asked for comment. For example, if an organization is involved in a major expansion that involves millions of dollars in construction awards and an expanded workforce, the media will probably want to talk to the mayor or city manager about its effect on the community. Your company won't be in good graces with city officials if you haven't engaged them in discussions before you break the news to the media."

The Community at Large

The purpose of the typical community relations department is to convey a company's benevolence, corporate citizenship, and social responsiveness. Key strategies range from pro bono activities and charitable contributions to relationship building with artistic, educational, and cultural institutions. In this way, companies integrate themselves into their local communities and surround their activities with a positive halo of goodwill.[9]

Community relations efforts generally encompass corporate volunteerism and charitable giving—efforts that impact community perceptions about the organization. Again, these efforts need to be strategic and aligned with the overall corporate vision and strategy. HR can play a role in establishing positive community relations. See "HR's Role in Community Relations."

HR's Role in Community Relations

The experiences of several organizations in South Florida illustrate the role that HR can play in partnering with the public relations function to impact community perceptions. Alexandra Bassil leads the human resources/public relations practice at Bernard Hodes Group and was the project manager on a case study that brought HR and corporate communication professionals together from several South Florida corporations that wished to recruit diverse candidates.

Ryder, Royal Caribbean Cruises Ltd., Office Depot, Inc., NCCI Holdings, Inc., and Florida Power & Light Company wanted to position themselves as the diversity employers of choice in South Florida. They faced perceived and actual barriers to the recruitment and retention of minority candidates and were all working with a limited budget. Their goals were to both attract a diverse staff to the area and retain those employees in a cost-effective manner.

continued

The companies, aided by Bernard Hodes, formed a corporate recruitment alliance—the South Florida Avenue Coalition. The alliance was conceived with the idea that such a unification would prove more effective for exhibition at national professional association meetings, conventions, and career fairs— specifically those sponsored by Hispanic and African American associations. The coalition would also maximize exposure of Florida-based corporations while achieving cost benefits resulting from economies of scale. The group wished to create an interest in the cultural activities and family-oriented environment found in the area, propelling individuals to consider relocation and career opportunities in Florida.

Bernard Hodes coordinated the participation, design elements, public relations, and advertising for all events. The coalition attended and marketed its unified image at the 2000 and 2001 conferences of the National Black MBA Association (NBMBAA) and National Society of Hispanic MBAs (NSHMBA). It promoted the South Florida Avenue Coalition to conference attendees using special advertising and public relations activities and branded the companies as employers committed to building diversity. The booth space, advertising, and public relations initiatives displayed a consistent message, branding the coalition and its commitment to diversity.

The efforts paid off. The South Florida Avenue Coalition established strong relationships between the candidates, NBMBAA, NSHMBA, and the coalition companies. It also made eight hires by the first quarter of 2002 at a much lower cost than if it had used executive search firms. Even more notable was its ability to expand the reach of individual recruiters by sharing resumes collected at the conferences. Public relations tactics generated an estimated 2.1 million impressions and contributed to the overall diversity image of the member companies. The recruitment effort grew from five companies in 2000 to ten companies in 2001. New members included Burger King Corporation, Citrix Systems, Inc., JM Family Enterprises, Inc., and Sports Authority, Inc.

There are clearly strategic benefits from effective community relations efforts and a role for HR in the process. A survey conducted by the United Nations Development Program (UNDP), PricewaterhouseCoopers, the Confederation of Indian Industry, and the British Council evaluated the perceptions, drivers, hindrances, prevalent approaches, and issues of corporate volunteerism and future leadership affecting corporate social responsibility (CSR). Respondents indicated that a desire to be a "good corporate citizen" and to "improve brand image" drives CSR. Of those responding to the survey, 81 percent had defined ethics requirements, 76 percent had environmental requirements, 72 percent met all regulatory compliance requirements, and 76 percent had clearly defined health and safety requirements. Other key findings of the research are as follows:

- Social responsibility is not the exclusive domain of government, and "passive philanthropy" alone no longer constitutes CSR.

- The majority of the respondents ranked ethical conduct including compliance, transparency of business, and nation building among the definitions closest to their perception of CSR.

- The respondents considered business ethics, compliance with regulatory requirements, and consistency in value delivery as three of the most important factors that impact the social reputation of a corporation.

- Most of the companies surveyed include social responsibility in the corporate strategy, and its conceptualization and deployment in most cases is at the highest level in the organization. The top four influences on CSR strategy are management (according to 98 percent of respondents), the board and employees (over 80 percent of respondents), local communities (67 percent of respondents), and shareholders (61 percent of respondents).

continued

- CSR is perceived as a mechanism to proactively approach and address significant regulatory requirements. Accordingly, in pursuit of CSR, systems, policies, and guidelines are delineated for concerns such as health, safety, and the environment.

- Absence of clear linkage between CSR and financial success was identified as the principal barrier to CSR. Lack of mechanisms to measure, monitor, evaluate, and report the impact of CSR initiatives is also seen as a major barrier.

- Many companies see a great future for earning profits through ethical conduct of business; complying with regulatory requirements, with a greater emphasis on protection of the environment; and employee health and safety.

Volunteerism is a key element of many companies' community outreach efforts. A study by the Points of Light Foundation (www.pointsoflight.org) of chief executives of leading businesses with proven track records of social responsibility provided insights into how being a good corporate citizen influences business success. The report revealed that companies like GE, Levi Strauss & Company, Pitney Bowes, and Walt Disney Company agree that workplace volunteer programs, which encourage employees to share their time and talent, help businesses achieve company objectives and deliver on their values.

"It's important to truly understand your corporate values, to communicate them clearly to all your employees, and to live them. I personally believe that community service contributes to business success in many ways. I also believe that we have a responsibility to give back to the communities in which we live and work," says James H. Quigley, CEO of Deloitte, which sponsored the publication of the report.[10]

The report validated the findings of another study on corporate community involvement, the 2003 State of Corporate Citizenship survey, conducted by the Center for Corporate Citizenship at Boston

College and the Center for Corporate Citizenship at the U.S. Chamber of Commerce, which reported that more than 90 percent of respondents stated that they had increased or maintained their efforts to reach out to economically distressed communities over the past two years. Seventy-five percent of respondents believed corporate citizenship was driven largely by internal corporate values, 53 percent by customer feedback. Eighty-two percent believed that good corporate citizenship helps the bottom line.

Summing Up

Some important and consistent themes exist among all these audiences:

- Communication strategies should be strategic and should be aligned with the overall corporate mission, vision, values, and goals.

- Managing the relationship with these audiences will serve to support and strengthen your company's reputation and image.

- The basics apply: identify your key messages, understand the audience and its existing perceptions. Develop strategies and tactics to influence those perceptions favorably (see chapter 8).

- Collaboration and cooperation between HR and related functions can enhance the value of communication efforts.

Leveraging Chapter Insights: Critical Questions

- In what ways is your HR department currently involved in communication activities designed to improve relationships with and service to customers? What additional opportunities exist for this involvement?

- Do members of your HR department interact regularly with local, regional, or national news media? Think of three key

HR-related stories or issues that could help your company strengthen its image in your community. Are there any HR-related stories or issues that you would *not* want to be covered by the media?

• How could your HR department collaborate more effectively with other departments in your organization to improve communication efforts?

CHAPTER SIX

Communicating with Employees

Strategies and Tactics for Communication with Internal Audiences

Key Topics Covered in This Chapter

- *Employee communication as a process*
- *Leadership support through modeling and "walking the talk"*
- *The critical role of frontline management*
- *Encouraging two-way communication*
- *Steps in creating an effective internal communication strategy*
- *Strategies, techniques, and tips for effective employee communication*
- *Measuring employee communication efforts*

T HE BETTER YOU communicate with employees, the better your return on investment (ROI). So says Watson Wyatt, and it has the data to prove it. Its *Connecting Organizational Communication to Financial Performance—2003/2004 Communication ROI Study* indicated that a significant improvement in communication effectiveness is associated with a 29.5 percent increase in market value. Additional findings include the following:

- Companies with the highest levels of effective communication experienced a 26 percent total return to shareholders from 1998 to 2002, compared to a −15 percent return experienced by firms that communicate least effectively.

- Organizations that communicate effectively were more likely to report employee turnover rates below or significantly below those of their industry peers.

Organizations can communicate effectively with employees and drive business performance, Watson Wyatt asserts, by:

- Building a strong foundation of formal communication structure and processes, which rely on employee feedback and use technology to connect with employees effectively

- Dealing directly with the strategic issues of change, continuous improvement, and business strategy integration and alignment

- Creating real employee behavioral change by driving change in managers' and supervisors' behavior and by creating a line of sight between employees and customers

To be effective, says Shel Holtz in *Corporate Conversations,* "employee communication must achieve the following three results, which are critical to an organization's success:

1. "Employees represent the company to external audiences in a manner consistent with the image the company's leaders want the outside world to see. They walk the talk. They are brand ambassadors. Their behavior represents the ideal that company leaders desire. Instead of covering breeches of ethics or wrongdoing by employees, the press winds up covering employee involvement in the community or tales of employee innovation.

2. "Employees produce quality work that satisfies the needs of customers. They innovate and collaborate to produce what the company needs them to produce, helping the company achieve competitiveness and profitability.

3. "Employees don't quit to go work someplace better. Companies that experience high turnover (or 'churn')—particularly among higher-level staff and key contributors—struggle to find the talent required to execute the company's plans."[1]

Good communication, says Kathryn Yates, head of the global communication practice with Watson Wyatt, goes beyond "just transferring information." Good communication, she says, "really inspires people to do things differently or to think differently." To achieve these ends, says Yates, communicators need to take some cues from their marketing colleagues—"you really need to deploy sophisticated marketing techniques of audience segmentation, developing compelling messages and creative design. All of those things have to come into play because, of course, we're all incredibly sophisticated consumers."[2]

In an SHRM/*USA Today* Job Satisfaction Poll of both HR professionals and employees (see figure 6-1), the importance of communication between employees and management was ranked as either very important or important by 98 percent of all HR professionals and 96 percent of all employees.

Communication plays a critical role in conveying an organization's commitment and credibility to employees. In an era when

FIGURE 6-1

Importance of communication between employees and management

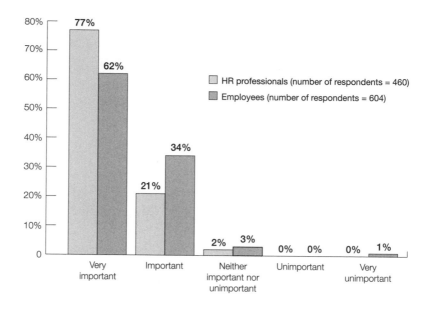

Source: SHRM/USA Today Job Satisfaction Poll. Used with permission.

corporate credibility is increasingly on shaky ground, this role becomes even more meaningful to corporate communicators.

In August 2002 SHRM and the Council of Public Relations Firms conducted a survey of both HR professionals and employees to address the question, How well are organizations demonstrating their commitment and credibility to employees? Results offer an overview of the similarities and differences between these two groups and provide solid guidance for the focus of employee communication activities. Key findings were as follows:

- Overall, it appeared that HR professionals had a slightly more positive attitude about their organizations' communications (95 percent). However, a majority of employees (82 percent) also indicated that their organizations were always or usually open and honest.

- Both HR (63 percent) and employees (59 percent) considered appreciation to be shown at good or very good levels. The fact that employees appear to be satisfied with organizational efforts in this area indicates that communication programs associated with showing appreciation are working.

Both groups indicated the best ways for companies to strengthen credibility among employees are to share both good and bad news as promptly and as fully as possible and to increase two-way communication between management and employees. Interestingly, employees appeared to more strongly believe that each method of communication presented could help strengthen credibility among employees.

Employee Communication as a Process

There's not a company in the world that doesn't need to concern itself with communicating with employees. The larger the organization, of course, the more complex these communication issues become. At some point, the issues may become overwhelming. Consider, for example, the communication needs raised by issues such as mergers and acquisitions, downsizings or plant closings, benefit changes, product defects, and so on. Even absent these situation-based impacts, companies need to communicate with employees about goals and objectives and business results. Companies that communicate effectively find a positive correlation between these activities and the satisfaction and productivity of their staff members.

Employee communication—just as any other type of communication initiative—starts with a strategy. Communication shouldn't occur haphazardly. It should not be event focused—an e-mail to announce a new product introduction, a flyer to promote an employee event, an intranet posting to announce annual benefit enrollment.

Communication is a process, not an event. Unfortunately, in many companies, employee communication becomes little more than a series of unrelated and uncoordinated events. Communication happens, but its overall value to the organization is questionable.

Employee communication should be undertaken strategically and coordinated centrally to ensure that messages are appropriately linked with corporate strategy and conveyed appropriately. Simply sending out messages to employees regardless of how frequent, how helpful, or how well received is not strategic and is not likely to generate the desired results. Without coordination, messages can have unintended consequences.

Consider an employee on the front line of a typical organization. The employee is bombarded daily with messages from a variety of points within the organization. Without centralization and coordination, a department whose manager "loves to communicate" may inadvertently develop an image as a "very important area of the organization" simply because of the sheer volume of communications generated. Left to their own devices, department managers—and their staff—may also inadvertently generate messages that fail to support, or may even detract from, the organization's mission, strategies, or desired image.

"HR plays a really critical role in communication," says Larry Smith of the Institute for Crisis Management. "From our perspective, internal communication is probably more important, more often, than external communication. I see companies that spend a million dollars on an external PR campaign and ignore the internal audience. One unhappy or misinformed employee can undermine or destroy a million-dollar campaign pretty easily."

An effective, and strategic, employee communication plan starts by responding to the question, What do employees need to know to support the organization's goals and direction? It's that simple—and that complex.

The complexities come into play both because the employee audience at most organizations is not homogeneous (it represents multiple, distinct segments) and because most organizations have a myriad of messages that a myriad of people (depending on their perspectives and areas of influence) all feel are *the most important things to communicate.*

The corporate communicator's role in the process is, therefore, made much more straightforward if the organization already has a well-developed strategic plan that clearly outlines the organization's goals and objectives and provides direction on "the most important things." However, even if your organization doesn't have such a plan, there are steps that can be taken to impact the effectiveness of employee communication and to ensure that these efforts are process focused—not event focused.

Addressing the Challenges of Effective Employee Communication

Even at the smallest organization and even with top management support, the task of communicating effectively to employees can be complex. Communication challenges mirror societal, industry, and organizational challenges. The environment in which you do business changes, and as those changes occur, communication needs shift. New threats appear. New challenges are presented. New issues arise. A change in upper management—particularly at the very top of an organization—can cause a shift in organizational culture. A merger, buyout, reorganization, or downsizing can challenge even the most skillful communicators. Just one manager who fails to "live by" the corporate communication model can have a dramatic negative effect on trust—and can threaten even the most skillfully planned and carefully executed communication efforts.

Fortunately, even though the challenges are great, certain commonalities and a measure of consistency can be found in organizations that are known for effectively communicating with their employees.

It Starts at the Top

The role of HR and corporate communication is to take the messages that have been framed by upper management and ensure that they are communicated frequently, consistently, and effectively throughout the organization. While those in a corporate communication role can help frame and guide those messages, they do not "own" the messages—leadership does. That means that even if you're not fully in agreement with the direction the organization is taking, your communication efforts must nevertheless support that direction. Communication is not the "tail that wags the dog."

The first step in developing an effective internal communication strategy is to clearly understand the communication goals and key messages that the organization wishes to communicate.

Prepare Employees to "Hear" the Messages

While top management is clearly the critical "first step" in any effective employee communication initiative, both HR and corporate communication staff play pivotal support roles. It's not enough to have top management articulate messages to be sent to employees if the employees aren't prepared to receive the messages.

Karen Horn has extensive experience as an employee communicator and says that she has found that at least 70 percent of what employees want to know has to do with their own work unit—the day-to-day issues that have a direct impact on employees' "life at work." Communicating the organization's "strategic goals" is important—but meaningful only if a connection is made between those goals and what they mean to an employee who has a job to do and simply wants to know that they're doing the right job, the right way.

Other intervening events or concerns can also impact the ability of employees to fully connect with the messages the organization wishes to send. For example, if employees are focused on concerns over being downsized, they are unlikely to be able to focus on corporate messages.

Maslow's hierarchy of needs offers a meaningful model to illustrate the need for employees to have their basic needs met before they're able to move on to higher-level issues. Roger D'Aprix has developed a tool for training managers in how to help employees move from those lower-level needs to a point where they're ready to hear the organizational messages. The training leads management through the process of recognizing and responding to some fundamental questions that employees have on the job. The first three questions are "me based": What's my job? How am I doing? Does anybody care? Until these three questions are addressed, employees cannot move on to the next levels of D'Aprix's model. The fourth and fifth levels are more "we focused": How are *we* doing? Where do we (our team) fit in? And, finally, step six: How can I help?[3]

The challenge for corporate communicators is translating those "corporate messages" into meaningful pieces of information that will resonate with employees.

Modeling the Culture—"Walking the Talk"

Culture isn't built through memorization of mission, vision, or value statements. Frontline managers may be able to reiterate the organization's value statements, but if their actions don't support those words, they are probably sending mixed messages to employees. For communication efforts to be effective, the organization—in particular, both top and frontline management—has to demonstrate through word, deed, policies, practices, and procedures that it is "walking the talk." A disconnect between your formal communication and your actual practices will undermine even the best-planned communication efforts.

One of the best ways to establish trust with employees is through direct communication. Face-to-face communication builds trust and credibility. Of course, it is not always practical, or possible, to connect face-to-face with employees. The challenge, then, is how can you establish relationships between upper management and line employees in an organization that employs several thousand people in many diverse locations? Technology has made this possible—whether that involves satellite broadcasts, Webcasts, or online forums and chat rooms (see chapter 9).

Providing Support and Training for Frontline Management

Frontline managers are critical to successful communication. The closer you are to the employees, the more impact your messages have. These managers shouldn't be left to their own devices, though. They need to be provided with the information, the tools, and the training and coaching to ensure that they're functioning effectively in their role as a communication conduit to employees. Strong communication skills are not necessarily skills that all managers have. Nor do managers always define *communication* the same way employees do.

While at GE Capital, Karen Horn says, "we saw a huge gap between how employees defined communication and how managers defined communication." When managers were asked to define communication, they pointed to tools or events like newsletters, meetings, and so on. Employees, on the other hand, viewed communication as a process—how they got the information they needed to do their job. Employees were interested in the answers to questions like What is my job?, How am I doing?, How are we doing?, and Where are we going?

"If managers are the ones who lead communication and they think it's something different than their customers (the employees), we have a conflict," Horn says. To bridge the gap and provide managers with the information they needed to fulfill their role, GE Capital developed a "toolkit" that Horn says included "some pretty simple tools." While simple, the toolkit had an impact. It gave managers information on how communication is really defined—from the "employee as customer" standpoint. And it gave practical information on how to communicate effectively—from a process standpoint.

Multiple Messages in Multiple Ways

Once is not enough. For your communication to have an impact, employees need to hear your key messages over and over again through multiple sources. That reinforcement and repetition will eventually result in the outcomes you're looking for.

Encouraging Two-Way Communication

There is, typically, no shortage of tools to convey corporate messages to employees. But even with so many tools, are organizations really communicating? In many cases they're not. Management sends messages down to employees. Employees attempt to send messages back up to management. Unfortunately, all too often, those messages are not part of a dialogue but part of the growing communication clutter that exists at many companies.

It's not enough to have the tools. It's not enough to craft messages that support company goals and share those goals with employees. It's not enough to offer feedback mechanisms.

What's required to encourage employees to talk to you?

- **Desire.** They need to believe they have something of value to say—something that's related to organizational goals and mission.

- **Opportunity.** This is where the tools come in. But in addition to the tools that technology makes available—like e-mail, intranet forums, and phone-in comment lines—employees need opportunity for face-to-face feedback.

- **Trust.** Without a climate of trust, employees are highly unlikely to share their thoughts and ideas. In an era of downsizing, reorganizations, mergers, and acquisitions, employees are often afraid to say what they think.

How can you encourage employees to provide honest and appropriate feedback? How can you encourage them to engage in meaningful discussion with your company? By creating the desire. By providing the opportunity. By building an atmosphere of trust. And to ensure that all the pieces of your communication efforts are working effectively, by monitoring and measuring employee opinions and attitudes.

HR plays a major role in this process, either through an employee communication function that is part of the HR department or as a partner with the corporate communication department. Actions speak louder than words. How your organization responds to employee feedback will directly influence the type of feedback you receive. If employees learn that even their most critical comments will be responded to promptly, honestly, and without rancor, they will begin to trust. If the opposite occurs—if their feedback is ignored, if the organization's responses are superficial, or if they experience, or feel that others have experienced, any type of retribution—they will not feel free to provide honest feedback or information.

Developing an Employee Communication Strategy

Developing an effective employee communication strategy involves a step-by-step process that ensures that your frontline messages are aligned with organizational goals and direction.

Follow these steps to create an effective internal communication strategy:

1. **Build the business case.** Employee communication starts at the top. The CEO and executive leadership set the stage for communication through their words and deeds. As a communicator—whether in the HR structure or in a corporate communication environment—if you can convince top management that communicating with employees is a critical organizational priority, the tough part is over. How do you convince senior executives that strong internal communication is in their best interest? From a dollar and cents standpoint, an image standpoint, and a competitive perspective. To gain senior management commitment, focus on the business reasons for enhanced employee communication. Use survey data from your organization and gather examples and information from other sources, such as the Watson Wyatt research, to substantiate the need to consider employee communication a critical part of the organization's communication efforts. Contact communicators in other organizations—you'll be surprised at how willing most are to share information and experiences that can help you build the case for a strategic internal communication plan.

2. **Gather broad input.** These efforts should be directed toward some identified end result. In short, you should have a "plan." A good starting point in developing an employee communication plan is having a series of discussions with certain groups within the organization: the CEO, the vice presidents, the managers, and, finally, employees themselves. These discussions or inputs might be one-on-one conversations, small focus groups, or formal surveys.

3. **Identify gaps.** The input you receive will help you determine where gaps exist between what management wants employees

to know or believe and what employees actually do know or believe.

4. **Develop an action plan.** Your plan will consist of objectives and tactics to help you meet those objectives. A challenge at this stage can be making sense of all of the information you've gathered and determining high-level priorities and key messages. Your challenge will be to find common points of recurrence from the information and to focus on what employees really need to know to do a better job, not just on information that is nice to know.

5. **Gain management commitment to the plan.** Neither HR nor corporate communication, alone or in concert, can achieve success with an internal communication plan if that plan doesn't have support from management.

6. **Implement the plan.**

7. **Measure results!**

Chapter 8 offers a process for preparing communication plans that can be used with any request for communication, regardless of the scope of the issue.

Meaning Through Measurement

Angela Sinickas is a communication consultant and expert at measuring the impact of communication efforts. Ideally, she says, corporate communicators need to "be able to show that communication made some kind of difference that affects the bottom line. To do this, we need to measure the impact our communications had on changing employee behaviors that have a bottom-line impact."

She offers a ten-step approach to connect communication with changes in audience behaviors that can help demonstrate that bottom-line impact.

1. Identify the bottom-line HR goals, initiatives, or programs for which communication might have the greatest potential impact.

2. For a particular goal, determine which groups of employees could take different types of actions that would better lead to the goal. For example, those with children, those close to retirement, those who are vested, those who are under age thirty.

3. For each stakeholder group, study available statistics to understand what actions those employees are currently taking, and determine with other HR staff what employees should be doing ideally. Get specific. How many married employees whose spouses also have health coverage are opting out of your medical plan? What percentage of employees over age fifty-five have more than 50 percent of their retirement accounts invested in the company stock? What percentage of accidents are occurring for different reasons among various employee groups, and which ones are resulting in the greatest amount of benefit payments and lost work time?

4. Conduct focus groups with the members of an employee group whose behavior you'd like to influence. Discuss with them several topics:

   a. Why they do what they do currently.

   b. What it would take for them to start taking the new actions you've identified.

   c. What types of knowledge or information they would need to be able to change their behavior.

   d. Their preferred ways of receiving this information.

   e. What attitudes might affect their behavior. Ask this in terms of "If you had all this new information, is there anything else that would still keep you or other employees from taking the new actions?" At this point, you'd be probing for "belief blockages" that could inhibit their behavior. For example, they might say, "What I have now has been working OK; why change what isn't broken?"

   f. What it would take to change their existing negative beliefs on the topic, if anything, including which other people might influence their opinions.

5. Conduct a survey of a sample of your targeted employees to identify the current baseline levels of knowledge and attitudes on the topics you identified in focus groups as being critical to the desired behavior change.

6. Start tracking on a frequent basis the HR measures of the behaviors—both desired and actual.

7. Design your communication campaign to integrate the knowledge and belief messages you identified as critical to the behavior change. Use the ideal communication approaches the focus groups listed as the best ways to gain the needed knowledge and change their beliefs.

8. Do minisurveys of employees' knowledge and attitude levels on the key messages—timed to coincide with your communication interventions.

9. Chart the changes in employees' behaviors versus changes in their knowledge and attitudes, indicating the timing of your communication interventions. You might also measure desired behaviors that were fine to start with to make sure they haven't accidentally been negatively affected.

10. Quantify the financial value of the change in behaviors—and take full credit for it![4]

To be effective, employee communication needs to be part of a carefully considered process, focused on achieving clearly identified, *measurable* results. It is not difficult to communicate effectively, but it does take some thought, a clear focus on objectives, an understanding of the tools available to communicate your messages, and a strong partnership between you and your internal customers.

Communication is a constant challenge because both the external and internal environments within which we operate are changing constantly. The people we communicate with are changing too. As a communicator, you have a job that is never done. Nor will you ever achieve 100 percent success. You can, however, approach the communication challenge from a continuous improvement perspective by establishing specific goals and objectives, measuring outcomes, and making changes in your strategy and approach because of what you learn.

"Most companies over the years have been pretty good at communicating with external audiences," says Horn. "We aren't, typically, as advanced with our internal audiences. You can tell people the business strategy all day, but fundamentally, you need to have people understand *why* and focus on what you want them to do. You get their commitment by getting them to understand the what and the why."

Special Opportunities in Employee Communication

The organization's relationship with employees leads to a variety of unique situations requiring well-planned and appropriately delivered communication.

Communicating with New Employees

The first days and weeks that a new employee spends at your organization are critical. First impressions *do* count. When a new employee joins your organization, you have an opportunity to "make or break" the relationship. What new employees experience in their first days on the job will determine whether their tenure with your organization is long or short, positive or negative. What employees really *need* and want to know during those critical first days is often very different from what their organizations focus on.

Employees first need to know about the issues that impact them individually and to feel secure on a personal level before they can look beyond their needs to the needs of the department or organization. That's why the first day on the job probably isn't the best time to talk, in any detail, about the organization's strategic goals, budget, or competitive strategies. The new employee simply isn't ready to hear this information.

Orientation, therefore, can be viewed as a process that extends from the specific (Where should I park?) to the general (What are the organization's long-range goals?). Employees are first interested in "the things that affect me, personally." Next they want to know about "the things that affect me as a member of my department." Finally, they are interested in "the things that affect me as a member of the organization."

You can set the stage for employees' initial experience with your organization even before they walk through the door on their first day. Consider some of the basic bits of information that can be extremely important to new employees:

- Where should I park?

- What should I wear?

- Where should I report?

- Who should I ask for?

- Where are the restrooms?

- Who will eat lunch with me?

The more you can do to respond to some of these questions, the more relaxed and comfortable employees will be. Having a sense of "belonging" is important to new employees. Be sure that they have a "home," a place to sit, and a place to put their "things." Provide the initial tools and supplies they will need to do their job. Something as simple as having a name tag or nameplate in place can send a very positive message to new employees and make them feel welcome.

Once new employees "settle in," the following questions become paramount:

- What are my work hours?

- What time do I need to report to work?

- Will I be expected to work overtime? To work evenings? Weekends?

- Will I need to travel? How often? Will I be expected to make my own travel arrangements?

- What if a business trip interferes with my personal or family plans?

- How flexible are my work hours—if I need to take time off to attend a child's school event or take my dog to the vet, can I do that?

New employees will also need to learn about "how things get done." For example, they will be concerned about administrative issues—like how to use the telephone and the computer. These may seem basic, but consider that the employees may have been used to an entirely different system. Also recognize that they certainly can't know about your organization's idiosyncrasies—for example, how do you want the phone to be answered? It is frequently these "little things" that create stress and uncertainty for new staff people—and it is also these little things that are often overlooked. What approval processes should new employees be aware of? Can they sign off on invoices? Up to what dollar amount?

New employees want to begin working as soon as possible. They want to quickly become involved and feel some sense of contribution. The first big question new employees have is, "What, exactly, will I be doing here?" That question encompasses a variety of issues, such as:

- Who will I be working with?

- Who are the people I need to get to know in the department and in other departments?

- What kind of work will I be doing?

- Where will my assignments be coming from?

- How will my work be judged?

- How does it fit in with what the department does and with the organization's goals?

- Who are the "movers and shakers" in the organization, and how can I become one of them?

- Are there opportunities to serve on special committees or task forces, and how can I find out about them?

- If I have ideas, suggestions, or concerns, what channels exist to share those concerns?

- How do people prefer to communicate in this organization? Face-to-face? By e-mail? Phone?

- And, finally, how does what I do in this department impact the organization?

Only after employees' need for individual information is satisfied will they be able to look beyond their own interests to the interests of the organization. What are the organization's mission, vision, and values (and how do I—and my department—fit into this?)

- Do we have a strategic plan? What does it entail?

- Who are our competitors?

- How are we positioned relative to our competitors?

- What are the major external issues that impact us?

- Do we have "strategic partners," and who are they?

- Are we financially sound as an organization?

- What are our priorities?

- What are our long-range goals?

- What are employees rewarded and recognized for? What are they ostracized for?

Be attuned to new employees' need for information and individual capacity for learning. Some new employees may want to move quickly beyond the basics to learn about the broader issues affecting the organization, while others may have many more questions about the daily nitty-gritty that will affect their individual work lives.

Engage new employees in meaningful conversation, don't just talk "at" them. Establish a dialogue. Offer ample opportunity for new employees to ask questions, share perspectives, and gather information. Designating a contact person or mentor to help new recruits through the early stages of employment can be a good way to provide the individualized attention each employee needs.

Keep in mind that in the early days that employees spend in a new job, the little things are foremost in their minds. The *organization* wants new employees to know many things—but don't move too quickly to these issues. Make sure that you have first addressed all those things that *new employees* want—and need—to know.[5]

Employee Suggestion Programs

Suggestion programs proliferate in corporate America—but too many of these programs are poorly managed and not effectively tied to the strategic needs of the organization. Consequently, employee input tends to focus more on complaints than on useful suggestions, management staff resent the time they must spend responding to what they often perceive as "worthless" input, and those managing the program feel overwhelmed by the administrative burden of gathering, logging, and responding to the comments they receive.

What makes a suggestion program successful? A number of things. Successful employee suggestion programs are:

1. **Supported by upper management.** As with any major initiative, without the support of upper management, even the best-run program is destined to fail.

2. **Developed with clearly defined goals and objectives.** What results do you want to obtain through your program? A program designed as a way to "manage the rumor mill" will look very different from a program designed to help the company save money on expenses.

3. **Easily accessible by all employees.** For your program to be useful, employees need to have ready and convenient access. This may mean that you offer a number of alternatives for submitting suggestions: traditional suggestion boxes, a sugges-

tion "hotline," e-mail suggestions, and so on. Consider all employees when establishing your program.

4. **Easy to use.** A four-page form that must be filled out and submitted in triplicate will probably not generate an overwhelming amount of input. If your objective is to limit suggestions and to educate employees on preparing sound business cases, that may be all right. But if your goal is to involve as many employees as possible and to generate numerous ideas, keep it simple.

5. **Low risk.** Employees are often hesitant to share their ideas. They may feel that nobody cares, that their ideas will be considered stupid, or that somebody else may have already thought of the same idea. They may fear that they will somehow get in trouble for making a suggestion that may step on someone's toes. Or they may fear retribution from their direct supervisors. For all these reasons, you might allow employees to submit ideas and comments anonymously.

6. **Easy to administer.** Many programs fail simply because the administrative burden is too great and the time and effort to maintain the program is viewed as excessive.

7. **Responsive.** Quick follow-up to any suggestion or comment submitted is a must for any program. The follow-up can be as simple as "We've received your suggestion and will evaluate it within the next thirty days." Ultimately, employees need to hear whether their ideas have been acted upon and need to see tangible evidence that their suggestions are valued and are making a difference.

8. **Measurable.** To continue to generate management support for your employee suggestion program, you need to develop some means of measuring the value the program provides.

Suggestion programs can be a simple way to generate employee feedback if done effectively. See "Strategies for Successful Suggestion Programs" for some tips to enhance the value of this communication tool.

Strategies for Successful Suggestion Programs

- Be specific in terms of what types of ideas you want from employees, and provide guidelines to help them submit suggestions that are focused and clearly presented.

- Make it easy for managers to respond. The burden on management to respond to suggestions can be overwhelming. The administrators of the program can help ease this burden by developing FAQ lists, drafting suggested responses to certain comments, and so on.

- Share suggestions and responses with the staff at large. A simple Q&A format in your employee newsletter can be a great way to do so. This helps cut down on duplicate suggestions and comments and offers an excellent way to educate and inform employees on issues they are concerned about.

- Manage employee expectations. Make sure that employees know what to expect when they contribute a suggestion. Where will their suggestion go? How long will it be before they receive a response?

Employees have suggestions, concerns, and complaints. If you don't have a formal suggestion program, you're just less likely to hear about them.

SOURCE: Lin Grensing-Pophal, "Suggestion Programs: The Good, The Bad & The Ugly," May 2000, www.shrm.org. Used with permission.

Techniques for Effective Employee Communication

Kathryn Yates, head of the global communication practice with Watson Wyatt, has more than twenty years' experience in communications and operations management. Yates offers ten tips for effective employee communication:

1. **Never start at the beginning.** It's important, Yates says, to start with the end result in mind. "Too often," she points out, "people jump into a communication project without considering what it

is that they're trying to accomplish." Whether you're working on a simple communication task (introducing a new employee, for example) or implementing a major communication initiative (communicating with employees about a pending merger), you need to have a clear idea of what your communication objectives are.

2. **Understand the business drivers.** Communicators need to understand how their communications fit into the overall business strategy. "If there is a fault I've seen in employee communication," Yates says, "it's often that the homework hasn't been done." Understanding the business drivers can also help HR professionals gain credibility with business leadership. Communication shouldn't focus just on the nice to know, it should focus on what employees need to know to help the business move forward.

3. **Integrate.** "Use every opportunity to put messages in a consistent framework," recommends Yates. For example, if you make a change in an employee benefit, explain how this change fits into the overall context of benefit administration. If you're introducing a new employee, explain how the new employee will contribute to the team and what personal and professional characteristics the employee has that mesh well with the organization's culture.

4. **Don't waste people's time!** Think carefully about the number of communication pieces distributed within your organization. "Target your message and your audience as much as you can," Yates says, "so you're not just blanketing people with information." Consider, also, that people receive messages in many different ways. Some prefer print, some verbal, some electronic. A mix of messages, strategically planned, can help ensure that all employees receive the information they need.

5. **Get real.** While it's okay to be positive as you frame your messages, it's critical that you be straightforward and clear. "Frankly," Yates points out, "credibility—yours and leadership's—is on the line." Sometimes you have bad news to convey. Be accurate, honest, and direct—don't sugarcoat.

6. **Listen as much as, or more than, you speak.** "This isn't rocket science. It's sitting down and saying, 'How much do I

really understand my audience?'" Stephen Covey, author of *The 7 Habits of Highly Effective People,* says, "Seek first to understand." This is good advice for communicators. By understanding the needs of your audience, you can better design messages that will be meaningful and impactful.

7. **Prioritize your messages.** Focus on a few key points or you'll risk losing the attention of your audience, whether you're providing the information verbally or in writing. If you try to convey too much, you will end up conveying nothing. Be selective.

8. **Consider an internal review board.** A group of influencers within your organization can provide a great opportunity to test your messages before rolling them out to the entire company. Yates warns, however, not to use this internal review board merely to get agreement on what you've already done. "You need to really want to understand what they say—they're not always going to agree with you," she says.

9. **Don't fall in love with your communication product or process.** It is quite common for communicators to create a newsletter that they think is wonderful, or a headline that they feel is clever, or an Internet page that they believe is cutting edge, only to discover that the tools they created didn't achieve the goals they had intended. Don't fall in love with your communication products, Yates warns. Instead, she recommends, "fall in love with the result."

10. **Measure and monitor your effectiveness over time.** "Everybody says this, but very few people do it," Yates says. Measurement helps you understand whether your messages are getting through, helps you determine how credible you are, and indicates the effectiveness of your communication tools.

Building strong relationships between the organization and its employees requires trust. Organizations that communicate honestly with employees are able to establish the trust required to deliver even negative information as State Farm's experience indicates. See "Being Brutally Honest with Employees."

Being Brutally Honest with Employees

A common complaint of employees is that their organizations don't communicate honestly with them—that they sugarcoat negative information or bad news. It's a valid concern. Organizations—and their communicators—*do* have a tendency to "spin" bad news. Some organizations, though, have discovered that by telling employees the real story, however disconcerting that story might be, those employees can become important ambassadors.

State Farm Insurance is one of these companies. In an article in its employee publication titled "Over the Backyard Fence: Seven Talking Tips on State Farm's Tight Spot," State Farm didn't mince words in addressing record losses and declining customer confidence. Management acknowledged that customers were "shopping around" and brought employees into the discussion—arming them with key messages to share with their friends and neighbors "over the backyard fence."

The article raised and then responded to questions like "How did State Farm get into this situation?" "Is this a State Farm problem or an industry problem?" and "What's the long-term direction for State Farm—grow or shrink?" For every question, employees were given a brief response. For example, to the question "How did State Farm get into this situation?" employees were given this response: "In a word: Record losses in 2003—claim costs have escalated, our rates weren't adequate, and our investment income was down." Additional detail was provided, along with explanations and definitions of industry jargon.

Employees represent an organization's frontline point of contact with the external audience. Arming them with straight answers to tough questions can significantly extend the impact and effectiveness of formal communication efforts.

SOURCE: State Farm Insurance, "Over the Backyard Fence: Seven Talking Tips on State Farm's Tight Spot," *The Heartlander* (Bloomington, IL: State Farm Insurance, September 2002). Used with permission.

Summing Up

- Studies have demonstrated that effective employee communication has a positive impact on an organization's bottom line.

- Employee communication is a process that starts with a strategy, is centrally coordinated, and responds to the question, What do employees need to know to support the organization's goals and direction?

- Frontline managers are critical to successful employee communication and must be trained and given the appropriate tools and resources to support the organization's messages.

- To be effective, employee communication needs to be part of a carefully considered process, focused on achieving clearly identified, *measurable* results.

Leveraging Chapter Insights: Critical Questions

- Much research suggests that effective employee communication can have a positive impact on the bottom line. Can you think of ways that employee communication has had this positive impact in your organization?

- Why is it important that employee communication be considered a process rather than an event? Are there examples in your organization of event-related communications that might be made more effective if considered as part of a broader process?

- How do your senior leaders impact the communication climate at your organization? In what ways do their activities or actions hinder communication? In what ways do their activities or actions aid communication?

- Does your organization have an employee suggestion program? Is it effective? Why or why not?

CHAPTER SEVEN

Issues Management and Crisis Communication

Dealing Proactively and Effectively with Issues and Crises

Key Topics Covered in This Chapter

- *The difference between an issue and a crisis*

- *Developing an issues management plan*

- *Types of crises and how to anticipate and respond*

- *Steps for communicating during a crisis*

- *Dos and don'ts for effective media relations*

I S IT AN ISSUE or a crisis?

Tim O'Brien is a principal of O'Brien Communications in Pittsburgh, Pennsylvania. A number of years ago, O'Brien worked with a corporation that owned a manufacturer of electric blankets. At that time, a writer for a national publication had written an article about electromagnetic fields (EMFs) based on a study that suggested a correlation between people with certain types of cancer and the fact that their homes were located near large power lines. "The writer—and only the writer," says O'Brien, "with no studies to back up his position, drew the conclusion that if EMF was bad around big power lines, then maybe other things we use in our daily lives might also hurt us—like electric blankets.

"My client suddenly had an issue to deal with that was created by this article," says O'Brien, adding that even though the company dispelled all the claims according to the facts, the article led to an almost two-year battle. The issue led to related concerns of how sales would be affected, how employees at the company would be impacted if sales declined, how to deal with employees who had concerns themselves about whether the product they were making could harm others, and so on.

The concern over EMFs and the relevance to electric blankets was an issue. The Chapter 11 bankruptcy that the company ultimately found itself in was a crisis.

O'Brien has handled both issues management and crisis communications, and says, "To be sure, there is often some crossover on these topics, but the best way to describe it is that crisis communication is usually centered on a specific situation or development that may or may not occur, but could still threaten the ongoing operation of a business or organization. Issues management, however, is a situation where a specific issue, or perhaps the perception of an issue, has the potential for long-term and negative implications for an organization."[1]

For example, he points out, a labor strike for the National Hockey League is a crisis. But when the strike is over, a key issue that is identified may be whether the fans will pay to see professional athletes they perceive to be arrogant, insensitive, and overpaid.

The destruction of the World Trade Center in New York City on September 11, 2001, was a crisis. The resulting impact on the travel industry because of consumer concerns about terrorism and safety was an issue that emerged from this crisis.

Issues Management

Identifying issues and responding to crises are two very important responsibilities of corporate communicators. But there is a related and equally important role for HR professionals to play.

Often, even though an issue may have a "public face" to it and an obvious impact on customers and other external audiences, says O'Brien, one of the first audiences you have to appeal to is your employees. "If you can't win the support of your own people, how are you going to win the support of those outside the organization?" O'Brien asks. HR professionals can find themselves involved in any number of company issues simply because of their role with the employee audience, he says. Because of this, he asserts, it's critical that HR professionals become sophisticated about issues management.

The HR function is an integral part of issues management principally because of its role with the employee audience. Organizations would be hard pressed to identify many issues that *would not* impact human resources. In fact, says O'Brien, "You can't effectively handle any issues management program without the involvement of HR, legal, oftentimes finance and the CEO. Those people are almost always involved in whatever you're dealing with."

For example, suppose emerging global competition is an issue facing your company. HR's involvement would relate to the potential impact on employees in terms of the need to search for staff with different skill sets or the need to prepare for organizational restructuring.

In the food industry, an important issue over the past several years has been a significant increase in consumer adoption of low-carb diets. This shift in consumer preference impacts sales, which impacts profitability, which ultimately impacts employees.

Expansions, plant closures, consolidations, new product innovations and shifting consumer demand are all examples of issues that will have employee impacts. "Companies that don't effectively manage issues are going to run into serious problems," says Mary Heimstead, a PR consultant with experience as both a reporter and a corporate communication professional. "They will be paralyzed by a 'head in the sand' or 'no comment' mentality that will chip away at the company's credibility."

The ability of an organization to "control" an issue, says Sherry Devereaux Ferguson in *Communication Planning,* is impacted by a number of factors:

- The more central the beliefs housed in the issue, the more difficult it is to effect changes in position on the issue. Central beliefs (e.g., the belief that abortion is wrong) will be resistant to change.

- The larger the field of influence, the less controllable the issue.

- The greater the number of dimensions to the issue (social, political, technological, economic, and legal), the less controllable the issue. Environmental issues, for example, have an impact on almost every area of our lives, Devereaux Ferguson points out.

- The more an issue is event driven, the less controllable the issue. The terrorist attack on 9/11 is a good example of this.

- The greater the power capability of the stakeholders that oppose an organizational stance, the less controllable the issue.

- The greater the number of stakeholders in the issue, the less controllable the issue.

- The more polarized the stakeholders, the less controllable the issue.[2]

Despite the obvious complexity and what may sometimes seem to be insurmountable hurdles, the process of issues management is fairly straightforward. It involves:

- Identifying the issues that impact your organization

- Conducting research in the form of surveys, focus groups, and simply walking around and talking to people

- Analyzing the impacts of perceptions and behaviors

- Prioritizing and ranking issues and subissues

- Identifying key messages and communication vehicles

- Implementing communication programs

Following a process like this, says O'Brien, may lead you to find that what you thought was a simple issue is something else entirely. For example, a number of years ago, O'Brien was working with a company that had struggled through a long history of labor problems. Managers had been quick to blame the "union mentality" for making things difficult. However, ultimately, says O'Brien, "we learned that the company's workforce had a legitimate literacy problem. Hourly workers, who were deficient in reading and comprehension skills, were simply taking the word of their union leadership on negotiations. They weren't able to read the company's letters, memos, and correspondence on all of the issues. So while we initially thought the problem was wages, benefits, and job security, we found that better communication had to start with a better-trained workforce in the area of literacy."

As a result, says O'Brien, when the strike was over, the organization implemented a literacy program, simplified company communication to the appropriate levels, created new communication vehicles, and provided literacy training "in a way that would not embarrass workers."

The following items should flow from a comprehensive strategy for issues management, says Heimstead:

- Risk assessment of issues

- Key messages for each issue

- Individual, yet integrated, communication plans that focus on key audiences such as investors, employees, community, and news media.

Some companies, says Heimstead, approach issues management with a department model. "Overall issues are outlined in a comprehensive strategic plan, but pieces of the plan are worked by the department most knowledgeable and most affected by the issue. For example, a utility may be plagued by frequent and long outages, creating customer complaints to state regulatory agencies. Who best to work the issues management plan than the most knowledgeable field department in conjunction with corporate communication, HR, and others?"

Many companies, Heimstead points out, "have wisely recognized that some changes require professional guidance. For example, a company that plans to change its pension program or time-off policies should rely on outside assistance. A consultant can help measure the level of internal resistance to such changes and help manage the issue."

Research is a critical part of the issues management process. HR's area of concern will lie with the employee audience. Related audiences include employees' families and retirees. "HR has to be concerned with their audiences—employees, families, and retirees—and, within those audiences, with specific segments (e.g., hourly employees, managerial staff, etc.)," says O'Brien. "Every group has a different self-interest so you have to determine what is most important to them. Research serves as a critical foundation. Once you've done the research, the mechanisms you need to put into place to address the concerns almost become obvious." So, for example, if an identified issue relates to the loss of key employees to competitors, and research indicates that employees are concerned because they "don't see senior

management enough," you know you have to get senior management out into the plant or out into the field more often. If the concerns are that "we don't believe what senior management says," you
have to do certain things that reinforce that senior management
means what they say and will do what they say.

A defined process for addressing issues management can help ensure that the proper inputs have been included and that all constituents
understand the issues and their role in responding to these issues.

At Conectiv Power Delivery, Timothy Brown, director of corporate communication, uses a matrix or grid to help identify the
central issues that the organization will address and to develop a plan
for addressing those issues. The matrix is reviewed and modified
annually. The approach was recommended by Peter Stanton, APR,
president of Conectiv's PR firm, Stanton Communications, and involves these steps:

1. **Carefully review the previous year's plan.** "We strive for
   continuity from year to year," says Brown, "which is important
   since many of the same goals, strategies, and tactics carry over."
   For example, he says, an advertising campaign meant to reinforce the company's commitment to providing reliable service
   was explicitly designed to run over a three-year cycle. By in-
   corporating elements and lessons of previous plans, Conectiv
   ensured that it was speaking to its customers in a consistent and
   credible manner.

2. **Seek input from business leaders through a "stakeholder
   enrollment process."** Key leaders from Conectiv business units
   are asked about the major challenges they see in the industry,
   the company, and their business over the coming year. "By
   tapping our leadership's perspective," says Brown, "the stakeholder enrollment process ensures that the annual communications plan supports existing business goals."

3. **Carefully review broad strategic issues facing the industry.** As
   part of this process, Conectiv looks at a variety of information,
   including general and trade media articles about developments in

its industry, and studies and reports from national trade associations. "In 2003," says Brown, "our research made it clear that the fallout from California and the Enron debacle had raised many questions about our industry's credibility for our customers, shareholders, employees, and the general public."

4. **Thoroughly analyze customer inputs.** Conectiv uses its annual customer survey as an important input to its matrix. Survey results are synthesized to determine key drivers of customer satisfaction: reliability, price, value, and customer service. "By assigning each key driver a specific value based on its relationship to overall customer satisfaction, the metric we ultimately use to benchmark success," says Brown, "we're able to weigh the relative value of different messages in moving customer satisfaction." Conectiv also uses this research as a tool to benchmark the effectiveness of its communication plan, building in specific customer questions about the impact of various communication vehicles."

Issues management, says O'Brien, "is not as tricky as some people might make it sound. You simply need to do research, prioritize issues, develop responses to those issues, communicate your responses, and maintain communication over time."

Despite an organization's best efforts at issues management, "things happen." Those things can be called "crises."

Crisis Communication

At about 11:00 a.m. on a December morning in Boston, in 2000, a forty-two-year-old software tester at Edgewater Technology, a software development and consulting firm north of Boston, went on a shooting rampage. Armed with an AK–47 assault rifle, shotgun, and semiautomatic pistol, and apparently upset over the possibility of losing some wages to pay for back taxes, he killed seven coworkers. At about 1:00 p.m. that afternoon, the receptionist at the Institute for Crisis Management answered a frantic call from the vice president of corporate communication. "Are you watching CNN?" the VP yelled into the phone. This is how HR can become involved in crisis communication.

Larry Smith is president of the Institute for Crisis Management, in Louisville, Kentucky. The institute identifies four basic types of crises that every organization will face:

1. **Perceptual crises.** Nothing has really been done wrong, but the public perceives wrongdoing, so the damage is just as real. A classic example: Procter & Gamble's (P&G) "man in the moon" logo, which has been touted from time to time as proof of the company's tie to Satanism. Despite evidence to the contrary, the company has found itself needing to respond to this "perceptual crisis" for decades. In fact, as recently as August 2000, a federal appeals court ruled that P&G could pursue its business-defamation lawsuit against independent distributors of Amway Corporation products who were accused of spreading a rumor linking P&G to Satanism. You can't plan for a perceptual crisis, says Smith, but you have to manage it when it happens.

2. **Bizarre crises.** As with perceptual crises, you can't plan for bizarre crises. These are the unexpected situations such as the one in which NBC ultimately terminated Marv Albert hours after a plea bargain cut short a trial about his lurid sex life. Albert was fired by NBC and resigned from his job as an announcer for the Madison Square Garden Network after pleading guilty to assault and battery of a longtime friend for an incident that occurred in a hotel room.

3. **Sudden crises—fires, explosions, workplace violence.** This type of crisis, says Smith, can be planned for—not the specific event but the impact. For example, many organizations have written plans outlining specific steps to take in a natural disaster, and they conduct drills annually to ensure preparedness.

4. **Smoldering crises.** The Institute for Crisis Management's founder, Robert Irvine, defined this type of crisis in 1990 as, "Any serious business problem which is not generally known within or without the company, which may generate negative

news coverage if or when it goes 'public' and could result in more than a predetermined amount in fines, penalties, legal damage awards, unbudgeted expenses and other costs."[3] Some examples could be an OSHA violation, an investigation by a federal agency, and customer or employee allegations of improper conduct.

It is this last type of crisis, says Smith, that is most prevalent. "We monitor fifteen hundred print business publications from around the world and track negative news coverage of all kinds. Year after year after year, almost three-quarters of all crises that affect the business world are what we call the smoldering kind. They start out small, usually internal, and are things that somebody should be paying attention to and recognizing to have potential damage that then could be managed or dealt with and would never become full-blown crises."

HR professionals, says Smith, "can play a significant role in spotting, fixing, or getting the right people on top of these kinds of issues so they never have to become real crises." Many of these "smoldering crises," he points out, are "people issues—discrimination, sexual harassment, age discrimination, gender discrimination. Those are the kinds of things that HR should primarily be involved with and on the lookout for."

Anticipating and Preparing for a Crisis

Your new billing system is implemented and seems to be working well. A month into the conversion, the system goes down, leaving customers with no access to current billing, and so on. As customers call the company, they learn that the "system is down" from frontline company associates. The media become aware. Even a billing system problem can become a crisis for a company, particularly a company that provides emergency services. There's also the issue of unbilled revenue, which can emerge as a financial crisis to a company as well. This is the type of situation, says Heimstead, that companies need to be prepared for.

Crises can be large or small, but even small crises can disrupt your business operations. A robbery, a fire, the bankruptcy of a key vendor—each of these could be considered a crisis, depending upon the extent of the impact on your operations.

We're all familiar with these well-known crises:

- Wendy's "finger in the chili"

- Tylenol tampering

- *Exxon Valdez* oil spill

- Columbine shootings

- Corporate scandals—Enron, Tyco

- Martha Stewart's insider trading

Every organization should prepare a risk analysis for a potential crisis, says Heimstead, even those crises not directly affecting your company. "What if a neighborhood evacuation prevented you and other employees from reaching your office and critical files of information? How would you operate? Do you have a back-up location? Do you have files backed up and in a secure location?

"Who would speak on behalf of your organization if the CEO is unavailable? What's your company's succession plan in case your CEO suddenly dies? What's your plan for getting the CEO or alternate chief officer to the scene of a crisis? How have you prepared your official for handling the media during a crisis?"

HR has a significant role to play during a crisis, says Heimstead. "Depending on the situation, there might be a need for grief counseling or alternate ways of reaching employees with critical information. What will the fallout from the crisis be? How will HR help communicate and manage it?"

Sometimes a crisis strikes close to home, but HR departments also can help manage a crisis that has a ripple effect on other companies. For example, Heimstead points out, Florida energy utilities have been affected by hurricanes. But because of a mutual-aid assistance program, other utilities traveled to Florida from distant states to help restore gas and electric service. "The HR and corporate communication departments of those utilities providing help were of great service by communicating what was occurring," says Heimstead. "Information had to be managed concerning the logistics of equipment, trucks, and staff. Families had to be reassured that their spouses would be gone only a certain number of days. Employees had to be reassured that they would have food, water, and a place to sleep when they arrived. Crews had to know that there would be a local contact to direct them when they arrived. Employees who weren't sent to the scene had to be kept informed of progress. And most importantly, the customers of any utility sending crews to the devastated areas of Florida needed to be assured that sufficient help would still be available in the event of storms or outages in their own backyards."

Every company—large and small—should have a plan to address crises, says Smith. In fact, he points out, "the smaller the company, the more you need to be prepared, because the more harm a crisis will do to you. Big companies tend to have enough cushion both in the bank and in other financial resources—and enough people that they can recover. Small and mid-sized companies don't have that financial cushion."

A good way to prepare for these types of situations, says Scott Sobel of Levick Strategic Communications, LLC, in Washington, D.C., is to "come up with the worst-case scenario, understand what the end-game might be and then work backwards from that through a logical model to see who the right person might be to speak—understanding where all the danger may be at the very end under a worst-case scenario."

If you don't have comprehensive plans around issues management, general communication, and crisis communication, get busy, says Heimstead. At a minimum, every plan should include:

- Executive summary

- Situational analysis

- Risk assessment

- Comprehensive strategy with individual plans for internal and external communications

- Core messages

- Communication principles

- Tactics for defined audiences

- Budget

- Timeline

- Evaluation

- Lessons-learned briefings

Specific tactics to consider, suggests Heimstead, include:

- A steering committee or department model to work the plan and ensure consistency of message

- Fact sheets, white papers, position papers

- Presentations

- Publications

- Internet

- Media outreach (briefings, editorial board meetings, advisories, news releases)

- Videos

- Direct mail

- Newsletters

- Town hall meetings

- Advertising

- E-mail

- "Setting the Record Straight" feature on the Web or elsewhere to curb rumors and inaccuracies

The key takeaway message: don't leave a crisis to chance. Every organization should be prepared for certain predictable crises: the death of a key executive, product tampering, a natural disaster, and so on. Spending time preparing for and practicing a response to these types of predictable crises will also provide you with valuable background if an unanticipated crisis occurs.

How to Communicate During a Crisis

The FBI is at your doorstep.

Your CEO has just been arrested for embezzlement.

One of your employees has robbed a local bank.

What do you do now?

- **Don't panic.** While crises demand a timely response, they do not require an *immediate* response. It's critical that you take some time to ensure that your initial statements are appropriate and well reasoned. Respond to media inquiries promptly—but on *your* timeline. While a "no comment" comment should always be your last option, a "no comment" is *always* better than a response that has the potential to damage your organization's reputation. Take the time you need to be appropriately prepared.

- **Gather internal stakeholders to develop a response plan and key messages.** Call a group of key players together, as appropriate given their roles within the organization. For example, if you're the senior HR professional in your organization and you've just learned that a senior manager has been charged with sexually harassing an employee, it might be appropriate for you to contact people in legal, corporate communication, and senior leadership roles to develop a strategy and communication approach. Other situations (a product recall, for example) might most appropriately be handled and led by the corporate communication or public relations departments.

- **When responding to questions from the public or the media, be sure that you are responding to *your* questions**

only. Be keenly aware of what information is yours to share and what information belongs to someone else. Don't repeat someone else's information, or *you* become the spokesperson. For example, if one of your employees is charged with em- ployee theft, you may have a copy of the police report. The report, however, belongs to the *police department,* and the police should comment on the investigation, not you. Don't even re- iterate the information contained in the police report. If you do, it becomes *your* statement, and you risk violating the em- ployee's privacy or making a misstatement. Know what's yours and respond to *only* those questions that are truly within the purview of your organization.

- **Never speculate.** If you don't know for sure, say so. If you're uncertain of the appropriate response or all the details, don't venture a guess. Offer to find the answer and the appropriate spokesperson.

- **Control the message.** Information should be shared on a "need to know" basis only, even among your communication and HR staff. This gives them less opportunity to inadvertently share confidential or inaccurate information.

- **Make sure that communication and other informed staff members clearly understand the importance of their role in respecting and protecting confidential corporate informa- tion.** They may be held to a higher standard than other employees and need to be above reproach. Even when they're repeating information that they've read in the newspaper, for example, there's the potential that if the statement is coming from them they will be quoted as "the source."

- **If inaccurate or misleading information is reported by the media, don't automatically move to correct that information.** Consider carefully before responding, weighing the value of issuing a correction that could give the story a "longer life" against the potential for damage from the misleading informa- tion. Other options are available to you to communicate "your side" of the story. (See "Threat Assessment—Managing Media Demands.")

- **Tell it all. Tell it now.** Don't let stories drag on because you haven't been forthcoming with information that you thought "would never become public." When a crisis occurs, operate from the premise that the media—and the public—will ultimately find out all the details. You are best served if you share information early and completely. Some well-known examples of the implications of *not* doing this include the President Clinton/Monica Lewinsky scandal and the Martha Stewart insider-trading case.

Selecting the right spokesperson in a crisis is critical. Contrary to what you might think, in most cases the CEO is *not* the right spokesperson. "When choosing the correct spokesperson," says Sobel, "you have to understand the legal ramifications of that person's comments." In the most sensitive situations, he suggests, it's a good idea to consult with a legal adviser. "Do you want a CEO to allude to some specific financial or personnel or operational matter that could have liability implications down the road and have them talk about it in general when, during a court action, there would be an assumption that if they could speak about something in general, they knew things specifically?" Cases in point: Enron and WorldCom.

Sometimes, says Sobel, a spokesperson may be selected simply because of "deniability." "If there's no expectation that they know everything and a reporter asks a tough question, they can say, 'I'll have to find out about that and I'll get back to you.' Whereas," he points out, "a CEO or some other expert in the company doesn't have that pad of time and luxury because a reporter—or any audience—would expect that that person would know that information."

Whoever you select for your spokesperson, make sure that they have been properly trained and coached to respond to the media or other public audiences. Again, operate on *your* time. While you need to be responsive, you shouldn't feel pressured into a response that you are not prepared for.

Advice for Handling Issues and Crisis Communication

Sherri A. Fallin is CEO of Duffey Communications, Inc., in Atlanta. In her work with companies in a variety of industries, Fallin says she has discovered a "universal truth"—"companies will either spend money up front to address crises head-on, or they will spend the money to earn back their reputation and revenues." She's seen companies make a number of mistakes in developing crisis management plans:

1. **Developing a crisis plan for a worst-case scenario and not being prepared for the more-likely-to-happen situations.** When developing crisis plans, Fallin says, "executives should focus on planning and preparing employees for those scenarios that are most probable in the context of their industry, location, and geography."

2. **Not having the appropriate safety nets in place to identify and address a situation before it escalates into a crisis.** Workplace violence and product safety are two areas, Fallin notes, where crises can be prevented if steps are taken proactively to identify areas of risk.

3. **Assuming that the company spokesperson can respond appropriately in a crisis without media training.** "Training new executives and determining when new messages to take to the public are needed should be an exercise that executives participate in at least annually," says Fallin.

4. **Not providing employees with the information they may need to respond to inquiries both in and out of the workplace.** When crises occur, says Fallin, the typical response is to "circle the wagons." While this is appropriate in certain cases, she says, "it is more important to prepare your front-line employees with information that they can use to respond to inquiries from vendors, friends and family members." The information doesn't have to be detailed, she says—"bullet

points or a letter from the president of your organization will often prevent damaging rumors resulting from internal gossip."

5. **Developing a crisis plan and putting it on a shelf without testing its feasibility.** Taking time to test the plan, says Fallin, is important. "Take a day or half-day and put your plan through the paces, involving the multiple departments that would have a role in responding to a crisis situation, including legal, operations, and communications."[4]

You can't possibly prepare for every issue or every potential crisis. But regardless of the issue or crisis—large or small—there are a number of important steps you can take to minimize damage to your organization's reputation and credibility. See "Threat Assessment—Managing Media Demands."

Threat Assessment—Managing Media Demands

Rick Chambers, a PR professional, almost dropped his soupspoon. Had he heard correctly? Over an otherwise enjoyable lunch, an editor from a local newspaper was demanding an interview with his company's CEO, who was based elsewhere, for a series of stories noting the one-year anniversary of the local firm's acquisition. For many reasons, Chambers felt that an interview would not be helpful, and since this was a local story, he offered the editor access to local management. But that wasn't good enough.

"If you don't give us the CEO," the editor announced, "we will report that he refused to talk to us and to the community." Chambers put down his spoon and tried to maintain his composure. "I'm not sure," he said in a calm voice, "but that sounded to me like a threat." The editor brushed off his concern but didn't retract the statement. Chambers left the restaurant deeply bothered by the exchange.

Recognizing that he might be overreacting, Chambers talked to other PR professionals, hoping that someone would have a different take. But no one did. He raised his concern twice more with the newspaper, only to have it dismissed again.

Although his company's local presence remained strong following the acquisition, Chambers learned that this was not the story the newspaper planned to tell. Much of its coverage all year had been negative, sometimes even petty, he felt. The anniversary gave the company an opportunity to bring a new perspective, and he had gone into the lunch meeting hoping to map out a way he could work with the paper to tell an accurate story. While Chambers admits that he might have produced the CEO had it not been for the editor's ultimatum, he now felt that doing so would set a bad precedent. On the other hand, he realized, refusing to cooperate would leave his company's perspective out of the coverage.

He needed a third option and fortunately, with a lot of support, came up with one. It involved three strategies that proved to be effective:

1. **Communicating directly with the public.** "We created a four-page color brochure about our local operations and mailed it to 102,000 households in the area. The brochure included brief summaries of our local divisions and their global connections, details about our local philanthropy, names and titles of local leaders, and an invitation to submit questions and comments. Most important was a personal message from our CEO to area residents acknowledging the difficult transition year and thanking them for 'welcoming us as friends, colleagues, and partners.' We distributed the brochure two days before the newspaper's anniversary stories appeared. The cost was minimal—about 35 cents per brochure, including design, printing, and mailing. The feedback from the community was overwhelmingly positive."

2. **Treating the threat as a separate issue.** "Several reporters worked on the anniversary stories, and all of them made reasonable requests for interviews and information. We decided to separate the threat from their requests. Over

continued

several weeks, we provided a huge amount of background material on the company and its local presence, answered scores of questions, arranged interviews with local managers, and offered significant access to our facilities. The messages were consistent and clear: Our local operations are important, our commitment to the community is strong, and we are poised for potential future growth."

3. **Addressing the threat specifically.** "Shortly before the newspaper ran its anniversary stories, a reporter asked me for a formal statement explaining why our CEO did not grant an interview. I waited until the day that the brochures were mailed with the CEO's personal message to the community. Then I arranged to have a copy hand-delivered to the newspaper with a cover letter. In the letter, I repeated my belief that the interview request was made in the form of a threat and that I refused to present such a threat to our CEO. I also pointed out that in spite of the ultimatum, we had provided the newspaper with extraordinary access to people, facilities, and information, reflecting 'a fair, reasonable, and cooperative relationship' that I hoped we would maintain in the future."

Ultimately, says Chambers, his organization was able to reach the public directly with its messages, influence the newspaper's coverage, and deal aggressively with the threat. "The editors could not accuse our CEO of refusing to speak to the community—he did so through the brochure. They could not accuse us of stonewalling—we cooperated extensively except where we felt we'd been threatened. As a result, the level of access we gave the newspaper resulted in a series of largely positive, fair, and accurate stories." And, he adds, the relationship with the newspaper that made the threat has steadily improved. "Although the editors objected to our interpretation of the threat, they honored the way we dealt with it because our approach honored them and their interest."

Have a Plan

First, you should know who in your business will be responsible for communication in a crisis (see chapter 2). If your staff is extremely small, or if you simply don't have talent on-site to assume this role, you may wish to consider researching the availability of public relations or communication firms that could fill this role in a crisis. Your crisis plan should list all the key people in your organization, with phone numbers where they can be reached at any time. This information should be provided to key members of your organization, and they should be instructed to keep it readily available both at work and at home.

Certain people on this list might also be assigned various responsibilities for participating in communication. For example, you may have one person assigned to communicate with the local business community, one person assigned to respond to media inquiries, one person to focus on employee needs, and so on.

While this plan must, by definition, be general, it should provide enough structure that it could help lead anyone in your company through a process for responding to a crisis.

Practice Your Plan

Large organizations invariably have quite extensive crisis communication plans, and they test those plans regularly. Small companies can do the same. Simple "crisis drills" can be designed to "test the system." Whether announced or unannounced, these drills can give employees the opportunity to see how well the plan might work, to modify the plan by adding elements that were not previously considered, and to reduce stress and uncertainty about "what would happen if something *really* happened."

Nurture Ongoing Positive Media Relations

The media can be an important ally at a time of crisis. Local media can help to communicate important messages to the public and can play a role in helping to share your story. Of course, the media can also create stress and uncertainty for companies not used to dealing with reporters who can sometimes be aggressive and "out for a story."

When you're dealing with the media, the best defense can be a good offense. Establishing relationships with key media representatives and nurturing those relationships on an ongoing basis can serve you well in a crisis. Your messages will be more credible, particularly when your business may be somehow at fault, if you have already developed a trusting relationship with the local media and if media representatives know you can be relied upon to provide immediate and accurate responses to their inquiries.

While your organization is likely to have a specific area or individual responsible for media relations, you may also wish to develop strong media relations skills among key HR staff. Media training can provide the confidence and background required to present the organization effectively.

Have Tools for Immediate Communication

Your organization likely has a number of standard communication tools for communicating with key audiences. For instance, you may use e-mail to communicate with employees. You may have an Internet site. You may have an employee newsletter. These are all tools that can be used to communicate during a crisis. Having templates available can help ensure that you're able to get the word out quickly and effectively. A banking institution, for example, might have a specific process and templates to respond to a robbery.

In addition, you may want to consider other means of getting information out quickly in a crisis. A "calling tree," for instance, can be a good way to inform employees of a crisis during nonbusiness hours. A database of key contacts (including e-mail addresses) can also be helpful to get information out quickly and consistently. Again, while your organization may have tools like this at a corporate level, the HR area can also benefit by proactively considering its own need to communicate with various constituencies during a crisis.

Learn from Others

There is nothing more instructive in the field of crisis communications than learning from both the successes and the failures of other companies that have found themselves the "victim" of a crisis. Be alert to how others handle crises. Learn from their experiences, and use their experiences to strengthen your own crisis communication plans.

Steps to Take in a Crisis

- Put your plan into action! Now is the time to dust off your draft crisis communication plan.

- Get the facts. Gather the team of individuals you've identified as quickly as possible to review the situation. Get answers to the "five Ws": who, what, when, where, why.

- Determine the extent of damage or impact. Fortunately, in most cases that you are likely to deal with, the extent of damage will not be catastrophic. Stay calm and focus on actual impact.

- Assign a spokesperson. Identify the *one person* who will share information about the event with the public and the media.

- Develop key messages. Come up with two to three simple statements focusing on what has happened, how you feel about the event (typically a statement of support or empathy for anyone who may have been harmed), and what your company is doing. Your initial message may be as simple as, "We are devastated by this event. We are still gathering information about what has happened and will be communicating further as soon as we have this information." Then do it!

- Identify stakeholders. Who are the key audiences you need to communicate with? Generally, these will include those impacted or harmed, employees, the community, and customers. Stakeholders may also include local business leaders, vendors, and certain affinity groups (PETA, for example).

- Communicate! Whatever you do, don't go into hiding. You need to get your message out there quickly—before someone else does.

- Address internal audiences first. This is the area where HR can provide the most impact and positive benefit to an organization during a crisis. The internal employee audience is critical. Their needs, concerns, issues, and questions should take priority because they are in a position to have a significant impact on the needs, concerns, issues, and questions of your external constituencies.

- Review coverage. Stay in touch. Know what is being said by the public, by the media, and by your own employees. Have "listening posts." Determine whether coverage is adequate and accurate.

- Communicate! Correct inaccurate information. Provide updates and status reports.

When communication professionals think of crisis situations, they often tend to view the crisis as an event. In reality, as Timothy Brown points out based on his experience, a crisis can extend far beyond the actual precipitating event. See "A Crisis Isn't Over Until It's Over!"

A Crisis Isn't Over Until It's Over!

How do you balance the needs of various publics? Start with a plan and remain flexible! In September 2003, Hurricane Isabel disrupted electric service to more than 40 percent of Conectiv Power Delivery's customer base. The company's director of corporate communication, Timothy Brown, was proud of the way his staff—and the entire organization—had responded to the crisis. A week later, though, says Brown, the team realized that the crisis communication challenge was really just beginning. Follow-up inquiries from customers, legislators, regulators, and media "demanded a more robust post-event communication plan than we had expected," says Brown.

Widespread power outages raised many questions: Why had service been out for so long? Had the company taken adequate measures to prepare? Why wasn't the company able to provide more exact time frames for restoring service? What impact did deregulation have on the frequency and duration of outages?

Conectiv's matrix communication plan provided a good foundation, but the communication challenge facing the organization after the hurricane required more. The matrix needed to be modified. Here's what Conectiv, under Brown's leadership, did to address the communication challenges it faced in the aftermath of the hurricane:

1. Listened to customers—early and often. Senior leaders participated in talk radio shows, the organization held town hall meetings sponsored by legislators, presentations were made to more than two dozen local civic associations, and a detailed customer survey was taken to quantify the level and nature of concerns.

2. Involved internal stakeholders. Buy-in from internal audiences was critical. "We simply could not communicate with customers without understanding clearly how our company was planning to respond to their concerns," says Brown.

3. Established an objective—communicating the steps the company was taking to meet heightened customer expectations.

4. Developed strategies to drive the plan, including educating customers about the physical constraints and cost consequences of meeting such unrealistic expectations as "100 percent power, 100 percent of the time."

5. Defined tactics that would be used to convey the messages to various target audiences, using the existing plan as a starting

continued

point and modifying existing tactics to incorporate new messages.

Important lessons can be learned from Conectiv's experience:

- The crisis isn't necessarily over when the crisis is over! Even though operational issues may be "business as usual," the corporate communication role will be ongoing.

- Listen—be visible, be accessible, be responsive.

- The customer isn't always right—sometimes customer expectations are greater than your ability to meet them.

- Don't create new strategies in a vacuum—use your existing communication plan as a foundation and build from there.

- Every crisis represents an opportunity for learning.

Summing Up

- The HR function is an integral part of issues management principally because of its role with the employee audience.

- Despite the obvious complexity and what may sometimes seem to be insurmountable hurdles, the process of issues management is fairly straightforward.

- Research is a critical part of the issues management process.

- There are basically four types of crises that every organization may face.

- Every company—large and small—should have a plan to address crises.

- Responding calmly and purposefully during a crisis will ensure that your organization can effectively manage its messages.

- The selection of the right spokesperson is a critical decision when you're dealing with issues and crisis management.

Leveraging Chapter Insights: Critical Questions

- Think of a crisis your organization has faced. What type of crisis was it? What issues resulted from this crisis?

- What role does the HR department play in issues management at your organization? How could that role be strengthened?

- What issues might your company face that would require the use of outside consultants? Why do you feel it would be wise to look for external help in certain situations? When might it not be wise?

- What are some crises that your organization could anticipate? Are plans in place to respond to these crises if they actually occurred? What role would you play in this response?

- Why is "telling it all and telling it now" a good issues management practice? Does your organization heed this advice? Why? Why not?

CHAPTER EIGHT

Developing and Implementing Communication Plans

A Process for Developing Effective Communication Plans

Key Topics Covered in This Chapter

- *Types of communication plans and their uses*
- *The benefits of communication plans*
- *Eight steps in the development of a communication plan*
- *Using a "planned response" to communication requests*

YOUR FINANCE department wouldn't dream of sitting down at the beginning of a fiscal year without a plan," says Kathryn Yates, head of Watson Wyatt's global communication practice. "Why in the world are 35 percent of our corporate communication functions sitting down without formal plans? If we want to be taken seriously as a business function—which I believe we are—then we need to behave like one."

Watson Wyatt's research, says Yates, has demonstrated that companies that communicate effectively achieve better financial results. Organizations that communicate effectively start by handling process issues correctly: they actively plan their programs, document their communication strategy, and coordinate their internal and external messages to eliminate confusion.

This requires, says Yates, that "every year the communication function (including all of the broad categories like HR, corporate communication and marketing) sits down and creates a formal plan that is strategic, that has tactics, and that examines how they're providing value to their various constituencies—the business and the employees."[1]

The foundation of effective communication, according to Watson Wyatt, consists of following a formal process, using employee feedback, integrating total rewards, and leveraging technology. From a strategic perspective, effective communication needs to facilitate change, focus on continuous improvement, and connect to the business strategy. From a behavioral standpoint, communication should drive supervisors' and managers' behavior and create "employee line of sight," meaning that employees should be able to clearly see themselves within the process and identify how their behaviors impact organizational success. Awareness that leads to action that serves to further the organization's goals should be the objective of communication. That's true whether the communication is directed toward employees, consumers, or shareholders.

Types of Communication Plans

In *Corporate Conversations,* Shel Holtz outlines two types of communication plans: general and special. The general plan, says Holtz, "is the roadmap for ongoing communication within the organization." It should cover a period of time from one to three years and should include the "communication challenges, media and messages for your day-to-day activities, including regular face-to-face meetings, publications, online communications and multimedia." In addition, says Holtz, some events might precipitate the need for a special communication plan, such as the following:

- Plant closing

- Layoff

- Acquisition of a company

- Bankruptcy filing

- Entry into a new line of business or market segment

- Labor conflicts

- A crisis, such as an explosion or a death on-site

- Reaction to adverse regulation or legislation[2]

Sherry Devereaux Ferguson outlines five types of communication plans in *Communication Planning: An Integrated Approach:* strategic, operational, work, support, and crisis communication plans.

1. **Strategic plans** "supplement a corporate or a business/ functional plan."

2. **Operational plans,** which are fairly general in scope, "specify how the organization will achieve its strategic objectives and establish the allocation of funds for different communication ventures."

3. **Work plans** are "an extension of operational planning" and are often performed in the same time period, but are more concrete and specific.

4. **Support plans,** the most common type, according to Devereaux Ferguson, provide for managing a specific activity, initiative, or issue. Examples might include a campaign to encourage people to purchase a new product, a plan to address a safety issue, or a plan to convey the organization's position on a specific issue. Support plans may be very brief—no more than one page.

5. **Crisis communication plans** (see chapter 7) are part of the organization's overall crisis management plan and outline the role of the communication function, including specific accountabilities and guidelines and formats for various communication tools (e.g., press releases).[3]

Steps to Develop and Implement a Communication Plan

While the types of plans may vary, the process steps are much the same. In fact, developing a marketing plan requires the same steps as developing a corporate communication plan or a crisis management plan. Each plan will share certain common elements, and the approach will be similar to that described in the following sections:

1. Situation analysis or background

2. Quantifiable objectives or goals

3. Target audiences

4. Key messages

5. Strategies and tactics to meet objectives or goals

6. Responsibility or accountability for completing tactics

7. Budget (as appropriate)

8. Measurement

The development of a communication plan—whether a general plan or a plan specifically addressing a particular communication challenge—is an obvious and appropriate opportunity to reach out and involve other communication constituents outside your organization. If you're a communicator within the HR organization, for example, and you are developing a plan to communicate with employees about a change in pay structure, you may find it helpful to involve communicators in the marketing environment who can provide perspectives and insights on market issues that might help support your messages. Communicators in the investor relations structure can help ensure that your messages are accurate and consistent with public messages.

Conversely, if you're a communicator in the marketing organization and you are developing a communication plan about the expansion of services to a new geographic market area, your colleagues in HR could provide insights on how employees might respond to these messages or what role employees might play in helping to convey the message.

Don't look just to the communication staff to participate in the development of your communication plans. A variety of inputs and insights—particularly from the target markets you will be communicating with—can help ensure the success of your plan.

Let's take a more detailed look at each step in communication planning.

Situation Analysis or Background

The situation analysis or background section of your communication plan should provide a high-level overview of the situation or communication need with sufficient detail that someone not directly involved would understand the issue driving the need for communication and the desired outcomes. This section should include any pertinent facts or data that would have an impact on the communication process—for example, areas of particular sensitivity, any anticipated negative responses from specific audiences, details on how similar issues have been handled in the past along with the results, and so on.

This area of your plan should identify any key cross-departmental impacts or inputs necessary to successful implementation, or point to any areas of concern regarding the need for consistency between internal and external messages or between various target audiences. It should also briefly address the desired outcomes of the communication effort.

Quantifiable Objectives or Goals

The next step in developing your communication plan is to identify objective or goal statements that indicate the "end state" you hope to achieve. It's critical that each of your objectives or goals have a specific, targeted "end point" or outcome. This helps you determine the amount of resources that must be allocated to achieve the goal and provides an indicator of success. A simple example will illustrate. Your best friend says that this year she'd like to have more money. You hand her one dollar. She now has more money. Chances are, though, that's not what she had in mind. When you're setting goals, state what you *do* have in mind, or you're likely to underachieve.

Specific, quantifiable goals are critical. Simply wanting to "increase awareness" doesn't provide enough specific direction to allocate resources—money and effort—appropriately. By how much? Your goals need to take into consideration where you are today and where you would like to be (*specifically*) so you can focus on closing that gap.

Your goal statements should be expressed in such a way that the desired end result is clear. The following are some examples of poorly expressed goals and how they might be modified to provide better direction:

(Poor) "Increase awareness." Not only is that statement not quantitative in terms of responding to the question of *how much* of an increase you looking for, but it also fails to identify among which audiences—*all* audiences, a specific geographic audience (e.g., employees at a certain branch location), or a specific demographic market (e.g., new employees to the organization). It also fails to identify the time frame in which you wish to achieve this goal. This month? This year? Next year?

(Better) "Ensure that all line-level employees at the XYZ plant have heard about and understand the implications of the XYZ initiative by the end of the first quarter."

(Poor) "Change negative perceptions that customers have about XYZ product." Again, this statement is far too general to provide good direction for the organization. Which customers? What is meant by "negative perceptions"? What do you want to change those negative perceptions to? By when?

(Better) "According to data from quarterly consumer preference research, achieve a 25 percent gain in perception of XYZ product as being 'best' within its product category." Now you know, specifically, what you hope to achieve through your communication efforts and what "success" will look like. Could you choose multiple customer segments? Certainly.

The point is that you should take the time to ensure that the goal statements you establish are actionable so that you, your communication colleagues throughout the organization, and your leadership know when you have achieved success.

A helpful acronym that you can use to evaluate the appropriateness of your objective or goal statements is SMART. The SMART acronym is used to develop goals that are most likely to achieve results—goals that are specific, measurable, attainable, realistic, and time framed.

- A *specific* goal is one that clearly identifies an end point. "Raise positive employee perception about our products" is not a specific goal. "Raise employee perceptions about product X from _____ to _____ by year end" is. Be specific by stating *exactly* what it is you wish to achieve.

- A *measurable* goal provides a way for you to know whether you have hit your target. Employee satisfaction scores, for example, that clearly specify the level of increase desired are measurable.

- Goals need to be *attainable*. Suppose you indicate that you wish to influence all employees to agree that an impending merger is a benefit to them and the organization by year end. That's specific. It's measurable. But in an environment where employees are concerned about job security and resistant to change of any kind, 100 percent acceptance is probably not attainable.

- Even if your goal is attainable, it may not be *realistic*. For example, suppose your goal is to train your sales staff on a new product management software program in three months, but you're also introducing several new products during that time frame and increasing sales goals among this same group. This would not be a realistic goal.

- Finally, goals need to be *time framed. When* will you achieve the goal? This week? Three months? One year? Longer?

The development of goals or objectives is a process that involves discussion and careful consideration of the multiple impacts that affect your activities. It can be frustrating to realize that a legitimate goal cannot be achieved because of internal constraints on resources—budget, staff, and so on—in spite of an obvious need, but if that is the reality of the environment in which you operate, those factors need to be taken into consideration.

Target Audiences

Given the goals you've identified, what target audiences will you need to impact to achieve those goals? Remember that your challenge will be finding a balance between exerting more effort than is required to communicate to various audiences and not exerting enough effort to impact the appropriate audiences.

A good starting point in identifying target audiences is to consider the various stakeholders that the message impacts. For instance, a communication plan about a plant closing would impact a variety of constituencies both internal and external:

- Managers or supervisors

- Employees at the plant

- Employees at large

- Senior leaders

- Community leaders

- Local media (and potentially regional or national media)

- Board members

- Customers

Each of these segments could, potentially, be broken down even further. When deciding how narrowly to define your target audience, consider the following:

- Will different key messages need to be delivered to each group? For example, employees at the plant will have different questions or concerns than employees in other parts of the organization. But individual parts of the organization at large may not have different communication needs, and they might be considered as a single audience.

- Are there specific requirements because of the relationship between your organization and the audience? For example, certain large customers may require a personal visit or call, while other customer segments could be appropriately communicated with through a letter or an e-mail announcement.

Another consideration when you're identifying target audience segments is the order in which they need to be communicated with. The previous list, which was not presented in any particular order, could be reordered from first to last group to contact, as indicated by the numbers in parentheses:

- Managers or supervisors (3)

- Employees at the plant (4)

- Senior leaders (2)

- Employees at large (5)

- Community leaders (6)

- Local media (and potentially regional or national media) (7/8)

- Board members (1)

- Customers (7/8)

Or it might be ordered in some other manner. The order will depend on the individual needs or issues that each segment represents, legal requirements (publicly held companies must communicate certain messages publicly before sharing them with internal staff), and practical concerns (certain customers may be difficult to reach, an in-person meeting might be preferred but not possible given time or budget constraints).

Key Messages

Each identified target audience has different communication needs. The content, order, and number of key messages are likely to vary by group. In general, the fewer and more specific your key messages can be, the better. Three key messages are a good number to aim for—more than that will broaden your focus and minimize the impact of your communication. Each message may also have submessages or support points that should also be documented to help ensure consistency and to avoid missing a critical point when you're communicating with various audiences.

Some key messages related to specific HR communication needs could be the following.

INTRODUCING A NEW BENEFIT PLAN

- Our company will be introducing a new benefit plan designed to decrease costs and increase coverage options.

- The benefit plan changes will be primarily administrative—employees will be only minimally impacted by these changes.

- This change is part of our ongoing objective of providing competitive benefits that meet employee needs.

RESTRUCTURING A DIVISION

- After six weeks of study and discussion between all affected leaders and staff, the marketing division is announcing a major restructuring.

- This restructuring is designed to provide better, more accessible service to internal stakeholders.

- While reporting structures will change, there will be no layoffs or movements into lower job grades as part of this restructuring.

Strategies and Tactics to Meet Objectives or Goals

Objectives or goals identify the end points you hope to achieve. But you need to go beyond these broad objectives to identify specifically *how* you will achieve those end points. This involves developing strategies and tactics.

Strategies are broad statements of activity. Tactics are more specific statements of activity that are actionable. When identifying strategies and tactics, you should be realistic. There is probably a wide array of activities that you *could* undertake to achieve your objectives, but those activities may be hampered by budget and staff resources. You may wish to start this process by brainstorming all the various activities that you might undertake, and then review those activities and prioritize them according to both the potential for having the most impact and the availability of resources to accomplish the tasks.

Some strategies and tactics related to specific HR communication needs could be the following.

INTRODUCING A NEW BENEFIT PLAN

Strategy: Ensure acceptance and understanding among staff of the benefit plan changes.

Tactics:
- Survey staff to determine current level of acceptance or understanding.
- Identify gaps between current and desired state.
- Hold town hall meetings.
- Distribute brochure or newsletter updates outlining changes to plan.
- Send mailing with specific details to employee homes.
- Survey staff to determine whether acceptance or understanding has been positively impacted.

RESTRUCTURING A DIVISION

Strategy: Minimize employee departures related to concerns over restructuring.

Tactics:
- Establish schedule of one-on-one meetings between supervisors or managers and all staff within the division.
- Identify areas of concern and misconception.
- Schedule regular town hall meetings to provide opportunity for Q&A during restructuring.
- Create online newsletter for impacted staff to keep them informed of restructuring efforts.

Responsibility or Accountability for Completing Tactics

Having a plan is a good first step. Assigning accountability for the accomplishment of that plan is critical. Unless specific areas of the organization—and individuals within those areas—recognize that they are being held responsible and accountable for completing specific tactics that drive your ability to achieve your strategies and objectives, you will not achieve your desired results.

Assigning responsibility involves more than simply putting department or individual names in your plan. You need to ensure that you have buy-in and commitment from the departments and individuals you have listed. This may involve discussion at the senior management level of the organization and negotiation between organizational leaders to gain agreement on where the company's efforts should be focused. It should also involve, of course, conversation with the departments and individuals named, to ensure that they understand the expectation, realize the impact their involvement has on the achievement of the plan objectives, and are personally committed to helping to achieve those objectives.

Budget

In addition to identifying the people resources needed to achieve your communication plan objectives, you may also need to address the budget resources needed. While some communication plans will require no additional budget and can be accomplished with existing staff within standard work hours, other plans will require additional staff (overtime efforts, freelancers, or consultants) or the development of communication materials (newsletters, Web content, video, mailings, etc.). All these costs should be documented in the communication plan to provide an overview of the total cost for the communication effort and to give anyone in a position to approve or dismiss the plan a clear idea of the resources required to achieve the identified results.

Receiving approval for your communication plan budget will be based primarily on your ability to justify the expenditures that you're requesting. That means doing your homework in terms of providing background information that may include details on the outcomes of previous efforts, the impact to the organization of *not* achieving success, and the actual costs of the various communication activities you are proposing.

Measurement

A communication plan should be a "living document" and an opportunity for organizational learning. When you develop a plan, you should also identify specific ways in which you'll determine the effectiveness of your activities—your ROI. (See chapter 4.)

A "Planned Response" to Communication Requests

Your R&D department wants to improve organizational awareness of its product development efforts. So the department head gives you a call and says, "I'm sending over a list of all of the new products we've developed in the last twelve months—could you take care of sending this out to all managers?"

Inwardly you groan. Why don't they "get it"? But you think better of sharing your thoughts and ask, "How about getting together to discuss this further so I can help you come up with a communication plan?"

This is an example of a situation where what Devereaux Ferguson defines as a support plan would be appropriate. Communication is a process, not an event. Unfortunately, your internal customers may fail to appreciate the strategic value of communication and look for a quick fix. While these types of requests don't warrant the same type of commitment of time and resources as you would devote to your overall corporate communication plan, "planning before you do" is still important.

The following is a ten-step process for responding to a request like the preceding one. In fact, this process could be used with any request for communication, regardless of the scope of the issue.

1. **Understand the purpose of the communication.** Communication, regardless of the issue, should be designed with some end in mind. It should be implemented expressly to achieve some result. That result might be increasing awareness, or generating some action, or educating employees about a particular

issue. Regardless of the purpose, communication shouldn't just "happen." If you can't determine a *reason* for communicating, maybe you shouldn't communicate!

2. **Encourage your internal customer to get together for a discussion of the issue.** This isn't always an easy task. Everyone is busy, and often your customers will just want you to "do something." To overcome resistance, you need to present some solid benefits of taking the time to step back and think about the best way to address the issue. If possible, share examples of communication efforts that have failed because of inadequate planning and preparation. Impress upon your internal customer that their perspectives and insights will be critical to you in moving forward with communication. Ask provocative questions that demonstrate the need to get together for further discussion—that is, "How will you know whether your communication objectives have been met?"

3. **Gather additional input.** Depending on the complexity, sensitivity, or controversy of an issue, you may need to gather additional input from others within the organization. You may wish to poll employees to determine their current level of knowledge about an issue. You may wish to hold focus groups to uncover potential biases or misperceptions. You may need to research the issue or topic through external sources—media coverage, Internet, and so on. The more you know about an issue, the better you'll be able to present it knowledgeably and accurately.

4. **Identify key audiences.** The audience is not "everybody." Communication, to be effective, should be targeted. For example, if you need to communicate about budget cuts, the information you share with managers will be different from the information you share with frontline staff or customers. Even among employee groups, variations may require different messages or different communication tools. For example, off-site staff may not have ready access to the company intranet and

will need to receive hard-copy information, information by phone, and so on.

5. **Create key messages.** What *key* messages do you wish to convey? Be succinct and focus on "need to know" according to the outcomes you're looking for. Don't try to convey too much, or you'll confuse your audience. Hit the high points.

6. **Develop a timeline.** The order in which you inform key audiences can be critical. For example, if you put a notice in your employee newsletter about a benefit change before you have informed managers about the change, managers may feel undermined and at a definite disadvantage when it comes to addressing employee questions. Carefully consider which audiences need the information first, which may need it concurrently, and how long you can afford to wait between each step to ensure that the information won't begin to leak through unofficial channels.

7. **Develop a plan.** According to the audiences, messages, and timelines you've developed, prepare a written plan that outlines, specifically, the communication tools and processes you'll be using. The plan should include the background, key messages, and target audiences you've identified. You'll also want to specifically detail the tactics you will use to convey your messages. Some important elements to include are audience, tool, timing, who is responsible, and cost, if applicable. A simple table format can be a good way of presenting this information, as shown in table 8-1.

   Share the plan with your internal client, making revisions as necessary, before developing a final document. This plan then becomes your blueprint for moving forward and not only helps you maintain focus but provides a good organizational tool to ensure that you don't overlook any key steps in the communication process. The plan is also something of a "contract" between you and your internal customer, outlining what you have each agreed to in terms of messages, tools, budgets, and, as applicable, outcomes.

TABLE 8-1

Sample communication plan

Audience	Tool	Timing	Responsible	Cost
Management staff	Monthly management meeting	Nov. 5	Corp. comm. mgr.	N/A
All staff	Brochure	Nov. 12	Ad agency	$5,000
All staff	Intranet announcement	Nov. 12	Corp. comm. staff	N/A

8. **Start inside first.** Your employees are an important audience for your communication messages—even for marketing messages about your products and services. The more *they* understand, the more they can help you accurately share your messages with other, external audiences.

9. **Use multiple tools, multiple times.** Sending out a memo to announce a major corporate initiative is communication. But it's probably not *effective* communication. Advertisers recognize that their sales messages need to be repeated multiple times before they make an impact. The same is true of any kind of communication. In addition, you need to use multiple tools or methods of communicating. Some people will pay more attention to an e-mail message than a memo. Some people may not read your internal newsletter. Some may rely exclusively on your corporate intranet. *Repetition* is not a dirty word when it comes to communicating effectively. In fact, when you start to hear employees say, "I already heard about this," you'll know your message is starting to get across.

10. **Think "circular."** To develop a communication plan that will produce measurable results you need to, as Stephen Covey says, "start with the end in mind." Where do you want to go? What results do you want to obtain? The next obvious question is, How will you know when you have obtained those results? If you're attempting to increase employee awareness of your

organization's benefits, you may decide to do a baseline survey to determine employees' current level of awareness. Not only will this provide you with information against which to measure future results, it will also let you know which areas need to be emphasized and which do not, allowing you to better prioritize your efforts. Once you know where you want to go and where you are now, you need to fill in the gaps by identifying the communication tools you will use to increase awareness among the various audiences you have targeted.

To be effective, communication needs to be part of a carefully considered process, focused on achieving clearly identified, *measurable* results. It is not difficult to communicate effectively, but it does take some thought, a clear focus on objectives, an understanding of the tools available to communicate your messages, and a strong partnership between you and your internal customer.[4] Watson Wyatt's "Steps for Conducting Communication Audits" provides a useful framework for planning a communication effort (see appendix G).

Summing Up

- The foundation of effective communication consists of following a formal process that is connected to the organization's business strategy.

- There are different types of communication plans, but the purpose of each is to connect messages with audiences in such a way that specific actions or outcomes are achieved.

- Communication plans cover eight areas: situation analysis or background, quantifiable objectives or goals, target audiences, key messages, strategies and tactics to meet objectives or goals, responsibility or accountability for completing tactics, budget, and measurement.

- Goals should follow the SMART model. Goals should be specific, measurable, attainable, realistic, and time framed.

- A planned approach to responding to requests for communication assistance will ensure the appropriate use of resources and an optimum outcome.

Leveraging Chapter Insights: Critical Questions

- How are communication plans used in your organization? After reading this chapter, what suggestions would you make to improve the use of these plans?

- Consider a communication need you are currently facing. How could you use the eight-step process of developing a communication plan to address this need? Which of these steps do you feel is most critical?

- Do you feel a formal communication-planning process would result in a better outcome? Why? Why not?

- Which of the five types of communication plans identified by Sherry Devereaux Ferguson are you most familiar with? How have they been used in your organization? By your HR department?

CHAPTER NINE

Tools of the Trade

The Use and Benefits of Various Communication Tools

Key Topics Covered in This Chapter

- *Key questions in formulating a communication strategy*

- *Verbal communication tools—pros and cons*

- *Written communication tools—pros and cons*

- *Electronic communication tools—pros and cons*

T HE COMMUNICATOR'S TOOLKIT is large, with a multitude of tools to choose from, either alone or in combination. The selection of the appropriate tool for the audience and issue being addressed is critical—as is a solid understanding of how to maximize the effectiveness of each of the tools available. The challenge for communicators is selecting from among this wide variety of tools the "mix" that will be most effective in a given situation. The use of the term *mix* is purposeful—and meaningful. Just as in the world of mass media advertising, in corporate communication it is the combination of various media that will achieve maximum impact and not, necessarily, the use of one tool alone.

Consider your personal experience with communications from your organization—a new product introduction, for example. Suppose that new product introduction were communicated through an e-mail to managers. Would that serve to sufficiently inform the organization? Or suppose the communication occurred through the employee newsletter. Would that be more effective? Or perhaps the information were posted on the company intranet. While each of these examples might be appropriate ways to communicate the information, they are unlikely to have as much impact independently as they would if they were used in combination.

HR faces communication dilemmas frequently, particularly when dealing with internal audiences—benefit communication, policy communication, or perhaps communication about a merger, consolidation, outsourcing, or downsizing initiative. The challenge facing the HR communicator is selecting from among these various tools the combination that will most effectively address the needs of the target audience and achieve the desired communication outcomes or actions.

Leonard Lee is president of Perfectense, a public relations and marketing firm in Minnesota. Asking what the "best tool" is for communication, he says, should be the last question communicators ask as they're developing communication strategy. "Fly swatter or elephant gun? It depends on what you want to do and who your target is."[1]

The key questions in formulating a communications strategy are, he says, as follows:

- What is the corporate culture of the organization?

- How are employees used to receiving information?

- What is their accessibility to these tools (maybe they don't all have e-mail or Webcast access; maybe they have round-the-clock shifts, so multiple town hall meetings would be necessary; etc.)?

- Are there existing channels of information such as unions, work groups?

- What is the message? What is its criticality?

- How thorough is the depth of understanding you are trying to achieve?

- Are you trying to engender action on the part of recipients?

- How familiar are people with the background—is this similar to previous messages or expressing completely new concepts?

Communication tools can be broken down into three categories:

1. Verbal

2. Written

3. Electronic

HR practitioners have the opportunity to take advantage of these tools to maximize the impact of their communication. The

HR department might hold town hall meetings (verbal) to share information with employees; it might produce an internal employee newsletter (written); or it might manage an intranet (electronic). Having a good understanding of the various tools available, their benefits and drawbacks, and how to use them most effectively will serve the HR practitioner well.

Verbal Communication Tools

Communication, at its most basic level, occurs between two people. MSN Encarta refers to these interactions as "dyads" and says, "Some dyads exist over a long period of time, as in a marriage or partnership. Communicating well in a dyad requires good conversational skills. Communicators must know how to start and end the conversation, how to make themselves understood, how to respond to the partner's statements, how to be sensitive to their partner's concerns, how to take turns, and how to listen. Together, these abilities are called communication competence. Shyness or reluctance to interact is called communication apprehension. Persuasion is the process of convincing others that one's ideas or views are valuable or important."[2]

In the workplace, communication occurs in a variety of settings at a variety of times. From the simple interaction between two individuals, verbal communication can become quite complex—and easily misinterpreted. Group dynamics—often referred to as "politics"—make communication challenging in even the most open, trusting settings.

Still, says Roger D'Aprix, "face-to-face communication is the most effective way of communicating with individuals." Communication professionals agree with him wholeheartedly. It is the relationship between direct supervisor and employee that is frequently pointed to as most critical in an organization, and that is precisely because of the opportunity for direct, one-to-one communication.

Verbal communication allows for two-way sharing of information. "Many of the tools commonly referred to as 'communication'—memos, email, voicemail, intranet postings, newsletters," says

D'Aprix, "are one-way communication tools. Although they are certainly useful, they do not, in and of themselves, mean 'communication' has occurred. By themselves they do not allow you to check for understanding, to decipher various interpretations or to solicit feedback."[3]

Yet, while communicators agree that verbal exchange is a powerful medium, you need to be aware of some downfalls when determining which tools will be most effective for your communication "mix."

"Certainly the upside of one-on-one communication," says Leza Raffel of the Communications Solutions Group, "is that you get away from that corporate wall that management is lecturing top-down and we're not in a position to respond. You definitely have a stronger one-on-one interaction. The problem is that you lack consistency in that approach. If someone in upper management is making the rounds talking to individual employees, the chances that the message articulated is going to be identical each time is slim to none—things will get lost in the translation. You'll end up with people interpreting things differently because they're not hearing the whole story or management is not communicating the whole story."

One way of helping to minimize this variation is in the preparation of "speaking points," or guides that are provided for internal spokespeople with the expectation that these guides will direct their discussions. Still, as you might imagine, some variation is inevitable.

In addition to direct, one-on-one interactions between managers and employees, for example, group meetings are another commonly used verbal communication approach. These meetings can certainly be effective, particularly, says Raffel, if your goal is to inform, persuade, explain, motivate, prompt action, or provide a sense of direction. "You get group buy-in. You have consistency of the message now because you're talking to everybody at once, and you can frame the message in a very positive way. You can control the message." These meetings are especially useful, she says, during times of change. "Companywide meetings are valuable because employees are given a sense that management values them sufficiently to take time to talk to them directly and to respond to their questions or feedback."

The problem, she says, is that "in that environment people are often reluctant to ask questions because they're in a large meeting." In addition, she points out, these large group meetings require that staff is taken off the job to participate, so there's an impact on productivity. Table 9-1 highlights the differences between face-to-face communication approaches.

Written Communication Tools

The commitment of words to written form is ancient. Papyrus was an early form of paper, made from grasses, that was used by the Egyptians. Later, in the second century AD, the Chinese wrote on silk fabric instead of wood and developed paper made from silk

TABLE 9-1

Differences between face-to-face communication approaches

Tool	Pros	Cons	Tips
One-on-one discussions	• Direct, personal. • Build relationships. • Allow for exchange of ideas and information.	• Difficult to ensure consistency of messages between senders and from one receiver to another.	• Raffel suggests developing "key communicators" within work groups —individuals identified as being responsible for sharing messages within their group.
Staff meetings	• Offer opportunity to provide the same information at the same time to a large group. • Allow for exchange of ideas and information.	• Some individuals may be intimidated by a group setting and hesitant to speak, share information, or ask questions.	• Minutes can help protect the integrity of the information, ensuring a record of what actually took place.
Town hall meetings	• Offer opportunity to provide the same information at the same time to a large group. • Allow for exchange of ideas and information.	• Some individuals may be intimidated by a group setting and hesitant to speak, share information, or ask questions.	• Meetings may be taped or broadcast via audio or video to allow greater participation among dispersed groups.

fibers. And from as early as the second century BC, Europeans wrote on thin layers of tanned and scraped animal skins called parchment with quill pens made from bird feathers. Until the 1400s in Europe, all documents were handwritten but, by the fifteenth century, demand increased for the ability to easily duplicate documents. An early version of movable type was first developed in China around 1045; in 1450 the German printer Gutenberg perfected movable metal type and introduced typesetting. The broad availability of printed documents and books increased literacy and learning, having a dramatic impact on the world.[4]

Today, typesetting has given way to word processing, and while not long ago many were predicting that print would eventually become obsolete, today most agree that while electronic communication may augment the printed word, it is unlikely to replace it anytime soon. "Some companies have eliminated print communications, believing they will save money by only communicating electronically," says Jane Shannon, a communication consultant and author. "It's a bad choice. You need a mix of communication vehicles that takes into account what each does best."

"I still think people want something tangible to hold in their hands," says Raffel. "Something they can take with them on the train. I'm hopeful that the electronic media won't replace the company newsletter. I think it's still important to have something tangible that's handed to you." These tangible materials may appear in a variety of forms:

> **Annual reports**—Publicly held organizations are required by the SEC to produce an annual report. However, while the SEC requires only that these organizations file a Form 10-K, most companies go far beyond that requirement to produce a report that serves, in essence, as more of a marketing document. For these companies, the annual report is about more than numbers—it's an opportunity to communicate and connect with shareholders and other key constituencies.
>
> Annual reports are big business. In its annual report survey results released in September 2004, the National Investor Relations Institute (NIRI) reported that the median budget

or midpoint of all annual report estimates provided was $103,500, including production and distribution of the report but not including postage. This represents a decrease from $124,900 in 2002 but is still a significant expense. The average cost per copy increased from $3.73 in 2002 to $3.91 in 2004. There was a significant decline in the average print run, from 95,600 in 1999 to 61,900 in 2004.

The strategic intent behind the annual report for most was to communicate corporate strategy (81 percent), to communicate the company's nonfinancial drivers (70 percent), and to comply with SEC regulations (68 percent). Departments most often responsible for managing the project are investor relations (59 percent), corporate communication (18 percent), and finance or treasury (11 percent).

Brochures—Brochures are print pieces that can appear in a variety of formats and sizes. They can be used to communicate internally (e.g., a brochure outlining employee health plan options) or externally (e.g., a brochure about a specific product). Brochures might be used to provide general background information about a company and its products and services or to educate or inform various audiences about a variety of issues.

Direct mail—Direct mail might take the form of a brochure, a flyer, a postcard, or even a letter that is sent through the mail to specific target audiences. Direct mail is generally considered a form of direct marketing, intended to elicit a response from a prospect for a company's products or services. However, direct mail might also be appropriately used to communicate with employees—to generate registrations for a company event, for example. Direct mail is designed to immediately attract the attention of the recipient, providing compelling information designed to generate a direct response—a phone call, a return postage-paid card, an online order, and so on.

Editorials and letters to the editor—When organizations wish to speak directly to the public in a news-related forum that offers greater credibility than a paid advertisement, the letter to the editor or editorial is often used. Letters to the editor are often sent by organizations in response to what they believe has been incorrect or misinterpreted material previously printed, or to expand on information shared during an interview that they feel wasn't adequately conveyed by the reporter. While these tools can offer an opportunity to set the record straight, organizations need to exercise caution in their response, carefully considering whether the potential value of correcting the issue in this manner outweighs the potential to drag the story out. Sometimes, PR professionals advise, it's best to simply let the story die rather than continuing to fan the flames by engaging in a dialogue in a public forum.

Fact sheets—Fact sheets are generally single-sided, 8½ × 11 inch documents that present information about an issue or a product in an abbreviated, easily scannable format. Public relations departments often use fact sheets to present an overview of key points relevant to their companies, which might include company name, address, contact information, business focus, a listing of products and services, locations, management team members, and so on.

Media kits—Media kits are used by public relations departments to provide information to the media about the company and news related to anything from new product releases to plant expansions or closings, to positions on issues. The media kit generally consists of a folder that contains a variety of background materials that might include relevant news releases, background information or a fact sheet about the company, biographies and photos of key staff members or spokespeople, product sheets or brochures, contact names and numbers, and so on. Media kits might be distributed via mail

or handed out at news conferences or other events. Many
organizations now have online media kits, giving reporters
easy access to this background information on the company
Web site.

Newsletters—The American Marketing Association defines
newsletters as "brief digests of important or noteworthy
information. A newsletter may be developed by individuals
for sale or distributed free by associations, professional soci-
eties, and companies as a method of reaching various publics
quickly."[5] Of source, newsletters are also widely used by
organizations as an internal form of communication to employees and may be produced in print or electronic format.
(See "Twenty-five Ways to Use Employee Newsletters.")
Internal newsletters are a common way that organizations
communicate with their internal constituencies—and they
are an effective communication source. Yet, like other communication tools, they are not without drawbacks.

"Internal newsletters are a great way to introduce a new
initiative," says Raffel. "They're a great way to let people
know about other things going on in the organization.
They're good for clarifying myths and inaccuracies because
you can hit them head-on."

But, Raffel adds, the internal newsletter shouldn't be the
sole source of information for staff. "Communication is one-
sided and doesn't allow employees to have pressing questions
and concerns answered immediately." That, says Raffel, leaves
room for misunderstanding and frustration. "The internal
newsletter is best used as one of several tools to circulate
information."

Simma Lieberman agrees. Lieberman is a communication
consultant and the author of *Putting Diversity to Work*. Too
often, she says, communicators will say, "Well, we put that in
the newsletter," when employees lament, "We didn't know
about that!" Simply putting a message in the newsletter is not
enough.

Twenty-five Ways to Use Employee Newsletters

Robert F. Abbott is the author of *A Manager's Guide to Newsletters: Communicating for Results* and has owned and operated The Newsletter Company since 1991. He has written and published employee, customer, and member newsletters for companies in a diverse range of industries and sectors. He believes strongly that newsletters are an excellent means of communicating with employees and that, if used strategically, newsletters can help organizations achieve business objectives. He offers twenty-five ways to "address problems or take advantage of opportunities" using employee newsletters:

1. Spread your organization's philosophy or vision.

2. Report changes in that philosophy.

3. Announce changes in policies or procedures.

4. Advise of changes in management or staff.

5. Recognize special contributions by employees.

6. Welcome new employees.

7. Report on changes in benefits packages.

8. Deal with frequent questions or complaints about benefits.

9. Remind employees of the value and availability of benefits.

10. Explain the introduction of new technology.

11. Upgrade job-related skills or expertise.

12. Introduce or encourage employee ownership stock plans.

13. Prepare staff for new sales initiatives.

14. Help employees handle sensitive inquiries.

15. Introduce new products or services.

continued

16. Explain how to sell new products or services.

17. Maintain contact with distant branches.

18. Improve health and fitness.

19. Greater safety awareness on the job

20. Explain the handling of customer complaints.

21. Provide information about customers.

22. Explain the rationale behind corporate advertising.

23. Gather ideas for productivity improvement.

24. Identify personnel for promotion.

25. Improve inter-office cooperation and coordination.

SOURCE: Robert F. Abbott, *A Manager's Guide to Newsletters: Communicating for Results* (www.managersguide .com/1.html). Used with permission.

News releases—A news release is a statement from a company about its products, services, or events sent to the news media in the hope that reporters will run a story about the company. The term *press release* is also used but is actually a much more narrow term, since the word *press* suggests print media, and news releases are, of course, distributed to broadcast as well as print media. A modern variation on the traditional news release is the *video news release,* or VNR, which is a publicity spot produced by a company to have the same look and sound as a news story.

The big benefit of written communication tools, says Raffel, is that "you don't run the risk that things are going to be miscommunicated." Once committed to writing, material is considered "fact." This demands, of course, that communicators remain vigilant about the accuracy of the material they produce. While verbal communication has impact, that impact is fleeting. The written word—inaccurately presented—can remain to haunt the communicator for years! Table 9-2 highlights the differences between written communication approaches.

TABLE 9-2

Differences between written communication approaches

Tool	Pros	Cons	Tips
Newsletters	• Portable. • Tangible. • Flexible—offer ability to include graphics and photos. • Offer ability to communicate a wide range of information in one compact format.	• Can be costly and time-consuming to produce. • Errors have a long "shelf life." • Gathering representative information from across the organization can be challenging.	• A "reporters network" of contact people from across the organization can help to provide "tips" on newsworthy issues. • Offering newsletters in both print and online formats can help meet individual preferences of staff.
Brochures	• Portable. • Tangible. • Ability to include graphics and photos.	• Can be costly and time-consuming to produce. • Errors—and outdated information—have a long "shelf life."	• A standardized process for production can help minimize errors and ensure timeliness.
Flyers	• Portable. • Tangible. • Quick to produce. • Good way to highlight key points or facts.	• Errors—and outdated information—have a long "shelf life."	
News ("press") releases	• Allow organizations to commit facts or key messages to a tangible format.	• The traditional "print" news release has become outmoded.	• "Electronic" news releases offer greater timeliness and direct reach. • When used as part of a "media kit" or distributed along with a three-dimensional piece (e.g., promotional item, marketing "hook"), can be very attention getting.

Electronic Communication Tools

When considering electronic forms of communication—particularly "new media"—you should remain grounded in your focus and remember that your objective is to *communicate*. You should never select a communication tool simply because it's new or trendy. There is certainly a place for electronic communication options, but your objectives, message, and audience need to be the basis for your selection of the appropriate communication tools. A variety of media are available:

Blogs—A relatively new entry to the communication world, blogs, or Weblogs, are ongoing information and communication about various topics of interest, running the gamut from blogs focused on specific companies and their activities to blogs that are nothing more than an individual's ramblings about his or her interests and thoughts. It is estimated that there are more than *ten million* blogs in the United States alone. Why the proliferation? Because they are easy and inexpensive to create.

Blogs allow users to:

- Create a searchable archive of content where every entry has a unique URL, which makes it easier to find through Google or other search engines.
- Promote ongoing, dynamic communication.
- Promote transparency—they can be open to the entire world, or they can be password protected to allow access to only a specific audience.

From a corporate communication standpoint, blogs might be promoted within an organization to allow employees with shared interests—whether on a business or a personal level—to interact. Companies that have been proactive in promoting blogs include Microsoft and IBM.

Like any form of communication, of course, blogs can create problems. Organizations need to establish guidelines and policies for the use of blogs and guard against such things as violating copyright and plagiarism, liability, and the release of proprietary information. The Electronic Frontier Foundation has released a free guide—*Legal Guide for Bloggers*—that offers information about appropriate and not-so-appropriate uses of blogs (see www.eff.org/bloggers/lg).

E-mail—E-mail offers the ability to communicate with individuals literally around the globe in a matter of seconds and at an extremely minimal cost compared to what has come to be known as "snail mail." Widely used—sometimes *overused,* e-mail has become an extremely prevalent form of business communication, giving rise to a number of questions about "e-mail etiquette." For example:

- Is it okay to use emoticons when sending professional e-mail correspondence?
- How long should your signature line be?
- How much of a previous e-mail should you include with your reply?
- Can you forward someone else's e-mail to a friend? To ten friends? To a newsgroup?
- Is it okay to include full text articles in your e-mails?
- What is spamming, and could you be doing it unintentionally?

These are just a few of the many issues that business people face when communicating online. While it is most often the Internet newbies who commit the most heinous online etiquette blunders, even old pros can find themselves inadvertently committing online faux pas. It is often the little things that cause the greatest problems. Online communication is no exception. Following are some "little things" that you should be aware of when communicating online.

- AVOID ALL CAPS. WHEN YOU TYPE IN ALL CAPS ONLINE, IT'S CONSIDERED SCREAMING. Also, reading text in all uppercase is difficult. If you want to emphasize a word or phrase, use *asterisks* around the word.
- Always fill in the "subject" line of the e-mail and be descriptive. This is particularly important when you're participating in newsgroups or message boards.
- Don't send unsolicited file attachments. Viruses are commonly carried through attachments, and recipients are hesitant to open these attached files unless they're confident that the source is safe. It's best to cut and paste the content directly into your e-mail to avoid this problem.
- When you reply to an e-mail, edit out those portions of the message you received that are not pertinent to your reply.

Don't delete the entire message, because the sender may not know what you are responding to. But don't send the whole thing either—it takes up unnecessary space and requires the receiver to read through a lot of extraneous material.

- Don't participate in e-mail "chain letters." These messages, containing "heart-warming stories," or "great jokes," or "dire warnings," proliferate online and can be extremely irritating to recipients. No matter how clever, unique, or touching you find them, don't pass them on!

- Avoid online "grudge matches." Even if you are the recipient of a rude or abusive e-mail, resist the urge to respond. The beauty of e-mail is that it can be eliminated with a click of the Delete button. Use it.

- Be cautious about the information you include in your e-mails and do so only with the knowledge that e-mail is not private. Your e-mail message can be readily forwarded on to others individually or through newsgroups and message boards.

- Respect copyright laws. Don't include full text articles in your e-mails (instead, include a link to that information if it is available online). If you quote from published material, always cite the source of that information. Don't forward e-mail you've received from someone else without their express permission.

- Use *emoticons* judiciously. Emoticons are symbols formed with letters on the keyboard and arranged in such a way that they represent various facial expressions. The most common is a smiley face, ☺, but there are literally dozens of others. While emoticons can be helpful for conveying meaning when you don't have the benefit of facial expression or voice inflection, don't overdo it.

- Keep your messages short and to the point—and proofread your messages! While e-mail is a very informal communication medium, sloppy e-mails reflect negatively on you.

- Be responsive. Check your e-mail regularly and respond promptly to the messages you receive. But don't be too impatient with slow response from others. Generally, forty-eight hours is a reasonable time frame within which to expect a response.

Too many people overrely on e-mail, says Lieberman. "No matter what you do, if people only get to know you by e-mail you'd better understand e-mail etiquette and e-mail language. I've seen so many miscommunications occur through e-mail— it's really a good avenue for misunderstanding."

E-newsletters—E-newsletters or e-publications are online versions of the more traditional print newsletter. Electronic publications are different from their print cousins in a number of important ways:

- Their production. E-publications eliminate the need for print production, saving time and cost, and providing greater flexibility in terms of making last-minute changes.
- Their delivery. E-publications are intended to be consumed somewhat differently from print publications. They are more transient in use from both the developer's and the consumer's perspective. They should offer a "quick read." While they provide the opportunity for the editor to link to more detailed content for that portion of the audience that wants more detail, they are generally lighter on copy and make more use of lists, bullets, and other "readability formatting options" than print newsletters traditionally have.
- Opportunity for immediate feedback and interactions through comments, online polls, surveys, and links to chat rooms.

Intranet—While Internet sites are designed to reach an external audience, an intranet is basically an internal Internet or Web site that is accessible only to employees. Intranets provide distributed access to a broad array of company information, interaction, and work flow processing (e.g., ordering supplies, submitting HR requests). See "HR and the Intranet" in chapter 10 for more information on how HR communicators might use an intranet to communicate to and interact with staff.

Just as with your Internet site, your intranet should be developed with a specific purpose in mind and should be designed to generate positive benefit to the organization through increased efficiency in communicating and sharing information as well as increased productivity through interaction and electronic processing of requests. "The intranet has a great capacity for facilitating the exchange of information during the introduction of a new initiative," says Raffel. "Whether you choose to keep employees apprised of changes through daily e-mail blasts or by establishing a Q&A component to your Web site, the intranet can be empowering to employees."

Internet—The advent of the World Wide Web, or Internet, has had dramatic implications on organizations and the public at large and has significantly changed the ways in which we interact with customers and the public, the way goods and services are exchanged, and the availability of information on a multitude of subjects in literally seconds. Internet technology has enabled interactivity, the efficient distribution of information, and the development of "community" between organizations and various publics. An organization's Internet site should be developed strategically, with content taking precedence over aesthetics. While your site should certainly convey and support the correct brand image for your organization, when it comes to determining the value of the Internet, it's outcomes—not looks—that matter. You should have specific goals and objectives for your site that go beyond simply "generating hits." These might include creating visibility for your company, strengthening your brand, or developing relationships with specific target market segments.

Streaming video—Streaming video is video that is displayed over the Internet or an intranet. When accompanied by sound, streaming video is referred to as *streaming media*. Streaming media technology allows users to see these images or hear the sound without having to download a large file.

The media is sent in a continuous stream and played as it arrives through the use of various technologies like Microsoft Windows Media Technologies.

Web forums—Forums (also called message boards, online forums, or bulletin boards) are online postings of comments, questions, and responses that relate to a topic of shared interest among a group of people. SHRM, for example, has a number of forums on topics like HR outsourcing, workplace law, and compensation and benefits. Visitors can read previous postings, leave new messages, and check back for responses to their messages. When you participate in a bulletin board discussion, keep the following points in mind:

- Make sure the forum you select is appropriate for you, particularly if you plan to be an active participant. While it is perfectly all right and quite common for participants to "lurk" (read the messages of others without actively posting), if you plan to be a participant, make sure that you "fit in," or other group members may become frustrated with you.
- Follow the rules of the group. Visit the FAQ (frequently asked questions) area before participating. This is where you'll find answers to basic questions about the site as well as tips and rules for participation.
- Remember that the messages you post to the group are public and will be read by all. Use tact and diplomacy in criticizing the ideas and comments of others. Personal attacks online are known as *flaming*. You do not want to be the victim or the perpetrator of a flame.

Webcasts—Webcasts might be thought of as programming through Internet transmission. They are presenter-led, Web-based events that include both visuals (slides, streaming video) and voice. Webcasts allow multiple people in many locations to view content that is being generated from a single source. They are less interactive than videoconferencing and are often recorded and made available on demand for viewing when convenient to the audience. Webcasts combine various communication options that might include facilitator-controlled PowerPoint presentations (for live Webcasts), streaming video or audio, chat rooms for live Q&A, and so on. Webcasts are sometimes combined with telephone conference calls to allow direct interaction with the facilitator of a live presentation. Webcasts also offer the opportunity for polling of participants, Web tours, demonstration of software applications running on the presenter's desktop, and the ability to record and store presentations for future use.

Electronic tools like Webcasting, says Raffel can be very useful in large organizations with multiple, dispersed audiences. Teleconferencing is another option.

Communication experts advise caution in considering the use of e-technologies. "In a world cluttered with modern technologies," says Kerry Patterson, coauthor of the *New York Times* bestsellers *Crucial Conversations: Tools for Talking When Stakes Are High* (McGraw-Hill, 2002) and *Crucial Confrontations: Tools for Resolving Broken Promises, Violated Expectations, and Bad Behavior* (McGraw-Hill, 2004), "too many people are defaulting to the easy and fast forms of communication such as e-mail, instant messenger, Blackberry technology, etc. They are bypassing the traditional channels, which are more effective in communicating sensitive or highly emotional messages."

We've all heard the stories about employees who receive notice of termination via e-mail. Whether that is apocryphal or not, it is certainly true that many businesspeople overrely on electronic media to communicate when a face-to-face interaction would be preferable.

Patterson says that deciding which tool to use requires evaluation of the message and the audience—for example, "Is it bad news?" "Is it highly emotional?" "Is this my initial contact with this person?" By first determining the content and then evaluating the audience, the appropriate communication channel will become more obvious and the result more appropriate. Table 9–3 highlights the differences between technology-aided communication approaches.

TABLE 9-3

Differences between technology-aided communication approaches

Tool	Pros	Cons	Tips
Voice mail	• Ability to communicate with people when they're "away from their desk." • Can retrieve messages from other locations.	• Temptation to avoid direct contact by letting calls "go to voice mail."	• Establish "voice mail protocols"—instructions on what voice mail messages should include—and how to leave efficient or meaningful messages for others.
Fax	• Ability to transmit information, including graphics, immediately. • Ability to enter "fax groups," eliminating need to enter individual numbers.	• Someone must be available to retrieve and deliver the fax. • Faxes considered "junk mail" may be ignored by receivers.	• "Fax alert" programs offer the ability to quickly communicate important, time-sensitive information to pre-identified groups immediately.
E-mail	• Quick. • Immediate. • Instant communication of "hot" news.	• May be overused. • Meaning is easily misconstrued, leading to miscommunication.	• Don't use e-mail for communicating sensitive issues. • Be aware that e-mails are permanent documents that can be easily and broadly shared with others.
Blogs	• Easy to create and update. • Connect a wide range of people.	• Raise issues of libel, plagiarism, and release of proprietary information.	• Develop guidelines and policies for employee use. • Establish processes to monitor blogs.
Intranet	• Broad access to a lot of information. • Ability for multiple content owners to post and share information. • Allows for interaction that can streamline work processes.	• Outdated or inaccurate information may proliferate if content owners do not keep material up to date.	• Content over aesthetics. • Use as a process improvement tool (e.g., making requests, submitting information).

continued

TABLE 9-3 (continued)

Differences between technology-aided communication approaches

Tool	Pros	Cons	Tips
Internet	• Can add, change, delete information quickly. • Very up to date. • Easy, convenient access.	• Can get "lost" in the clutter.	• Content over aesthetics. • Interactivity is key.
Webcasting	• Ability to bring people together from a variety of remote locations. • Easy to repeat after being offered for the first time.	• Lack of visual tie.	• When using tools like Webcasting or having online discussions, a clear structure for asking and answering questions can help manage the interactions.
Video-conferencing	• Ability to bring people together from a variety of remote locations. • Visual connection among people.	• May feel "distant." • Can become unwieldy when more than two groups are conferencing.	• Use to include staff that might otherwise feel "disconnected." • Don't use video-conferencing exclusively. Allow for face-to-face interaction on occasion.

Summing Up

- Communicators have a wide variety of tools at their disposal, each representing various pros, cons, and opportunities.

- Selecting from among the various tools requires an understanding of their uses, benefits, and drawbacks.

- Verbal, one-to-one communication is often cited as the most direct and effective form of interaction by communication professionals.

- Written communication tools provide value through permanency and the ability to ensure that a consistent message is delivered.

- Employee newsletters are a commonly used written communication tool that may also be offered through electronic means.

- Most communication professionals agree that electronic tools
are an augmentation to—not a replacement of—traditional
print media.

Leveraging Chapter Insights: Critical Questions

- When you consider the various communication tools currently
used in your organization, which are most prevalent: verbal,
written, electronic? What suggestions would you have for
increasing or decreasing the use of these types of tools to be
most effective? Why?

- As a communicator, which type of tool do you find most
preferable? Why? As an employee, what form of communication do you find most effective? Why? Suppose your answers to
these two questions are different. What impacts do you think
this difference will have on your communication effectiveness?

- In considering all the specific communication tools available to
you, which do you think are overused by your organization?
Which are underused?

CHAPTER TEN

Selecting the Appropriate Tool

Guidelines for Selecting the Right Tool for the Right Purpose

Key Topics Covered in This Chapter

- *The use of communication tools*

- *Key variables to consider when selecting tools*

- *The objective and its impact on tool selection*

- *The audience and its impact on tool selection*

- *The culture and its impact on tool selection*

- *Communicating multiple times in multiple ways*

- *HR and the intranet*

S INCE COMMUNICATORS have so many tools at their disposal, it can be instructive to look at how they use these tools across a variety of organizations. In a survey of 533 companies, including 47 *Fortune* 500 firms, Lawrence Ragan Communications, Inc., found that "an astonishing 41 percent of the companies surveyed said they didn't have a written communication plan in place." Without this formal road map, Ragan concluded, "these organizations tend to spend less on internal communication, do less with the communication tools at their disposal and grossly under use the CEO" in their communication efforts.[1]

Many companies had access to the variety of tools described in chapter 9 to communicate with employees, but the study found the tools are used less frequently in those organizations without formal plans. Figure 10-1 shows a graphical representation of the findings.

Norman Crouse, business consultant and author of *Motivation Is an Inside Job,* suggests that there are five key variables to consider when selecting the appropriate communication tool:

1. **Cost** (travel, staff time, etc.). Too many organizations, says Crouse, don't calculate the cost of staff time when they schedule meetings. Or if they do count it, they only take the raw hourly wage cost. "I like to use the cost of a fully loaded productive hour (take the hours in a work week and subtract out all the nonwork time like vacations, sick time, lunch, etc.). Then divide that figure into the fully loaded wage—including the cost of benefits, FICA, etc. When a client does this it usually

FIGURE 10-1

Use of communication tools

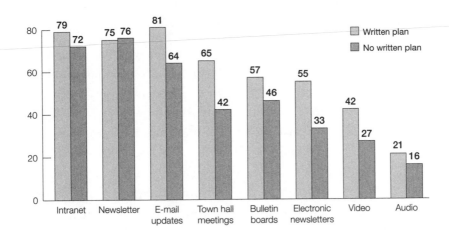

Source: *Ragan Survey of CEO Communications,* 2002. Used with permission.

shocks them how much money is running up on the labor meter during a meeting. That helps them evaluate the return on investment of having people get together."

2. **One-way versus two-way.** "If I'm going to bring people face-to-face for a meeting," says Crouse, "I have to ask myself what advantage is there to them being physically present. What am I going to do with them here in person that I couldn't do with them by e-mail? Typically, the answer involves some sort of iterative decision making or give and take. If I can't figure out why I need them together, I should use one of the other, less expensive, tools for communication."

3. **Timeliness of information conveyed.** "If I'm communicating something they need to know now and need to act on immediately," says Crouse, "then I'm going to choose a tool that allows me to send it immediately (think e-mail or instant messaging). If it's merely something I want them exposed to, then I will choose something like a newsletter or a poster."

4. **Learning channels** (visual, auditory, kinesthetic). The more important the message, says Crouse, the more learning channels should be utilized. "So, for a mission critical message I'm going to use many tools that involve all the channels," he says.

5. **Long-term relevance of information.** If the information is something that will have long-term relevance and should be available as a reference, says Crouse, "I am going to want to put it into a tool—manual, intranet site, etc.—where it will be available on demand. The challenge with this is to keep the versioning in control. If I send out an update to a manual how do I ensure someone inserts the update into the manual? Many organizations use electronic storage like an intranet site or online knowledge base to combat this versioning challenge."[2]

What works and what doesn't? "Everything," laughs Francesca Karpel of Network Appliance, Inc. In all seriousness, though, she says, what works depends on your objective and your audience.

It's hard to say which tool is "right," agrees Kathryn Yates of Watson Wyatt. The "right" tool depends on your ultimate objective, your audience, and the culture and history of your organization.

The Objective

The most important thing to consider, says communication consultant Simma Lieberman, is "what's your message and what are the results you want from that message so you can select the best way to get those results."

Karpel agrees. "The first thing to consider when selecting a tool is what's your objective? What do you want to accomplish? Once you've defined that, then you can make the right choices." So, for example, she says, "if you just want to inform, you might use a broadcast medium. If you want to have a dialogue, then you need some verbal interaction. If you want people to feel something, then you probably want to use a medium where you can convey emotion."

In selecting the appropriate communication tools, says Yates, the first step is knowing what you're trying to accomplish. The second is considering your audience segment and the best means of reaching or influencing that segment. "What do you want to have happen? Who is it that has to know about this? What kind of commitment level do you need from that audience?" So, for example, if you need your leadership team to support some new initiative, you will need to use a different level of communication and different tools than if you simply need to inform a group of employees about an "FYI" item.

The Audience

Charlie Melichar is vice president of PR at Colgate University. "As a professional communicator," says Melichar, "I have a wide variety of communication tools at my fingertips—e-mail, Web, Webcast/conference, videoconference, meetings, etc.—and I've found that the choice of tools must be guided by the needs of the audience and the context of the message. E-mail, for example, is the best tool for quickly sharing facts and brief information, but it provides no context and important messages can easily be misinterpreted. Similarly, certain audiences that are 'in the loop' via a newsletter or other communication vehicle might need some one-on-one time with the CEO or another executive to provide them with some reassurance that their issues are being handled effectively." The bottom line, says Melichar, is that "communicators need to have just as firm a grasp of their audiences and their needs as they do the various communication vehicles they have access to."

The demographics of your workforce and the specific audience you're attempting to impact will play a key role in the selection of communication tools or tactics. "A younger generation will enjoy more entertainment and live, busy media," says Karpel, "while someone fifty-five or above might not want that—they might prefer to be able to read a print publication or a very simple Web page." Demographics in terms of the professional mix of your organization also come into play. "Folks who are in engineering and the sciences like more explanation, they're more analytical, they're also more likely to be early adopters of technology," says Karpel.

"You really have to know the demographics of the people you're talking to," Lieberman adds. Location of staff is obviously an issue when you're selecting communication tools. "If everybody is in the same building," says Lieberman, "you're not going to use videoconferencing."

Careful consideration of the audience can have a significant impact on the success of your communication efforts, as Karpel points out. When planning a significant change in health care options with a very small window of time for the open enrollment period—two weeks— Karpel started at the back end, with the needs and concerns of the audience, in coming up with communication options and messages.

Karpel explains, "We recognized that there was the potential for tremendous resistance because of the uncertainty about 'is my doctor covered?' We figured that would be the area for the greatest resistance. We planned the communication around this and took steps to make it easy for employees to get the answer to that question. The benefits team identified the doctors that would be out of network that our employees had used and put together a list of a couple of hundred names to give to the medical, vision, and dental providers to see if they could start soliciting these doctors to become part of the network. We created an online form that an employee could link to and drop in the information about a doctor to say, 'please have the new company contact my doctor to see if he/she can become part of your network.' We also created a template of a letter that individual employees could send to their doctors requesting that they become part of the network. The insurance providers had Web sites where the lists of doctors in the network were provided.

"We took all of these actions so that in our general communications we could allude to them and tell people we understood that a very high percentage was included, but for those of you with concerns these are the steps you can take. We provided them with a substantive way of responding to a need that we addressed."

In addition to these steps, says Karpel, a very ambitious communication plan, developed in cooperation with the insurance providers, included information on the various Web sites, 800 numbers for preenrollment questions, open house fairs at cafeterias in major locations, Webcasts for employees not able to attend the fairs, and a series of e-mails during open enrollment, including reminders sent only to those people who had not yet made their enrollment selections.

"What was most important," says Karpel, "is we thought in advance about what would be the greatest challenge for people and what would cause the most concern and then we took steps to address those concerns." The net effect, she says, was a very successful open enrollment period—"We actually got people enrolled more quickly than we had in the past."

The Culture

Your organizational culture, says Yates, will also dictate the tools you select. "The right tool for a Palo Alto high-tech company may be the wrong tool for a Cleveland-based manufacturing company." In addition, Yates says, it's important to understand the history of the use of various tools within the organization. What's worked in the past? What hasn't? "Maybe you have to grab attention with something entirely new—or maybe you need to use a traditional vehicle."

"You want to make sure that you don't put the wrong level of formality in your communications," says Leza Raffel of the Communications Solutions Group. "The company size and the cultural environment are going to be critical in terms of determining how you want to communicate."

Karpel agrees. "If you're in a company that has always had a newsletter, to take that away might be taking away a link that people feel is really important. But, if you've never used print, and you've got a young workforce, you might not need to go there."

Multiple Times—Multiple Ways

The tools used need to work in combination, Karpel says, emphasizing that communicators should consider how to maximize the effectiveness of these tools through their interplay. For example, she says, if your CEO sends an e-mail message to all staff, that same message might also be posted on your intranet site. Within the message there might be a link to another page that provides more detailed information, or to various FAQ pages geared to specific audience segments.

At Network Appliance, she says, messages are "cascaded" through the organization in a planned manner to ensure the right audiences receive the messages in the appropriate order. For example, she says, "we might advise an executive team in a meeting of something that's happening and then an e-mail might go out to a broader group of managers telling them what's going to be coming for all employees so they can prepare for that. Employees might get another e-mail or be directed to a Web site with more information."

Careful coordination and timing requires planning but results in more effective communication. If you're having a town hall meeting to announce a new initiative, for example, says Raffel, communication should be coordinated so that when staff return to their offices, they see posters on the walls in the hallway, in the restrooms, and so on. They might receive a follow-up e-mail and more information through interoffice mail. Their managers and supervisors might be provided with talking points to share that reinforce the town hall messages.

Communicating about your tools and their purpose is another important step for HR and communication professionals to take, says Lieberman. "You need to market your tools—to let people know the importance of them." So, for example, you may want to make it very clear to staff that information about benefit changes will always be explained through the "HR Newsletter" or that responses to employee suggestions will always be found in the "Ideas" forum on the intranet.

For HR professionals, says Karpel, looking for help among communication colleagues can be a good place to start when thinking about the use of various tools. "I would always recommend that they find someone with communication expertise. It's well worth the time spent touching base with a communicator."

HR and the Intranet

The company intranet is generally considered to be a communication tool—a method of sharing information with employees. Certainly, an HR intranet site can aid in providing information to employees, and providing information is a worthy goal. But just as Internet sites evolved beyond "brochureware," so must HR intranet sites evolve beyond being viewed as only a communication tool. HR communicators should look to the intranet as a means of saving time (which ultimately saves money) and improving service to employees.

Consider the use of your intranet site in terms of not only sharing information but also increasing efficiency, streamlining operations, and increasing value to your internal customers. You can do that in a variety of ways:

Online employee handbook. In the "old days," keeping employee handbooks updated could be a tremendous administrative and logistical task. Changes would be made to the original, copies made and distributed, and fingers crossed in the hope that managers and employees would dutifully update their three-ring binders. Today, employee handbooks (along with policy manuals and other documents) can be easily maintained and updated online, ensuring that employees and managers have ready access, at all times, to the most accurate and up-to-date information.

FAQs. In many organizations, the HR department is the "catchall" for questions from employees. Many of those questions are repetitive. In large organizations, responding to the same question several hundred times can be a drain on resources. But tracking and categorizing those commonly asked questions and putting them on the HR home page, where they can be searchable by key words or phrases, not only cuts down on calls to the HR department but provides great service to employees as well.

Employee activity calendars. The intranet makes it easy
to maintain a calendar of events viewable by all staff and
easily updated by HR personnel. Events could range from
employee social activities to organizational meetings to educational offerings and other company activities. For organizations that participate in various fund-raising efforts, calendars
can be a good way for employees to promote these events
and ensure that they aren't competing with too many other
offerings.

Forms. First-generation intranet sites frequently contained
forms online that employees could download and fill out.
That's a step in the right direction. But making those same
forms interactive goes one step further. Interfacing the data
that employees enter on the form into other corporate systems goes further yet. Some examples:

> **Name or address change forms.** Instead of calling HR
> or filling out a form and sending it to HR, what if
> employees could pull up a screen to make changes to
> their name, address, and so on and then with a click of a
> button automatically update all internal databases that
> contain the information?

> **Personnel requisitions.** Are managers required to fill out
> forms to request replacement or additional personnel?
> Why not make those forms interactive?

> **FMLA requests.** While it will take more than an online
> form to simplify the requirements of complying with the
> Family and Medical Leave Act (FMLA), making this
> form interactive can help cut down on the administrative
> burden.

> **Leave requests.** Funeral leave, jury duty, leaves of ab-
> sence—all these requests can be streamlined and simpli-
> fied by enabling employees and managers to process the
> "paperwork" electronically.

Other requests. Take a look at the myriad forms that cross your desk every day. How many of these forms could be automated?

Employee evaluation. Processing evaluation forms online streamlines the process not only for HR but for managers as well. Another option is to automate 360-degree feedback, with forms automatically sent to appropriate individuals, who fill in their ratings. The ratings are then compiled and reported to the supervisor—electronically. And of course, the data can be readily stored in that format for easy access and review later.

Job postings. Consider moving toward the online receipt and processing of applications for open positions. With some slight modifications, the same process that is used for processing external applications can be used with internal staff. Employees can be kept up to date on positions they may be interested in, while managers will have online access to information about the status of a job opening, the ability to view resumes and applications online, and the ability to work through—and document—the entire hiring process electronically.

Payroll. Is your payroll system automated yet? Consider a system whereby employees enter their time worked and time off and send the information electronically to managers for approval, and then the data is automatically uploaded to the payroll system, where payments are processed.

Online benefit enrollment. The annual benefit enrollment process can be a paper-pushing nightmare. But the intranet can automate this process. Combining both the information sharing aspects of the intranet with the ability to process transactions can greatly ease the chore of benefit enrollment and give staff enhanced access to information and illustrative examples about the benefits available to them. Online benefit calculators can help employees choose among various options or model the impact of various elections.

Connecting Employees Through an Intranet

When it comes to the introduction of an intranet, you can't just build it and expect them to come! When Weber Shandwick, a leading PR and communication management firm, introduced an intranet site—i.connect—to its global employees in 2003, it knew that it would take a series of planned communications, and a little "buzz," to make the site a success.

A "virtual tour" helped introduce employees to the site, taking them through i.connect's features. Branded mouse pads were distributed to all employees, worldwide, on the morning of the launch. A series of weekly e-mails with the subject "Using i.connect" promoted and highlighted various features of the site and provided instructions on how to use those features. Clickable links in the e-mails led to feature stories on events in global offices.

Weber Shandwick also recognized that once employees came to the site, it would take fresh information and useful content to keep them coming back. The home page is updated weekly with news from offices around the world. Features include

Education and training. What if employees could review course offerings and availability and register online? What if they—and their managers—could log on at any time to view an up-to-date record of the courses they've taken and to ensure that they've completed any mandatory training?

Logo goods online. Does the HR department in your organization have responsibility for the sale and distribution of corporate logo items for use by employees or for distribution to various goodwill efforts? Wouldn't it be nice if these products could be ordered online, just as we've all become familiar with ordering from various Internet-based e-commerce sites?

"Global Voices," a periodic thought leadership piece from senior management, and "Faces of Weber Shandwick," a weekly Q&A providing a lighthearted look at the personal and professional backgrounds of mid- to senior-level professionals. The site also provides centralized access to human resources, benefits, and learning and development programs, including a catalog of courses and online registration for both classroom and virtual instruction. All relevant materials for the company's Performance Management Process—an employee review system that allows employees to map out their professional goals—are also provided online.

The efforts have paid off. Nearly all of Weber Shandwick's employees use the site regularly. Following the launch, the average monthly rate was more than 84,000 visits and more than 225,000 page views.

Key takeaways: you can't just develop an intranet site and expect employees to find and use it. You need to support your site with a communication plan focused on benefits for staff, and deliver on your promises with pertinent, fresh content that provides value for employees to keep them coming back.

Reward or recognition programs. Many companies have programs whereby employees earn points from managers and fellow employees in recognition of their efforts "above and beyond the call of duty." They can then "spend" these points for movie tickets, corporate logo items, days off, and so on. This process could readily be automated, allowing employees to send points online as well as to spend the points they've earned.[3]

The experiences of Weber Shandwick demonstrate the value of strategically introducing an intranet to employees. See "Connecting Employees Through an Intranet."

Summing Up

- Organizations with formal communication plans tend to make broader use of the variety of communication tools available.

- In selecting the appropriate tool—or mix of tools—the first step is identifying your objectives or goals. What do you want to accomplish?

- The demographics of the workforce and the specific audiences you wish to influence will drive the use of specific communication tools or tactics.

- Organizational culture will have an impact on the use of various communication tools and should be considered when you're identifying tactics.

- Communication tools need to be used in combination and with repetition to ensure maximum impact.

- The intranet can provide a wide variety of communication opportunities—and process improvement options—for HR communicators.

Leveraging Chapter Insights: Critical Questions

- How does the audience for a specific communication impact the selection of a communication tool? Do you feel that your organization currently does a good job of selecting the appropriate tool for each audience? Why or why not?

- In what ways does the culture of your organization impact the tools used to communicate with employees? In what ways does the culture of your HR department impact the ways you communicate with employees?

- How effective is your organization's intranet? How could its effectiveness be improved? Are there specific functions that your HR department could benefit from?

CHAPTER ELEVEN

Handling Challenging HR Communications

Insights for Dealing with Common yet Challenging Communication Situations

Key Topics Covered in This Chapter

- *Compensation and benefits communications*
- *Communicating about health care plans and options*
- *Communicating with employees in remote or off-site locations*
- *Communicating during relocations*
- *Downsizing or corporate acquisition communication*
- *Budget cuts or bankruptcy communications*

HR COMMUNICATORS might face a number of particularly challenging, yet common, communication situations, including compensation and benefits, health care plans and options, employees in remote or off-site locations, relocations, downsizing or corporate acquisition, and budget cuts or bankruptcy. In each case, HR communicators should use the same process or method for developing and disseminating messages as they would use in any other situation. The basics remain the same—the devil, as they say, is in the details of communicating difficult messages and the increased need for attention to detail to ensure the proper sequencing of messages. Those nuances, along with tips and suggestions from communication experts, are presented in the sections that follow.

Communicating Pay

A 2002 *WorkUSA* survey conducted by Watson Wyatt indicates that the percentage of employees who say they understand how their pay is determined is at its lowest level in a decade—40 percent. The cost to employers? Employees who don't understand how they are paid are less satisfied with their jobs. HR professionals can improve retention and productivity simply by better and more frequently communicating to their workforce how their organization determines pay and salary increases and bonuses. Experts recommend that communicators keep compensation simple and easy to understand and that they "market" the plan to employees.

"Generally, people don't understand how they get paid and don't understand the connection between their pay and rewards," says Frank Roche, a principal in the communication practice at Mercer Human Resource Consulting in New York, where he leads the Performance Measurement and Communications Group.

According to a 2002 Mercer study on workers' attitudes about their jobs, little more than half understood how pay was determined, and only 28 percent said they were personally motivated by that knowledge because, the study concluded, workers don't clearly see how the quality of their work affects their pay.

The Mercer research shows some startling effects on job satisfaction when pay issues aren't clearly understood or clearly tied to performance. For example, of those employees who said they understood how pay was determined, 74 percent were satisfied with their jobs. Of those who did not understand how pay was determined, only 42 percent were satisfied with their jobs. And of those who said they were paid "fairly," 85 percent were satisfied; of those who felt they were not paid fairly, only 47 percent said they were satisfied with their jobs.

The "really good companies," says Roche, are starting to pay more attention to these issues and are improving how they communicate messages related to pay and incentives. "There's not as much money to go around, equity is going away, merit increases are down and bonuses have, in some cases, gone away or have been fairly dramatically reduced."[1]

Ace Hardware is one company that has experienced a change in its compensation philosophy. Laurie Nicolazzi, a senior compensation analyst with Ace Hardware Corporate Compensation in Oak Brook, Illinois, says, "When I came on board, communication was limited in regard to salary information. In 1997, we said, 'We're opening that door.' We became much more forward with the information that we gave our management and supervisory teams. We said, 'If you're a manager of this organization, then this is something you need to do your job effectively.'" The managers can then accurately engage in dialogues with their employees about compensation and how their performance and the company's performance affect it.

"Opening the door" to fully disclose more details and information about compensation plans is a worthy goal, but it's not always an easy process. Compensation planning and pay administration are complex. Quite often, the focus of compensation communication is on the technical details of the compensation plan and pay systems. This technical focus, says Marc Wallace, a consultant with the Hay Group in Chicago, is not necessarily the best approach to take. "What's going to make a difference is the amount of effort you put into implementing and communicating the plan," says Wallace. "You can spend a lot of time behind closed doors figuring out the perfect plan, but if the employees who are participating in that plan don't understand it, then you're not going to see any of your expected impacts."

The companies that do well spend more time communicating the plan than worrying about the perfection of the design, he says. They're also comfortable with the notion that the plan is a work in progress that can—and should—be modified according to information gained through experience and feedback.

Brad Hill, a senior consultant with the Hay Group, agrees. "Statements that I designed earlier in my career," Hill admits, "dealt too much with the technical details from a compensation manager's perspective and didn't say enough about the individual's contribution to the business."

The key is to work with employees to develop focus, understanding, and, eventually, commitment. To do this, some companies are taking a less technical, more marketing based approach to compensation communication.

Joe Rich, copresident of Clark/Bardes Consulting, a compensation and benefits firm based in Marlborough, Massachusetts, says HR and compensation professionals could be much more effective if they learned a few lessons from their marketing colleagues. Communicating issues of pay to employees, he says, is no different from selling any other service. "Marketing people realize that understanding what a customer wants and then presenting what they have to

offer in (those) terms enhances the value. Compensation is no different. If you understand how people perceive pay as a 'good,' and how
it helps them meet their personal and family needs," says Rich, "you
have a whole different way of thinking about what compensation
communication is about."

Keeping it simple is one of several points that consultants and
HR professionals say are key elements of effectively communicating
issues of pay to employees. Others include:

- **Mission focus.** "We have to focus employees, first of all, on
  the things that are essential to the business's success," says Tom
  McCoy of T. J. McCoy & Associates, LLC, in Kansas City,
  Missouri. "Those are the measures. After we create focus, the
  next thing we need to do is create understanding—that's an
  educational process and it's an ongoing, continuous educational
  process. We really want to help employees understand the story
  behind the numbers. What's important to the company? What
  do those numbers mean? Where did they come from? What are
  the trends? How can I impact them?"

- **Transparency.** The more employees are informed about how
  the compensation plan is structured and what it means to
  them—the more *transparent* your organization is about its pay
  practices—the greater the level of trust.

- **Frequency.** In many organizations, communication about pay
  happens once a year. Instead, employees should be reminded and
  updated frequently about the pay plan and how the organization
  is doing. That could take place in a meeting, a monthly report, or
  an e-mail update. "My recommendation is that supervisors and
  managers use their measurement scorecard on at least a monthly,
  if not weekly, basis," says McCoy. "They should sit down with
  their employees to talk about those key performance measures
  which employees are incented on, and what they mean."

- **Management buy-in.** Companies that take the time to train
  their managers and supervisors on their compensation plans

before rolling out these plans to employees at large are more successful, says Wallace. "The best way to reach your employees is through your management team." At Ace Hardware, says Nicolazzi, meetings are held with supervisory and management staff several times a year to explain how the salary administration structure was developed. In addition, if concerns arise, meetings are held between the supervisor or manager and the employee, "so there's relationship-building and education involved," she adds.

- **Engage employees.** To engage employees, recommends Wallace, organizations need to "communicate a sense that they are a part of a broader team, that they are working toward a common goal." And, he adds, "it's not inappropriate to ask employees' opinions, find out what they value in terms of pay, what makes sense to them and what doesn't make sense to them." Ace Hardware surveys employees regularly, says Nicolazzi, asking questions about various facets of HR, including compensation. Results provide direction for future initiatives, including communication.

Are your compensation and benefit communication efforts working? It's relatively easy to measure the impact of compensation and benefits communications, says communication consultant Angela Sinickas, although she admits that she doesn't see many companies doing this. "You may have a campaign that includes print, online, telephone support meetings, and maybe not all of your locations are taking advantage of these tools. Normally you might see that as a problem, but I look at it as 'free research,'" says Sinickas. What these variances allow, she says, is the ability to compare results across locations or sites.

"We did this once at Hewitt," Sinickas says, "where we found there was a large difference in both the number of people enrolling in a 401(k) plan and the average deferral percentage based on whether or not their plant had meetings available." All it takes, she says, is making a correlation between the communication effort taken and the results—and comparing across different sites. "It's so easy to do. It costs nothing and it takes a tiny bit of time."

For example, the plans an employee signs up for impact the company's bottom line. Employees are faced with a variety of decisions—whether or not to cover the spouse or dependent in the plan, the level of coverage to select, whether or not to put money into tax-deferred to tax-free accounts, and so on. These decisions can have a big impact on the company. "If we can prove what communication efforts get people to make the 'right decisions,' it's very simple to calculate ROI," says Sinickas. "We can even calculate the cost of the entire open enrollment campaign against just a few outcomes with a financial value." And, she adds, "I can guarantee there will be a financial return." Plus, she says, "you don't have to capture everything, just the easy ones to measure, and you can tell that what you spent made a difference."[2]

At Williams, a Tulsa, Oklahoma–based company that moves, manages, and markets a variety of energy products, Marcia Mac-Leod, vice president of rewards and policy, says the company has struggled through some "financial issues," as have other companies in the industry, and has had to make some adjustments. One of the major changes has occurred in compensation administration. The new plan, MacLeod says, has a much stronger emphasis on pay for performance. "It's a massive cultural change," she says. The first step, says MacLeod, is building understanding. "Not acceptance, initially, but understanding. We're in the process of doing a good old-fashioned going around and talking face to face, first with our executive management, senior management, directors, managers, and then down to supervisors. We're giving them tools to enable them to create the messages—not just sending out brochures, letters or e-mails," she says.

Williams is also using the intranet to provide interactive formulas so employees can see how their incentive pay will work. "We're providing training about the new financial metrics," says MacLeod. "We're sending out quarterly information on how the company is doing and how that relates to their pay."

MacLeod explains that this effort is an attempt to "demystify compensation. I think a lot of compensation professionals want to keep it like a black box. We've worked very closely with the HR generalists and management to explain (market) survey data to them, to demystify it, to be very open and to let them be a part of the process."[3]

Communicating Health Plan Benefits

HR communicators are in a key position to impact employee education about health care options—and, consequently, to impact the costs of health care coverage for both the organization and its employees.

Carol Hadley is the director of employee benefits for Aurora Health Care in Milwaukee, Wisconsin. "Everybody knows that health care costs are rising," says Hadley. "The more informed a participant or an employee is, hopefully the better health care choices they can make. They can get the correct services at the right time and the right place—get them early if they need it and, in the long run, be healthier and keep costs down."[4]

Like Aurora, Jenny Craig International is also concerned about the health and well-being of its employees, says Roberta Baade, PhD, vice president of human resources. "It's what we're about," says Baade. Healthy employees result in a healthier workforce, she asserts. "It's in your best interests as an employer to keep your employees healthy." And, she adds, "we're asking employees to share more in the cost of their health care coverage, so they want to know more about how to utilize that care effectively."

The open enrollment period traditionally prompts the dissemination of information about health plan options and related health and wellness issues. "As we head into our open enrollment period, I start out by putting articles about the rising costs of health care and what's happening in health care out there so the folks will see pieces of information that *I'm* not writing," says Baade. Information is shared through the company intranet and print communication vehicles. "As we get closer to enrollment, we do streaming videos," says Baade. Videos are done once a week, with an introduction from

Baade and messages from each of her staff members. Information about enrollment is also sent to employees' homes.

"We take a lot of time when we make changes to our health insurance policy to try to explain to employees why we made changes," says Nancy Ayres, general manager and benefit decision maker at Clipper Belt Lacer, a small manufacturing company in Grand Rapids, Michigan, that among other things has turned its "smoking room" into a health care education and wellness facility. About 65 percent of Clipper Belt Lacer's employees are male, and the average age is a bit higher than forty-seven.

"You cannot over-communicate about benefit plans," emphasizes Baade. "And I don't mean just speaking in 'benefit-ease.' I'm talking about ways in which you can get your employees to understand what their coverage is, what to expect and where to go so they don't have those scary experiences when they go to the emergency room and someone says, 'You're not in the system.' We try to communicate as much as possible," says Ayres, "but in a lot of different ways because people have different learning styles." So, she says, Clipper Belt Lacer does a lot of the traditional communication tactics—bringing representatives from their health care providers in for "lunch and learn" sessions focusing on how to read food labels, how to reduce stress, how to exercise, how to eat better, etc.

Tracy Lewis, SPHR, is the HR manager for Kemin Health LC, a nutritional ingredient company based in Des Moines, Iowa, with operations worldwide. At Kemin, says Lewis, a number of activities help encourage healthy behaviors. Lunch-and-learn meetings are held each month, offering employees an opportunity to learn about various health-related topics while they enjoy a catered meal. Employees also have embraced the competitive aspects of being healthy. A competition based on pedometer use, for example, challenges employees to form teams and see how many steps they can take in a day. Prizes help offer encouragement and incentives for participation.

When it comes to healthy lifestyle messages, communication relies heavily on "walking the talk." Sometimes the cultural messages can be as influential as the tangible, if not more so. A healthy-eating message in the company newsletter loses its meaning, for example, if the vending machine is filled with candy bars and potato chips. Clipper has worked with its vendors, says Ayres, to reinforce healthy food choices by providing yogurt, fresh fruits and vegetables, and flavored water as healthy snack options for employees. "It's been extremely popular," says Ayres. A bulletin board also offers employees the opportunity to share healthy recipes.

What is the measure of effectiveness for these types of communication efforts? For employers, says Hadley, benefits lie in cost savings and a healthier workforce. "I think everybody believes that the healthier their employees are, the more they'll save in the long run. The healthier employees are, the more productive they are as well." And of course, educating employees about health care options and healthy lifestyles can offer value beyond the bottom line. To many it's simply the right thing to do—a win-win situation for all involved.

Communicating with Employees in Remote or Off-site Locations

Communicating with employees on-site is challenging enough. The complexity increases when employees are in remote or off-site locations. And of course, challenges are even greater when you're communicating in global organizations. Kathryn Yates of Watson Wyatt encourages communicators to "think globally, act locally." Global communication is becoming more and more important, she says, but communicators can't overlook the need to customize messages for the needs and culture of their "local/global" audiences. Just as when you're addressing any other communication challenge, the steps remain the same: identify and segment your audiences and develop messages that are most appropriate for those audiences; then deliver those messages in the appropriate mix and frequency to achieve your desired outcomes.

A number of steps can be taken to avoid breakdowns in information, trust, and connectedness between organizations and their remote workers, says Jathan Janove in the SHRM white paper "Management by Remote Control." These include:

- **Regular communication.** Managers and HR professionals underscore the necessity of continual communication "even when nothing is going on." Don't let problems serve as the only triggers for communication. Maintain a regular practice of staying in touch with remote offices or employees. Suggestions include having at least one e-mail exchange a day and at least one telephone discussion a week. One manager has employees do weekly one-page reports in which they describe what they accomplished the past week, the state of morale at their location, and their ideas for improvement.

- **Go to *gemba*.** Wes Schotten, senior consultant with the Hayes Group International in El Paso, Texas, preaches the concept of "going to *gemba*." As he explains, *gemba* is a Japanese word meaning "scene of the accident or crime." However, as construed by Japanese management, it refers to going to the heart of the matter on a regular basis to observe firsthand what is important. More Americanized managers might employ the acronym MBWA (Management by Walking Around, a concept introduced by management guru Tom Peters). Make it a practice to get away from the home office and go where remote offices, facilities, and employees are. Conduct these visits even when there appear to be no problems to solve. Be there for positive events such as employee awards, promotions, and the opening of new departments. While you're there, make a point of being visible. Don't slip past the receptionist and spend your time holed up in the local manager's office. Bear in mind, as one executive observes, it is often when things are going well and when numbers are up that the seeds for future trouble are sown. Excessive or inappropriate hiring, personnel issues, or the need for product or service innovations often get overlooked. Therefore, take inventory even when everything appears to be going well.

- **Periodic audits.** Paula Gabrault, a consultant with Reintjes Services in Kansas City, Missouri, urges managers responsible for remote sites to periodically audit compliance with company policy and applicable employment laws. Develop a checklist. Some of the items on it can be done by or with HR's help, such as whether I-9s are being properly processed for new hires or whether employees are being lawfully classified as exempt or nonexempt. Other items on which the manager should focus include checking whether employees at remote sites have received and understand important company policies such as internal compliance reporting options to the home office or company policy regarding handling customer accounts.

- **Technology.** In today's technological times, you can stay connected with remote employees in a variety of ways. These include Web conferencing, videoconferencing, and well-developed intranet sites. Your IT department (or, if you don't have one, a consultant) should explore what is available and what will work best. For example, one employer conducts regularly scheduled Webcasts in which the CEO and other senior executives simultaneously address dozens and sometimes even hundreds of employees in eighteen locations throughout the United States. Available technology also includes sophisticated monitoring devices. These can provide remote checking of e-mail, Web sites, and programs that employees access; when employees log in and out of their computers; and even their exact keystrokes. However, just because the technology exists doesn't mean you should use it. A cost-benefit analysis should be conducted, including factoring in time, price, effect on morale, potential legal issues involving privacy rights, and the qualifications of those who will do the monitoring. Some employers have discovered to their dismay that employees in the IT department who were supposed to be guarding against employees' accessing illicit material became consumers instead.

- **Training.** Training remote employees continues to be a struggle. However, several tools help. A plethora of video and computer-based training products exist or can be customized. Intranet sites can be designed to include interactive training modules that teach employees the rules, expectations, and job-relevant skills. Such tools should not, however, entirely supplant live training. Face-to-face sessions tend to have a more powerful impact. They also help reinforce the connectedness between home office and remote location. In addition to having managers, HR representatives, and others make periodic visits to conduct training sessions, employees can be brought to the home office or to regional gatherings for training and peer reinforcement. Although this can get expensive, it is an investment in the three ingredients of knowledge, trust, and connectedness. These sessions also can go a long way to increase the likelihood of early reporting of problems, as opposed to letting them fester and grow.

- **Employee selection.** Cherie Aldana, vice president of HR at PDI, Inc., in Upper Saddle River, New Jersey, stresses the importance of making good remote hiring decisions, especially of the person who will be reporting to you at the home office. Some employees are self-starters with strong internal motivation and good organizational and communication skills. Others, however, need the physical presence and structure of a tightly organized management system. The employee selection process for remote sites should, therefore, be tailored to assessing in which category the applicant fits. In the interview process, ask applicants to describe specific experiences that demonstrate their ability to show initiative and thrive in relatively free or lightly structured environments. The background-checking process should seek to verify such experiences.[5]

Employee Relocations

Mass relocations are most commonly referred to by relocation professionals as "group moves." Joe Benevides, senior vice president of global business development for Paragon Relocation Resources, Inc., in Rancho Santa Margarita, California, defines *group moves* as "any large-scale movement of employees from one location to another." While typical relocations, says Benevides, involve people who are "on career paths in a management or sales capacity," in group moves the involved employees are more likely to represent "a broad range of employees, in addition to the upper-level executives and salespeople. Literally," says Benevides, "you're seeing administrative folks as well and that raises some very unique issues and challenges, mostly dealing with policy."

"The whole process of group moves," says Benevides, "is a lot different than a typical relocation." One key factor, he says, is the "group mentality" that must be dealt with. "You're dealing with a large group of people who are all influencing each other. That's why it's important to put a positive spin on the process and to have a very cohesive communication plan so you can head off any negativity that might exist and get the retention rate up as high as you can."[6]

Craig Caruso is senior vice president at Lexicon Relocation in Jacksonville, Florida. The reason behind the move, Caruso points out, has a major impact on how employees respond to the move and to the opportunities that may be presented to them. "As you can imagine," he says, "if you're faced with an offer to move from Wisconsin to Dallas where you'll run an office or facility, and it's a promotion, that could be a very exciting venture. If you're told 'we're going to close your office in Wisconsin and offer you a move to Dallas and if you don't take it that ends your employment,' it sets that whole process off on an entirely different tone."

There are, of course, some benefits to a group move that don't exist in typical relocations. One of those benefits is that many of the established social connections that employees have can be maintained so they're not moving alone into totally uncharted territory.

For HR professionals, one key point in handling the people issues related to a group move is recognizing the varied needs of the affected employees. "Don't assume one size fits all," Caruso stresses. "You need to focus on the human element involved in this corporate decision and remember that you've got everyone from renters to home owners to families. You've got singles, children, extended families, spouses, dual-income families. We're all seeing that loyalty to the corporation is not quite what it used to be. Employees really have to think long and hard before automatically accepting a move these days."

Providing resources and information to employees to help them make the decision—and to navigate that decision once made—is an important detail. Jim Glickert was on the Boeing site selection team when Boeing was involved in a major relocation of staff from Seattle to Chicago. As director of HR for the Chicago site at the time of the start-up, he was also one of the two hundred employees to make the move—with his wife and four children in tow, the youngest only four weeks old when the move occurred.

As soon as Chicago was selected as the destination city, says Glickert, a relocation office was set up at Seattle headquarters. Next door was a room that was used as a library with information on the Chicago area. The library also served as the base of operations for a local real estate professional who was on-site to provide assistance. Every employee who accepted a job offer was assigned to a relocation specialist; they, and members of their family, were able to access the resources available as they prepared for their move.

Giving employees and their families an opportunity to see and experience the new location is a critical part of any relocation effort, but especially critical during a group move. To accomplish this, Boeing chartered an airplane for three trips to Chicago to allow employees and their family members or significant others to explore the area and make decisions about where to live.

Throughout the relocation process—from announcement, to transition, to the move and beyond—communication is critical. "Probably the two most important things in any group move," says Benevides, "are to be out in front of it and to do a lot of planning. Most of the planning," he adds, "revolves around a communication plan." That plan, he says, needs to ensure that people are well aware of the action plan, who will be offered positions in the new location, what their individual options are and what the severance options may be for employees who do not make the decision to move.

"My feeling," says Glickert, "is to communicate early and to communicate often." Boeing did communicate early—the announcement was made in March, giving employees notice even before a location had been selected. In hindsight, says Glickert, that may not have been the best approach. "It proved to be a particularly hard struggle because there were people that immediately started lobbying for different locations." Still, he says, early communication is important.

"It would have been helpful for us if we had known the city right off the bat," Glickert says, "but my personal feeling is you've got to communicate. If a decision has been made to move, I'd let people start planning. Not only is that the fair thing to do for those relocating, but for people that aren't going to make the move, it gives them the maximum amount of time to find something else."

At Boeing, initial meetings were held at corporate headquarters in Seattle. The chief administrative officer at the time led the relocation effort, along with the head of relocation and Glickert, who had taken over as director of HR for world headquarters. Glickert made these discussions more meaningful by preparing a series of maps that helped show people the relationship between downtown Chicago and various neighborhoods. The maps included information about housing costs, transportation options, and so on. "People really liked that," he says. "They could easily see how much it would cost to live and how long it would take to get to work. It was easy to see that if you were willing to commute an extra 20 minutes, for example, you could get a house for less money."

"The key thing is to communicate and give the transferees the tools they'll need to make a rational and informed decision," says Benevides. "Certainly you don't want people just signing up without even having seen the place, because it might not be a good fit for them. On the other hand, you don't want them to dismiss it out of hand because it might be the best thing that ever happened to their career or to their family."

For HR and communication professionals, the implications and responsibilities involved with a group move don't end once the affected employees have accepted the positions offered to them, or even when the last moving truck pulls away from the curb of the last relocating employee. In truth, the need for ongoing communication, support, and encouragement of staff—at the new facility and those who may have been left behind—may need to continue for quite some time. It's not an easy process.

It can, however, generate some very positive results, Caruso points out. "You're helping a family transition to a new location during one of the most stressful times of their lives. That can be very rewarding."

Gale Baird experienced relocation both as a manager and as an employee impacted by a corporate move. See "Mass Relocation at Louisiana-Pacific."

Mass Relocation at Louisiana-Pacific

Gale Baird, SPHR, relocated from Portland, Oregon, to Nashville, Tennessee, in a Louisiana-Pacific Corporation (LP) group move. Baird is the business HR manager for the oriented strand board (OSB) business team of LP, whose corporate headquarters relocated to Nashville in July 2004. The move was designed to bring all corporate resources together in one location.

LP made the formal announcement that it planned to consolidate corporate headquarters in Nashville on September 30, 2003. Four locations had been considered, including Charlotte, North Carolina; Richmond, Virginia; and Portland, Oregon, where LP's corporate headquarters had been located. As part of the announcement, LP indicated that it intended to retain a significant presence in the Portland area—approximately one hundred thirty positions. "People knew we were going to consolidate corporate headquarters," says Baird. "It was something that had been discussed as a topic for a number of years. LP had done some business restructuring and we knew we would get to a corporate consolidation at some point in time."

There's no doubt that group relocations are stressful for all involved. "It really tests our adaptation skills," says Baird. "How well do you deal with stress that's just not your typical work stress?" Relocating employees frequently find themselves in a new environment that can feel very much like an entirely new job.

"One thing that's difficult for some of the folks here is that our corporate headquarters is now located in a downtown area,"

continued

says Baird. "That's not new for the Portland folks, but it is very new for those who came from North Carolina and Texas and some other locations. It's a different place you drive up to when you go to work in the morning." And, she adds, "it lends to the feeling that you're working for a different company in a sense."

Employees who have remained in the old location must also deal with adjusting to a new environment and changing relationships, she points out. "You're working in an office that's no longer the center of attention as it used to be. There's a lot of energy around senior leadership. When those jobs depart, you're in a very different environment."

Consequently, says Baird, in addition to dealing with the employees who are relocating, "one of the issues you have to contend with is the morale and how people feel who are *not* moving." People factors come to play in terms of recognizing work/life balance for all involved. But, as she points out, "business has to go on." For LP, she says, "it was a very busy year—the building industry was very hot for the entire season and it didn't let up. People still had significant parts of their jobs to manage, even if they were driving through cornfields as they headed to Nashville."

There's the job—but there are also personal and, in many cases, family needs to manage. "You're furnishing a new house, trying to set up a new office, work with a new assistant, going through interviewing. It's a lot of activity that you do routinely, but just typically not all at once. I don't know how you can really anticipate what that piece of it feels like," says Baird, "until you're in the middle of it." But, she adds, "that doesn't mean that we can't all get through it."

Flexibility counts. In Baird's case, for example, while the new corporate offices opened on July 1, she didn't complete the actual move until the end of September, when the home she was building was ready to be occupied. "I didn't want to move twice, if I could help it and my manager was very understanding in being flexible with me on that."

Corporate Acquisitions and Mergers

In 2003 Hewitt Associates conducted a survey of nearly seventy CEOs, CFOs, board members, and vice presidents of corporate development and strategy to learn more about their companies' philosophy and practices surrounding restructuring efforts, including mergers and acquisitions, joint ventures, and divestitures. The results indicated that 53 percent of those surveyed planned on increasing merger and acquisition activity, and 49 percent planned on increasing joint venture activity over the next two- to three-year period. While optimism was high, risk factors were cited, including culture fit (25 percent), financial impact or ROI (23 percent), retention of key talent (16 percent), overpayment for the transaction (14 percent), and rapid implementation of the business plan (9 percent).

When asked how they could improve deals, 42 percent of respondents said more effective or efficient integration in the first twelve months was the area in greatest need of improvement, while only 12 percent selected thoroughness of due diligence and preliminary planning. When asked what deal practices they were most likely to change, the number one response (54 percent) was "start integration earlier."

Respondents felt that they had mastered the due diligence piece of the process but were struggling with execution and integration. Ideally, the two would be considered as part of a continuing process. Areas where deals are made or broken, said the study's authors, are those typically viewed as "soft," such as human capital management.

When respondents were asked about factors impacting the success of their deals, solid leadership and retention of key talent were cited among the top four, ahead of more traditional areas such as speed of integration, advance planning, and the experience of the deal team. Culture fit and retention of key talent were cited among the top four risk factors for mergers and acquisitions.

Another study—"HR Rises to the Challenge: Unlocking the Value of M&A," from Towers Perrin HR Services—reveals that companies that involve human resource experts early in the process of a contemplated merger, acquisition, or other restructuring improve their odds of a successful deal. There was widespread agreement among survey respondents, who included representatives from two hundred U.S. and Canadian companies that expect a rise in M&A activity in the coming years, that people issues are most critical during the first three to six months after a merger or an acquisition (see table 11-1). Further, researchers found that companies that felt fully ready to deal with M&A-related people challenges managed the merger's impact on employees much better than companies that said they were less well prepared. In addition, the financial performance of this group of companies, as measured by three-year total shareholder return compared to their relevant industry averages, showed that the "fully readies" are more likely to be higher financial performers as well, as described in the table.[7]

During a merger, internal communicators have a tremendous opportunity to use their talents, says Jody Buffington Aud, APR, principal and founder of the Prio Group, a Maryland-based communications firm specializing in internal communication and corporate communication management. She offers the following points for communicators during what can be a very stressful time:

- Know your senior management. First, understand that it's likely you are not working for one of the 5 percent of organizations that have a charismatic leader for a CEO. Understand that charisma does not equal good leadership, which numerous historical examples confirm. Knowing that your senior management has a vision and a plan to fulfill it is paramount. You

TABLE 11-1

Top issues three to six months after a merger

Ensuring effective leadership from top management	87%
Choosing the top team	85%
Communicating effectively with employees	75%
Keeping top talent	65%
Aligning the cultures of the organizations involved	47%

Source: Towers Perrin HR Services, "HR Rises to the Challenge: Unlocking the Value of M&A." Copyright Towers Perrin. Used with permission.

can help them communicate that vision in any number of ways that can make up for what one individual may lack.

- Understand that an organization's culture can be larger than any single human being in determining how that organization communicates. The more open and participative a culture, the more two-way the communication.

- Pay attention to the "little things." Essentially, mergers happen because someone—the CEO or board of directors—has a vision about how the company can improve. The problem is that the CEO or board members don't always have a firm grasp of what it takes to make a merger successful. They think, once the deal is signed, everything else will fall into place. If you understand employee attitudes, you know that it's the little things that make a difference. It may be as simple as "How do I answer the phone now?" or "When will I get new business cards and letterhead?" Most senior managers don't have the time or the inclination to think about the details. As an internal communicator, you should take the time to listen to the questions that employees are asking. Look for patterns and trouble spots and report to your senior managers the trends instead of details. You'll have a far better chance of getting someone to listen. Most important, be prepared with recommendations for how communication can make life easier for everyone.

- Be sensitive. When you're communicating to employees during a merger, you'll need to develop a heightened sensitivity. Change is much like the grieving process. People need to say goodbye to the old before they can adopt the new. Recognize this process, but don't contribute to it. Focus instead on developing strategies that satisfy employees' information needs at three different levels: (1) contextual—what is happening in the environment that has required change (in this case, a merger); (2) strategic—what the company goals are and how the company plans to reach those goals; and (3) personal—how these changes impact employees on a day-to-day basis.

From a communication standpoint, identifying the key constituencies or stakeholders in the merger or acquisition process is a good starting point for communication.

As organizations prepare for a merger or an acquisition, a transition plan can help ensure successful integration, says Al Himegarner in an SHRM white paper, "Mergers & Acquisitions: HR Transition Model and Issues to Be Considered When Companies Integrate."[8] The transition plan, says Himegarner, should include strategies for:

- Effective communication between integrating facilities so that the information required for the integration is obtained in a timely manner.

- Orientation of managers and employees at each facility about the history, mission, and culture of the other facility.

- Recognizing and addressing fears, hopes, and concerns of employees at each facility.

- Ongoing support at each facility to address emerging issues related to the integration.

A transition team can help aid in the process and can take on a number of responsibilities, including the following:

- Be visible and actively participate in the "welcome" meeting and information social event when integration is announced at each facility.

- Identify as a group the key activities and key information necessary for a successful integration, and assign responsibility for obtaining this information within an agreed-on time frame.

- Consider the impact of the integration on other departments at each facility, and immediately notify the leadership group of any potential problems.

- Coordinate the schedule of visits by the transition team members (or their designee) to each facility so that neither feels overwhelmed or abandoned.

- Provide a general orientation to the acquiring facility employees other than transition team members who will spend time at the new facility as part of the integration.

- Distribute a "who's who" directory of key contacts at the acquiring facility to managers of the new facility so they know who to go to if they have questions about processes or procedures during the integration.

- As a follow-up to distribution of the acquiring facilities directory, plan brief orientation and "how to" sessions for staff at the new facility with whom they will immediately interact.

- Identify a human resources representative to implement a plan to address individual employee concerns at the new facility, in cooperation with the new facility's human resources department, as appropriate.

- Develop and distribute a question-and-answer communication to employees and/or conduct monthly information meetings at the new facility.

- Provide regular progress reports on integration to both leadership groups.

And of course, there is a key role for the human resources department to play in communicating during mergers and acquisitions. See "How HR Can Assist in Mergers and Acquisitions."

How HR Can Assist in Mergers and Acquisitions

Responsibilities of the acquiring HR department, says Himegarner, include the following:

- Actively participate as member of the transition team.

- Sponsor programs for employees at the new facility to address resistance to change, grief processes, team building, and consensus.

continued

- Work cooperatively with the HR department at the new facility to provide separate orientation sessions for employees at the new facility so that their questions and concerns can be addressed outside the general employee orientation.

- Provide a "who's who" list of key HR contacts, with phone or beeper numbers, to employees at the new facility.

- Sponsor separate orientation sessions for managers and supervisors at the new facility to explain HR policies and practices.

- Assign an HR representative for the new facility to address emerging employee issues and remain involved through the integration process.

- Provide ambassador training for members of the transition team and their designees who will be spending time at the new facility.

Downsizing

Not so long ago, organizations preparing for restructuring and downsizing needed to respond to and satisfy the desires of only a limited number of constituents, say Ronald Adler, Donna Bernardi Paul, and Nancy Glube in an SHRM white paper, "Restructuring and Downsizing: Managing Disruption."[9] Today, that list has grown and includes:

- Employees, applicants, retirees, and unions

- Temps, independent contractors, and other contingent workers

- Stockholders, investors, lenders, and insurers

- Customers, vendors, strategic partners, and competitors

- Congress and state legislatures

- Federal agencies (EEOC, OFCCP, DOL, SEC, INS, and IRS) and state agencies

- Plaintiff lawyers, the courts, and juries

- Nongovernmental organizations, the press, and the public

These groups, the authors point out, have different and conflicting interests, making communication especially challenging. Their advice: "As a part of your restructuring and downsizing planning activities it is prudent to identify which groups will play a role in your decision-making process and which groups will most likely be affected by your decisions. You will then be able to evaluate each group's expectations and requirements and measure the impact of your decisions on these groups. For example, while Wall Street praises downsizing that produces immediate results and indicates that you are 'serious' about getting your expenses under control, government agencies emphasize statutory compliance and customers and strategic partners usually value maintenance of relationships."

The need to downsize ebbs and flows according to the economy and the supply and demand for various types of positions. There is no doubt that the need to reduce staff can have a devastating impact on an organization—both short and long term. While it would be unrealistic to expect that you could spin this negative situation into a positive, you can do some things to minimize negative impacts.

1. **Be up front and open.** Don't delay the inevitable, and don't attempt to keep it quiet until all the details have been worked out. Word will inevitably leak to staff, and you will be best served by communicating quickly and openly.

2. **Arm supervisors and managers with information.** Employees will look to their managers for answers; make sure the managers have them, even if the answer, for now, has to be, "We don't know yet." The key question on each employee's mind will be, "What does this mean for my job?" Prepare managers with messages, and coach them on their responses to questions.

3. **Be fair and consistent in your actions.** Don't view downsizing as an opportunity to eliminate dead weight. Have a planned approach for your actions that you can explain to employees

and that you will implement consistently throughout the organization.

4. **Be sensitive in your communication approaches.** Sending a letter to an employee's home is not a sensitive way to share news about a job being eliminated. Although these situations are uncomfortable, it is important to communicate directly with the employees affected.

5. **Treat affected employees well.** Plenty of notice, a generous severance package, outplacement assistance, and so on are all ways to soften the blow on affected employees—and ways to send a message to other staff that the organization is concerned and responsible.

6. **Don't forget about the "survivors."** Even employees who do not lose their jobs will have questions about how their jobs will change, and will feel unsettled and stressful about the impact of the downsizing on coworkers.

It can be tempting during a downsizing to "hunker down," resulting in a lack of information across the organization. While these communication issues are uncomfortable to deal with and stressful to deliver, it is critical that the lines of communication remain open and that information is shared honestly and consistently with all.

Budget Cuts

Wisconsin governor Jim Doyle has embarked on a massive budget-cutting initiative that has repercussions throughout the state at every level. Even small, local governments are feeling the pinch as city and county government and civic leaders discuss ways of eliminating the dollars that must be cut. Their recommendations are, perhaps not surprisingly, most often met with criticism and challenges from both staff and the public. In one television interview, a city employee lamented, "They need to ask us for our opinions—the leaders are too far away from what's really going on; they're not making the best decisions."

Sound familiar? Whether you work in a public or private enterprise, this type of comment is prevalent as organizations attempt to get back on track by doing what comes naturally: cutting costs. Too often, though, decisions are made at the top and, to those on the front lines, can seem ill informed—or worse.

"At one company where I consulted," says Paul Glen of C2 Consulting in Los Angeles, "the day after a poor earnings report and a negative article in the local paper, the cost-cutting response of the management team was to have all the water coolers removed from the offices. This was done first thing in the morning without announcement or explanation. The resulting distraction and morale hit were clearly more costly than the water."[10]

What are companies doing to *successfully* engage employees in cost-cutting efforts? Communicating. Take Synygy, Inc., in Conshohocken, Pennsylvania, for example. After celebrating its forty-fifth consecutive quarter of profitable growth, Synygy is certainly not worried about sending the message that it's going down the tubes. A provider of incentive compensation and performance management software, Synygy has just over three hundred employees, whose involvement in continual cost cutting has become embedded in the company's culture. Synygy's vice president of human resources, Ed Steinberg, SPHR, says that continually looking for ways to improve the bottom line is just "something we do."

Linda Haneborg is senior vice president of marketing and communications for Express Personnel Services in Oklahoma City, where she recently faced the task of implementing cost-containing measures to compensate for projects earlier in the year that put the department over budget.

Haneborg asked staff to e-mail their supervisors with two or three cost-containing ideas that could be implemented immediately. Solutions did not have to be limited to the employee's own area; this, Haneborg feels, allowed employees to "own" the cost-cutting objectives, rather than viewing cost-cutting as an issue for upper-level management only.

Jim Mooney, senior vice president of Farr Associates, a leadership and organizational development firm in High Point, North Carolina, supports the approach that Synygy and Express have taken. He encourages other organizations to "tap the motivations that exist in the workforce in people who want to do a good job, who want to give their best and who want to be creative. Lay out a challenge," suggests Mooney. "Tell employees, 'We need to learn how to succeed with the resources we now have.' Encourage people to look at processes, functions, interfaces they've been using for years and find ways to do them better and faster. And reward visibly every success story."

Theresa M. Welbourne, PhD, is the founder, president, and CEO of eePulse, Inc., and an adjunct professor of organization behavior and human resource management at the Zell-Lurie Institute for Entrepreneurial Studies at the University of Michigan Business School. She has done extensive research on "what drives firm performance," hypothesizing that the answer was "people." She found that she was right. Through her research, Welbourne has worked with companies that were training to grow, cut costs, and be more efficient. "What we were challenged with was: how do you get employees not just to be engaged, but to share information? If you could get the information that employees had about your business into the hands of your management team, they would make better decisions. Employees might see opportunities that you might never see because they're on the front line," Welbourne says.

Too often, companies overlook the value their employees can provide, believing them to be too far removed from the "real issues" and questioning their ability to really contribute to the strategic discussions that drive results.

It's true, says Elizabeth Gibson, PhD, an organizational consultant and coauthor of the book *Big Change at Best Buy* (Davies-Black Publishing, 2003), that employees "don't have the information about some of the systemic issues that can be behind the scenes." Still, she says, "employees, absolutely, should be involved in any cost-cutting initiative. They are close to the action and they see the immediate impacts." After all, Gibson points out, "employees won't be making the decisions—they'll be bringing the ideas." Haneborg agrees, suggesting that companies "bring back the suggestion box, whether it's by email or a more traditional version in the breakroom" to allow employees to submit cost-saving ideas—anonymously, if they prefer.

Laura Bryniarski, with Watson Wyatt in Chicago, likes the concept of "engaging" employees and all that it suggests. "In the past," she says, "employers would simply say, 'this is the policy change.'" Now, she says, employers are much more up-front with communication to employees about what's happening, and they're also pulling employees in to learn their opinions and priorities. They might, for example, let employees know that there will be a need to change benefit plans for 2006—and why—and then conduct a series of focus groups with employees to understand their needs and issues.

To get those ideas, though, employees must care about the organization and its future, recognize the role they play in positively impacting that future, and believe that their input will be heard and valued.

Gibson uses a "head, heart and hands" framework when talking about the employee engagement process—a simplified translation of "psych-speak," she says, for "cognitive, affective and behavioral." The point, she says, "is that to really involve people and engage them you need to pay attention to all three of these aspects."

The "head" is the why. "You need to translate the business case for cost cutting into terms that are meaningful to all employees," says Gibson. That may, she adds, require different translations for different functions or groups or levels within the organization.

The "heart" is "what's in it for me?" "Be explicit about the answer," says Gibson, "and find out what's meaningful to different individuals." When an employee comes up with an idea that's implemented, she says, "make them a hero—celebrate them."

The "hands" are, she says, "what 'good' looks like, or a model of the desired behavior." She adds, "Be prepared to describe, discuss and dissect any propositions that people bring you and be able to provide your own specific examples because they're likely to not be able to generalize to their own situation."

Let employees "in" on the situation at an early stage, says Bryniarski. "I think once you do a certain amount of due diligence and have an idea of what the scope of cost cutting will be, you need to start preparing employees for future exchanges. They don't need to know what the specific measures are yet, but if they can start gearing employees up for what's coming down the pipe they can begin inviting feedback."

It's important, too, that your expectations of employees are realistic. "Link the expected activities from the employee to areas where they really can make an impact," says Steinberg. "Don't ask for ideas about saving on the cost of construction if that's not their area of expertise."

Of course, one very effective way to engage employees is to answer the question of WIIFM (What's in it for me?). Giving employees a share in the profits, says Haneborg, can be an incredible incentive. "Our experience at Express over the last several years is that when employees see a quarterly swing in the wrong direction it's a strong incentive to pay attention to what we need to do to move in the right direction."

Education of staff so that they clearly understand what *profit* means for the company, is also important, says Haneborg. "So often companies concentrate on top line sales without explaining to employees how much is involved in overhead, salaries and fixed costs. Oftentimes, employees do not have a clue and all they see is that top line number."

For example, Haneborg says, employees often encourage management to hire more people because they feel overworked or that they need more help. "If they realized how these new hires impacted the bottom line—and their profit sharing—they might be more inclined to find a better way of doing something or to eliminate some of the work to make the company run more efficiently."

When engaging employees in any cost-cutting initiative, the credibility of the organization, its leaders, and management staff is on the line. Credibility, says Steinberg, "is not a key point—it's *the* point. If it's not a credible message, you're wasting your time. If people are reading in the newspaper about the success of your company and then you say, 'we're looking to save costs,' it's not going to work.

"In our situation, we were looking to save costs for opportunities to invest more into the organization. In a volatile economy we didn't want to go to the equity markets or rely on outside funding." Synygy's culture made this message not only credible, but actionable. "We've never been a fat organization; we've always been a fit organization," says Steinberg.

"My business has suffered from the same economy as everybody else," says Welbourne. Honesty, she agrees, is important. "People can be energized, but not happy," she points out, "but you can't cheer them up with fake news."

And, adds Steinberg, you can't go to employees with a message of "everything's okay, but we need your help. Employees today are very well informed and they see what's happening in other companies and in the economy."

Credibility extends beyond words, of course. You have to, as they say, "walk the talk." And sometimes negative messages can be sent inadvertently.

Consultant John Reddish tells firsthand of a situation that could have turned ugly, but for some quick thinking and damage control. Reddish had been working with a company where there had not been raises or cost-of-living increases in nearly two years. One day, the number two person in the firm (who happened to be the owner's son) drove up in a new Ferrari. "By 10:00 a.m. when I arrived at the plant," says Reddish, "everyone was in a foul mood. Noticing this, I asked one of the friendlier workers, 'why so glum?' He told me about the car."

Reddish did some investigating and found that the car belonged to the owner of a garage where the owner's son had taken his own vehicle for repair—he had been allowed to borrow it. "We decided to announce that he had been lucky enough to borrow the car for the day and that it would be open to sit in and inspect at lunch time," Reddish says. "Lots of employees came to explore and some even had their pictures taken at the wheel. The mood went from ugly to workable. The executive learned a valuable lesson that day, because it had never crossed his mind that he might be creating a problem." What signals might your company and its leaders be inadvertently sending to employees?

Following through on suggestions—*all* suggestions—is another critical component in ensuring successful communication during tough economic times. Not every idea is going to work, but you're making a big mistake, says Steinberg, if you're nonresponsive. An idea that misses the mark, he says, represents an opportunity to build understanding. "Unless you just want to increase effort, I don't think there's a benefit in the 'thanks, anyway' approach," he says. "Employees can only make improvements if they understand why this idea doesn't work so they can adjust that idea and fit it into something that will work."

Jim Bolton, CEO of Ridge Associates, a communication consulting firm in Cazenovia, New York, says that most managers don't communicate enough. What's worse, he says, is they fail to "take their employees' frames of reference into account when thinking about what and how they communicate." Usually, he says, management communication is a "party line broadcast—the same information is sent to all constituents." Rarely do managers adequately distinguish how different groups will react and respond to that message.

"Yet," stresses Bolton, "all communication is ultimately local— employees in field offices will react differently to an announcement of layoffs at headquarters than the people at headquarters. They'll still be affected and concerned, but not in the same way."

In addition to crafting messages to meet the needs of various constituencies, communication, says Bolton, needs to be a 24/7 responsibility. "It's impossible to manage communication up front," he says. "It's an 'in the moment' process. It's in listening to grumbling about having to use styrofoam cups in the breakroom and then using that as a chance to speak about the importance of cost-cutting—and that such decisions have saved jobs, etc.—that managers really get the core message across."

Some amount of dissension should be an expectation. You can't, it's true, please all the people all the time. Regardless of your best intentions and your careful attention to communicating with and involving employees in your cost-cutting efforts, you are bound to ruffle a few feathers, especially in the climate that most companies now find themselves in.

"I think companies need to be especially careful right now because there's such a high level of employee cynicism and I think it stems from distrust of senior management and their own personal fears about the economy and how it has affected them financially," says Bryniarski. "Companies need to communicate cost-cutting measures very clearly and in a non-inflammatory way." And, she adds, "they have to be prepared, in spite of their best efforts, for critical and cynical feedback—and prepared to somehow channel that feedback productively."

"Managers don't like to listen during tough times," says Bolton, "because what they're listening to is complaints, frustration and other negative issues that they often can't do anything about. But skillful listening helps relieve frustration and enables employees to be more productive. It also builds employees' loyalty over time and provides managers with important information—about problems they hadn't anticipated and hidden opportunities."

Mooney suggests that companies actively seek feedback—even negative feedback. "Provide a venting and morale-restoring forum for people who want to take advantage of it," he suggests. "Many companies use their EAP resource for this. Other companies do climate assessments. Regularly take the pulse by talking to people."

The bottom line, says Welbourne, is to "value employees." She adds, "If you value people, and show them you value them, they'll share information with you." This, she says, is supported "by study after study that I conducted while I was at Cornell. The one thing that predicted performance was the human factor—the degree to which companies valued their people." Get it right, she says, and "your employees will share information with you, you'll have teamwork, managers making better decisions and people that are more engaged. The net result is better long-term performance."

Summing Up

- HR communicators may find themselves facing a number of special, challenging situations—in each case, they can use the same communication planning process.

- Keep communication simple, frequent, and transparent—today's employees are intelligent and resent organization's attempts to "sugarcoat" tough messages.

- Effective communication with off-site staff is a key element in ensuring the success of these arrangements.

- Communication in any situation requires ongoing attention—the need doesn't end once the event has taken place.

- Involving human resource professionals at an early stage in any issue that impacts employees can help minimize unrest and disruption.

- Engaging employees means allowing and encouraging two-way communication and being responsive to employees questions and concerns.

Leveraging Chapter Insights: Critical Questions

- What is the greatest communication challenge that your HR department has faced? What was the response to the challenge? Was the outcome favorable or unfavorable? Why?

- Looking ahead, are there challenges on the horizon that your HR department is likely to face? What could you be doing, now, to improve the likelihood of having a positive communication impact?

- What are the specific challenges your organization faces related to communicating pay and benefit issues? How might a "mission focus" help address these challenges?

- Health plan costs are a common concern among organizations and their employees. What could your HR department do, from a communication standpoint, to address these concerns?

- Does your organization have employees in remote or off-site locations? What communication challenges does this present, and how are you currently addressing those challenges? What might you do to improve communication with these employees?

CHAPTER TWELVE

Enhancing HR's Communication Competencies

What HR Professionals Need to Know to Ensure a Role in Corporate Communication

Key Topics Covered in This Chapter

- *Guidelines for functioning effectively within the organization's communication climate*

- *Core competencies for HR professionals in today's corporate environment*

- *Tips for boosting communication skills and overall business acumen and credibility*

THE ROLE OF HR professionals has changed significantly over the past several years. From a focus on administration—benefits enrollment, payroll, employee records management—to a "seat at the table," today's HR professionals are finding themselves faced with the opportunity to fill an important strategic role in their organizations. The ability to communicate effectively—in individual and group settings and in verbal, written, and electronic environments—is critical. Regardless of the formal organizational structure, HR professionals can and should take steps to involve themselves in the communication process. By building core competencies, broadening professional networks, and developing a strategic rather than an operational approach to managing important issues, HR professionals can ensure their personal and professional success.

Communication Skills for HR Professionals

A 2003 SHRM *Undergraduate HR Curriculum Study,* based on a series of surveys that examined the HR curriculum for undergraduates and how well it prepares or does not prepare students for a career in HR upon graduation, looked at the views of HR students, practitioners, and academicians and their perspectives on the core competencies required in this field. The top three KSAs (knowledge, skills, and abilities) identified by survey respondents were interpersonal communication skills, employee law, and written communication skills.

John Clemons, ABC, APR, vice president for communications at Raytheon Technical Services Company, LLC, in Reston, Virgina, says that to be an effective corporate communicator, "you have to be flexible. You have to be a good negotiator. You have to be articulate. You have to understand the business. You need to be creative and innovative. You need to be willing to stand up for what you believe is right—backed by business reasons, not 'I think/I feel.' You need to be a strategic thinker. You need to have a full understanding of the available communication tools such as the Web, print, video, etc. You must be a good writer—you *must* be a good writer—you have to nail the basics." And, finally, he says, "this may not be on anyone else's list, but it's on my list. Have a sense of humor. Some of the things we go through or have to deal with would drive lesser professionals crazy."[1]

It's not uncommon for HR and communication professionals to feel frustration because they don't feel they are sufficiently involved in the strategic issues that impact their organizations. Instead, too often, they feel they are mired in paperwork, compensation studies, and benefit administration. Strategic involvement means that in spite of where the communication function resides within the organization's structure, the HR professional has a voice in the process and an impact on how messages are developed and delivered—externally as well as internally.

Gaining this level of strategic involvement is not an impossible goal, but it's not something that happens automatically. It's not an entitlement—it's an earned privilege. Involvement in the strategic issues of *any* organization only occurs as the result of demonstrating initiative, commitment, and an understanding of the organizational needs and issues that impact its success.

Whether you reside in the HR structure, the corporate communication structure, the marketing structure, or some other area of the organization, the following guidelines can help you position yourself to become more strategically involved in the global communication issues at your organization:

1. **Recognize that your purpose is to serve the needs of the organization, not the needs of your department or your**

position. The people who have strategic involvement understand the needs of the organization and put them first. Their
decisions are based on what is best for the company, not on
what is best for their department or for themselves, individually.
Taking that viewpoint is not always easy—and it's not always
popular. But if you aren't able to align yourself with the needs
of the organization, you cannot expect to be taken seriously.

This doesn't mean that you must be a "yes-person." It
simply means that when you present a proposal or frame an
argument, you need to do so in terms of how the organization
will benefit from implementing your suggestion. To gain strategic involvement, you need to have a broad business focus.

2. **Learn about your organization and industry.** How do you
   develop a broad business focus? By learning about your organization and your industry. If your expertise is limited to HR or
   to corporate communication, how can you expect that you will
   be treated seriously when it comes to making decisions that
   affect the entire organization? The most successful executives
   are those who have spent time in a variety of positions—
   finance, marketing, operations, and so on. What can you do to
   demonstrate your interest in the *entire* organization? Start by
   networking with coworkers in other departments and becoming involved in task forces or committees outside the scope of
   your traditional, assigned duties. Read trade journals about your
   industry. Learn everything you can about your organization and
   the issues it faces.

3. **Think of yourself as a consultant, not a decision maker.**
   Both HR and corporate communication are service departments. They're important service departments, but service departments nonetheless. What this means is that your role as a
   member of one of these teams is to provide advice to management based on your expertise and experience. That is what you
   are paid for. Senior management is paid to make decisions
   based on the advice they receive from various internal and

external advisors. Unless you are part of the executive leadership team, you are not a decision maker and should not be offended if your advice is not always taken.

Will this be frustrating from time to time? Certainly. But you will get much further in your career if you learn from the experience and consider how you could alter your approach or strengthen your position in the future, instead of feeling victimized or put upon because "they never listen to me."

This is not to say that you should accept decisions that are against your values or that violate the law. Those are different issues. If you find yourself in an untenable situation at any organization because you are forced to support decisions that you feel are morally or ethically wrong, you may need to move to another organization.

4. **Use data and objective information to back up your suggestions and decisions.** While it would be great if your opinion were so valued that no one ever questioned your judgment and always followed your recommendations, that's a highly unlikely situation to find yourself in. More likely, you will need to provide tangible evidence to back up your recommendations. You should not feel insulted by this, but should recognize it as part of your job and learn to leverage your power and authority with the value of information and data you can provide from both internal and external sources.

There are very few HR or communication professionals whose advice will have impact simply because of their stellar reputation. The longer you're with an organization and the more you can establish a record as being someone whose advice is pertinent and valuable, the more you will find that you become someone who is "listened to."

5. **Disagree privately. Agree publicly.** You will not always agree with every decision that your management or your organization makes. It is your right—and often your responsibility—to share your concerns with the appropriate people. But there is a

right way, and a right time, to do this. The right *way* is to present your opposing view respectfully and to back up your view with objective data and information. The right *time* is during the decision-making process. Once a decision has been made and communicated throughout the organization, it may still be appropriate to present evidence to management that the decision may have been in error. It is neither appropriate nor wise to express these views publicly. If you want to be considered part of the team, you need to support that team.

6. **Build relationships.** Strive for diversity in the relationships you establish. Get to know people in all areas of your organization. Seek out people with different opinions. Purposefully pepper your committees with individuals who have dissenting viewpoints. Cultivate contacts at all levels of the organization—and outside the organization.

   To lead effectively, you need to understand the views and needs of the people you deal with—not just people in your department and not just people who are above you on the corporate ladder, but people throughout the organization. The broader your perspectives, the more accurately you will be able to "read" the organization and make proposals and recommendations that are strategic and appropriate. And from a personal standpoint, you never know whose support may be important to you in the future—cultivating relationships can yield positive results at unexpected times.

Nobody is automatically afforded the opportunity to participate in the strategic decisions that impact an organization. Some are players. Some aren't. You have to *earn* the ability to become a strategic partner, and you do this by demonstrating your understanding of the broad business issues of your organization and how your role supports those business issues. You do this by backing up your recommendations with sound data. You do this by being willing to take an unpopular stand and by publicly supporting the organization even when you may not be 100 percent personally on board with a decision (as long as that decision is morally and legally appropriate). And you do this by establishing a wide range of personal and professional contacts both inside and outside your organization.

Where to Go from Here in Your HR Department

Don Herrmann, SPHR, recently joined a large and aggressively growing international technology company as its top HR executive, director of human resources. When he arrived "just a short year ago," he says, "we had just under thirteen hundred employees—today we have just under three thousand. Much of this growth was through aggressive acquisition." The HR department, when he arrived, consisted of five employees, including him. Four of those employees were "administrative types"—each had formerly been receptionists at the company's main desk. "My charge was to upgrade the talent of HR, upgrade the presence of HR, and, without trying to be leading edge, create an HR function that complemented the organization and its strategic goal of being a $1 billion corporation in 2008," he says.

Herrmann's first challenge was the competency within the department. "Frankly speaking," he says, "outside of good clerical skills, HR knowledge and competency was not available internally. A simultaneous HR audit showed extensive regulatory compliance concerns, infrastructure that was almost nonexistent, no budget, and strategic HR processes such as company benefits and compensation systems that were arbitrary, piecemeal, and, as I quickly came to realize, 'willy-nilly' in how they were both administered and applied."

Today, the HR department has grown to a team of nineteen—ten members of the team are degreed and/or certified HR professionals. Yet, he says, "communication remains the greatest challenge."

Through his experience, Herrmann has identified a number of skills that HR leaders need to ensure that the role they play is strategic and that they are moving beyond the traditional—yet no longer sufficient—operational, administrative role of the "personnel department."

1. Finance
   - The ability to read and interpret internal financial reports
   - The ability to develop ROI and cost-benefit analysis plans to support projects and decision making

2. Marketing
   - The ability to successfully package plans and proposals and get internal buy-in
   - The ability to successfully package and *sell* HR services to internal customers
   - The ability to develop processes that will influence external entities to become involved with your organization

3. Technology
   - The ability to effectively use standard, off-the-shelf productivity tools (Excel, PowerPoint, Access, etc.)
   - The visionary ability to see technology solutions for everyday workplace issues

4. Core HR competencies
   - The basics of compensation, benefits, employment law, and so on
   - The ability to keep those competencies current and forward looking

HR professionals, says Kathryn Yates of Watson Wyatt, need to be constantly rethinking how they are using their resources. "Technologies are changing," she says. "HR people need to consider how they will keep constantly refreshing their skills. One way, of course, is making sure you understand how the new technologies can support your communication efforts. While everybody these days has an intranet, how are you effectively using that tool? Have you gone to portal technology?"

HR professionals, says Yates, need to see themselves as an essential component in a much larger process—as integral to making that process work. "I think about it in terms of a manufacturing company where there may be one group that's responsible for a certain weld.

Even though that group has a specific function and responsibility, it can't lose sight of the way it connect or aligns with everything else. Even if you're not responsible for communication in your organization," says Yates, "you can support the effective implementation of your weld by viewing yourself as part of the whole. The power that comes from having everybody pulling in the same direction is outstanding and the waste in companies of well-intentioned, but misdirected, effort is a shame."

HR professionals, says Yates, need to position their value to support the goals of the company. "That doesn't happen," she says, "if you just perpetuate activity year to year without really looking seriously at whether the resources it takes for that particular activity are continuing to be valuable to the company."

For example, she says, a company that produces a beautiful, four-color employee magazine may ask employees, "Do you read this magazine?" or "Do you like this magazine?" and the answers may be "yes" and "yes." But, Yates says, these are the *wrong questions*. "The right question is whether things are happening in a way that the company needs them to happen to gain advantage in the marketplace or to make their goals and does this publication demonstrate that it's tied into that effort?" If not, she says, "it would be better to take that money and do something else with it. That's what HR and communications should be asking themselves every year."

Jane Shannon is a communication consultant and the author of *73 Ways to Improve Your Employee Communication Program,* which offers tips and insights that can help HR professionals boost their communication skills—and overall business acumen and credibility:

- **Volunteer.** "If there are holes in your experience, patch them up by strategic volunteering," says Shannon. "For example, if you don't have a lot of (or any) video experience, you could volunteer to make a video for your child's school. Or volunteer through a professional organization."

- **Ask great questions.** "Listen really hard to what someone is saying, and then ask the 'stupid' questions like: 'Why?' 'What difference does this make?' 'Who wins/who loses?' 'Why do we care?' Preface your first question by saying, 'This may seem like a basic question, but . . .' and just about every time, you'll receive compliments for asking really good questions."

- **Learn three important facts about your company and industry.** "Ask these questions: Who are your major competitors? What issues does your industry face? What regulations govern your industry? What does the investment community say about your company and others in your industry? What obstacles does your industry face and what can be done to minimize those obstacles?"

- **Define your job in the broadest possible terms.** "If you work in a corporation," says Shannon, "your job is to help move information up, down and across the organization to help the company succeed. Wherever you work, your job is to help management solve problems and remove impediments so employees can work productively."

- **Take an imaginary elevator ride with the CEO.** "The elevator door closes and the CEO turns to you and says, 'So, what have you done for our shareholders today?' Every day, you should have an answer to this question—and even if nobody asks, you may want to explain your job from time to time. That's why you need an 'elevator speech'—you need to be able to describe the value you add to your organization succinctly, in the time it typically takes to ride an elevator."

- **Demonstrate how your work contributes to company goals.** "Figure out a way to measure the focus and impact of what you do."[2]

Summing Up

- The top three KSAs for HR professionals are interpersonal communication skills, employee law, and written communication skills.

- Getting a "seat at the table" is an earned privilege—not an entitlement.

- HR professionals need a variety of skills to succeed in today's fast-paced and challenging corporate environment.

- In communication—as in all activities—a focus on measurable and demonstrable outcomes and the ability to demonstrate value to the organization will serve HR professionals well.

Leveraging Chapter Insights: Critical Questions

- What are your current communication strengths? Weaknesses? Commit to developing a plan to address your communication weaknesses to improve your ability to contribute to this area.

- What core competencies will be most important for you to develop over the next year? Three years? Five?

- When you consider the HR function in your organization, how strategic do you feel it currently is? Are there opportunities to increase its involvement in the organization's strategic processes? What role could you play in strengthening this impact?

Speech Preparation Tool

Rosemary Sheffield, Director of Customer Relations for Media Training Worldwide in New York, shares the following Speech Controller™ Questionnaire. The questionnaire can serve as a good starting point when developing key messages for any communication effort.

1. Your water-cooler message. In sixty words or less, what is the main message you want members of your audience to take away from your presentation?

2. List every major point you might like to communicate to your audience. Don't worry about how it sounds yet; just list the point in simplest terms. Use no more than eight words per point. Brainstorm as many points as you can; don't worry about order.

3. Reexamine all of your message points. Reflect on them. Now decide which are your five most important points. Put a check to the left of each message point of the top five.

4. If possible, list one point that is relative to each of the five message points.

   Message point 1:

   Message point 2:

   Message point 3:

   Message point 4:

   Message point 5:

5. In twenty words or less, provide a specific and concrete example for each one of your message points.

   Message point 1:

   Message point 2:

continued

Message point 3:

Message point 4:

Message point 5:

6. The single most effective way to get your audience to remember your key points is by telling a relevant story (it does *not* have to be funny). You can simply recount a conversation with a client, customer, or colleague. A message, resolution, setting, people or characters, problem, and emotion. Prepare a story for message point 1.

   Title for your story:

   Message:

   Setting:

   People/Characters:

   Problem:

   Resolution:

   Emotion:

   Prepare a story for message points 2 through 5. This is the outline for your presentation.

   Source: Rosemary Sheffield, www.mediatrainingworldwide.com. Used with permission.

What to Measure

Here is a "hit list" of the kinds of things about your publications and audiovisual programs that you might ask outside communication experts to evaluate.

Content

- Is it interesting?
- Is there enough variety?
- Does it reflect important issues to your company and audience?
- Does it appeal to audience self-interests so they keep reading or viewing?

Writing style

- Do leads draw readers in? Do lead styles vary?
- Are headlines, subheads, captions, quote inserts, and so on written to capture or recapture readers whose interest may be waning? Similarly, are visual clues and techniques in videos and slides serving a similar purpose?
- What reading level is the writing geared to? To what extent are jargon and acronyms used? Are these appropriate to your audience? For audiovisuals, is the script easy for the ear to follow or has it been written for reading?
- Is the writing tight or is the same information repeated endlessly?
- Are words spelled or pronounced correctly?
- Is the writing grammatical and punctuated correctly?
- Are enough concrete examples used to illustrate theoretical points?
- Are direct quotes interesting and meaningful? Do they sound as if real people actually said them? Are all the quotes from management or is there a mix reflecting all employment levels? When "talking heads" appear on video, are they at least saying something interesting or should the narrator have paraphrased the same content?
- Is the tone formal or informal enough for the audience?
- Is attribution for facts and opinions used enough or is the editor or scriptwriter writing as the "voice of the company"?

Overall design

- Is the balance between text and graphics right for the audience?
- Is color used to help the reader along or just to decorate the page?
- Does the design lead the reader through the content or obstruct the way?

continued

- Is white space used well or trapped in all the wrong places?
- Is the combination of type style and size used for the body, heads, captions, and other elements complementary or chaotic?
- In video, is music or other sound used appropriately or just as background wallpaper?

Graphic elements

- Are images sharp and in focus? Do shots show care in composition to help tell stories and intrigue readers or are they just "grip-and-grins"? Are they cropped to focus on the best parts of the picture or to fill the hole left by the length of the story? Are photo layouts planned for graphic impact or are they scattered across a spread like seeds in a field?
- Do illustrations truly illustrate or just decorate?
- Are bullets and tables used where possible or is text allowed to run in endless straight narrative?
- Are pie charts, bar charts, and other aids to interpreting numerical information truly helpful or impossible to make sense of?
- In videos and slides, is the size of graphic or text elements large enough to be seen and understood by your viewers?

Source: Angela D. Sinickas, "How to Measure Your Communication Programs," www.sinicom.com, 2004. Reprinted with permission. All rights reserved.

Sample Scoring Sheet for Objective Media Review

This sample scoring sheet can be used as a beginning point to assess your publications. You should adapt it to measure the specific aspects of your own publications and other communication tools that you would like to evaluate.

	Publication 1	Publication 2	Publication 3
Date issued			
Frequency			
Readability level			
Issuing department			
Creativity			
Writing			
• Organization			
• Writing clarity			
• Leads			
• Headlines			
• Captions			
Design			
• Impact			
• Consistency			
Graphics			
Photography			
Illustrations			
Graphs, charts			
Objectives			
Suited to audience			
Reflects company objectives			
Fits in media mix			
Overall			

Source: Angela D. Sinickas, "How to Measure Your Communication Programs," www.sinicom.com, 2004. Reprinted with permission. All rights reserved.

Diagnosis Tool for Internal Communication

Part I: Is communication needed?

If you answer yes to one or more of these, there is probably a need to communicate.

☐ Are you a new leader to a group?

☐ Are you leading an initiative that has been identified as critical to your company's meeting business objectives?

☐ If yes, have you communicated about progress or updates in the past thirty days?

☐ Are you about to make an organizational change (promotion, reorganization, departure of key player, etc.) that will affect others?

☐ Are you about to introduce a new policy, process, or relationship that will need introduction or explanation?

☐ Are employees asking questions about a change that has been implemented but not formally introduced?

☐ Has a corporate initiative been introduced that you need to "translate" for your team?

☐ Are external conditions (competitive, economic, etc.) causing concerns for employees?

☐ Is the rumor mill active and does it need to be defused?

☐ Has it been more than ninety days since you have communicated formally with your team?

Part II: Who is your audience?

Audiences can range from all employees to specific individuals. Check the boxes for the most appropriate audiences

☐ Entire company—global communications

☐ Specific geographic location—local communications

☐ Specific functional areas for a meeting—department or functional communications

☐ Executive team

☐ Project team

☐ Key stakeholders _____

☐ Specific individuals _____

☐ Other _____

continued

Part III: How can you shape your message?

Once you have identified your audience, you can focus on shaping the message. What is most important for your audience to learn and understand about the key messages?

- What is the [change or topic]?
- What's the business reason for the [change or topic]?
- How does the [change or topic] move [company] closer toward meeting strategic or business objectives?
- What do audience members need to know so that they are focused on the right priorities?
- What else is going on in the business that would make people question this [change or topic]? How can these issues be addressed to increase employee understanding and, as much as possible, agreement with [change or topic]?
- What do they need to know to do their jobs?
- What motivation or reassurance will they need?
- What do you want them to feel?
- What action do you want them to take?

Part IV: Select media and communication tools

Type of communication	Personal or impersonal	High-touch or high-tech	Factors for selecting or using
Personal conversations	Personal	Touch	Commitment to managing by walking around and listening
One-on-one meeting with immediate manager	P	Touch	Individual, requires discussion
Staff meetings	P	Touch	Keep relationships with immediate manager strong
Brown bags	P	Touch	Especially good for two-way communication
Town hall (site)	P	Touch	
Functional "all hands"	P	Touch or tech	Can create enthusiasm and personal touch when local site leader hosts Q&A for remote locations
Corporate "all hands"	P	Touch or tech	"
WFTH	Impersonal	Tech	Quick way to communicate consistent information with large group of employees
News items/intranet	I	Tech	
E-mail from functional leader	I	Tech	"
E-mail from CEO	I	Tech	"
Live Webcast	P	Tech	Can look camera in eye and communicate emotion with tone, so has high-touch effect with an impersonal media
VOD	P	Tech	"
Phone call	P	Tech	

Type of communication	Personal or impersonal	High-touch or high-tech	Factors for selecting or using
Video-conferencing	P	Tech	
CD	I	Tech	For information with longer shelf-life
Plan a cascade of communication	P	Tech or touch	Way to provide consistency along with higher touch to communication
Pulse survey	I	Tech	Way to get employee feedback on a specific topic
Training	Personal or impersonal	Touch or tech	Remember to have training updated to include key communication messages

Source: Francesca Karpel, Network Appliance, Inc. Used with permission.

Sample Communication Plan

Human Resources Recruitment and Retention Awareness

Communication Plan
[date]

Overview

The human resource department (HR) would like to improve organizational awareness of its efforts related to recruitment and retention. The department does not feel that employees and management are aware of the many activities and initiatives taking place in HR and would like to improve both awareness and perception.

Goal

To increase awareness and positive perception of HR activities related to recruitment and retention.

Key Messages

- [Company] is committed to the recruitment and retention of highly skilled and service-oriented employees.
- The HR department is actively involved in a number of initiatives to improve recruitment and retention activities.

Tactics

Description/Tool	Audience	Responsible	Comments
Baseline survey	All staff	J. Smith D. Jones	Develop a baseline survey designed to measure awareness or perception of identified recruitment or retention activities with the ability to break down results by demographics (i.e., employee, physician, management, department). Results of initial survey (to be repeated in 12-18 months) will be used to as a point of comparison to determine success of subsequent communication efforts.
Priority list	HR staff	J. Smith	Based on results of survey, prioritize issues to target those most needing communication or those that have the potential for the most positive impact if awareness is increased. Focus on top-level issues first.

continued

Description/Tool	Audience	Responsible	Comments
Communication or education within HR department.	HR staff	J. Smith	Significant staff changes in HR department mean that awareness of HR activities among staff may be low. Staff members need to have information about HR initiatives to share as they interact with staff throughout the organization to avoid eroding confidence in the knowledge or awareness of these "experts." This can be done in a variety of ways: 1. Identify key issues HR staff need to be aware of. What is the retention plan? How do the individual elements fit together? How do individual roles of HR staff members support these elements? 2. Establish and communicate expectations of HR staff (i.e., "you are expected to have a working knowledge of HR's recruitment or retention efforts," "You are expected to portray the department and its activities in a positive manner when interacting with other staff members," etc. Measure and evaluate performance against these expectations through standard review process. 3. Discuss issues at individual and staff meetings. 4. Cross-train staff members. 5. Utilize intranet for intradepartmental information sharing. 6. Recognize individual staff efforts related to understanding and communicating R&R issues.
One-on-one follow-up with individual departments or individuals	Identified target departments or individuals.	HR account managers	Based on survey results or anecdotal information, identify departments or individuals where perception or awareness is low. Target these departments for one-on-one meetings or interactions between department directors and appropriate HR representatives. Or identify strong supporters organizationally and enlist them as ambassadors for HR's retention efforts.
Interdepartmental relationship building or account manager meetings	All departments	HR account managers	Develop formalized relationships between HR account managers and assigned departments. Attend department meetings on a regular (quarterly) basis, share information through e-mail updates, etc.
Reports or updates on retention progress	All staff	J. Smith	Consider sharing statistical information about recruitment or retention results with employees. Much of the general communication could be done on HR home page, in employee newsletter, on HR bulletin board, etc.

Description/Tool	Audience	Responsible	Comments
Intranet FAQs	All staff	HR staff	The intranet has an FAQ function with a link to HR that could be strategically utilized to communicate information about identified areas where awareness or understanding is low.
			Q&A related to benefit changes or policy changes, etc. could be posted here. This would not only provide another communication option but could minimize calls to HR for frequently asked questions.
			Promote availability of these FAQs through employee newsletter, intranet, HR home page, one-on-one, etc.
Intranet forums	All staff	HR staff	Intranet forums can be a good way to manage employee expectations, monitor issues, etc. Consider posting messages inviting feedback on various issues, "planting" messages to aid in proactively addressing issues, providing positive perspectives, etc.
Intranet home page	All staff	HR staff	Intranet offers many opportunities to communicate and interact with employees. Consider daily (or weekly) "HR Updates" on the front page of site sharing information on retention activities, HR employee activities or achievements (i.e., certification, participation in HR conferences), retention results, media coverage, tips for using HR services, etc.
Employee newsletter		HR staff J. Johnson	Utilize employee newsletter to communicate identified issues (based on priority ranking).
Media contacts	General public	J. Smith	Be alert to possibilities for media coverage of retention activities. Media coverage can positively impact employee perception as well as general public.
Re-survey	All staff	J. Smith D. Jones	Do follow-up survey to compare results to baseline (12-18 months) to determine whether above activities had an impact on improving perception or awareness.

Source: Lin Grensing-Pophal.

Acquisition—Phases and Types of Communication

The following phases and types of communications may be needed depending on the size and scope of the acquisition. Use as a guideline for building a communication plan.

Contact information (name, extension, e-mail) for key players

☐ Executive Champion for Acquisition _____

☐ Team Leader for Deal _____

☐ Team Leader for Integration _____

☐ Team Leader for HR _____

☐ Internal Communications _____

Key messages

☐ Define key messages and align with external communicators (PR, IR, AR)

☐ Define name to be used to refer to new team internally _____

Prior to acquisition (Note: Legal disclosure as required to appropriate parties)

☐ Develop internal faqs

☐ Brief execs

☐ Brief VPs

☐ Brief/high-level summary for HR business partners

☐ Brief team of leaders/managers who will be welcoming new team(s)

☐ Brief managers on their roles (as appropriate)

☐ Invite to all hands (if needed for open communication, allay concerns)

☐ Begin building out internal Web content for acquired team/entity

☐ Post any internal Web content about acquisition (link to intranet announcement)

☐ Identify any internal issues acquisition may raise that need to be addressed (off-shoring)

☐ Create executive champion video-on-demand message(s) (to either or both companies)

☐ Review internal communication plan

☐ Other

Initial announcement

To employees of "acquiring company"

☐ Executive champion's announcement to global "acquiring company" audience (e-mail directing to intranet news)

☐ Executive champion's announcement to the functional team(s) to which the new team(s) will be reporting

☐ Executive champion's greeting the newly acquired team

☐ Functional all hands? (List specific functions and reasons)

☐ Site all hands? (List specific sites and reasons)

☐ Small group meetings for teams

☐ E-mails to functions and/or groups announcing the change and its effect on the organization as well as asking existing "acquiring company" team to welcome newly acquired team from functional leader if function directly affected by acquisition

☐ Other

To employees of "company to be acquired"

☐ Invite employees to attend all hands meeting (personal invite/e-mail to all or only those moving)

☐ Executive champion's announcement to the functional team(s) to which the new team(s) will be reporting

Final signing (deal close)

☐ Celebratory event for newly acquired team (and significant other)

  ☐ Order logo-imprinted champagne flutes, shirts, etc.

☐ Send photos of new team and celebration to be included in next all hands meeting

☐ News item on intranet linking to press release

☐ Other

During integration

☐ Move new employees into new hire/assimilation system

☐ Fold communications with new employees into ongoing functional communications

☐ Fold communications with new employees into ongoing corporate communications

☐ Pictures in pre-meeting; mention in all hands meeting

☐ Other

Source: Francesca Karpel, Network Appliance, Inc.

Steps for Conducting Communication Audits

Core Audit

- Audit Planning Guide (Project timeline)
- Communication Materials Checklist
- Executive Interview Guide
- Focus Group Discussion Guide
- Say/Do Analysis Process
- Mapping Communication Process
- Message Delivery Matrix
- Intranet/Internet Assessment
- Content Analysis Protocols
- Robert Gunning Fog Index
- Communications Message

Comprehensive Audit

- Audit Planning Guide
- Communication Materials Checklist
- Executive Interview Guide
- Focus Group Discussion Guide
- Say/Do Analysis Process
- Job Shadowing Process
- Communication Effectiveness Survey
- Process Map
- Message Delivery Matrix
- Intranet/Internet Assessment
- Content Analysis Protocols
- Robert Gunning Fog Index
- Readership Survey
- Communication Message Alignment
- Stakeholder Analysis
- Demographic Profiling
- Integration Process Assessment (M&A situations only)
- Communication Strategy Planning
- Communication ROI Benchmarking
- Alignment
- Stakeholder Analysis

Audit Survey

Instructions: Please indicate your answers by circling the number that best represents your opinion on a scale of 1-10 (1-Poor, 5/6-Average, 10-Excellent). Please answer *all* questions to the best of your ability. Feel free to add suggestions for improvement in the "Additional Comments" areas at the end of each section by indicating the number of the question you are referring to, followed by the suggestion or comment regarding that question. Answers will remain confidential and will be used for the sole purpose of improving current communication-related processes within your company/organization.

Internal Communications

1. With regard to "internal" communication, how would you rate the effectiveness of communicating by telephone (i.e., convenience; using this method as a means of informing others of, or obtaining information for yourself; connecting with others in a reasonable length of time)?

   1 2 3 4 5 6 7 8 9 10

2. With regard to "internal" communication, how would you rate the effectiveness of communicating by e-mail (i.e., convenience; using this method as a means of informing others of, or obtaining information for yourself; connecting with others in a reasonable length of time)?

   1 2 3 4 5 6 7 8 9 10

3. With regard to "internal" communication, how would you rate the effectiveness of communicating through meetings (i.e., convenience; using this method as a means of informing others of, or obtaining information for yourself; connecting with others in a reasonable length of time)?

   1 2 3 4 5 6 7 8 9 10

4. With regard to "internal" communication, how would you rate the effectiveness of communicating through your company/organization's intranet (*a Web-based tool used only within your company/organization's infrastructure*) or your intranet's message boards (i.e., convenience; using this method as a means of informing others of, or obtaining information for yourself; connecting with others in a reasonable length of time)? Note: If your company does not utilize an intranet or you do not have access to this tool, circle "1."

   1 2 3 4 5 6 7 8 9 10

continued

5. With regard to "internal" communication, how would you rate the convenience of obtaining accurate and complete employee benefit information (such as procedures for accumulating annual leave, or information about sick leave, comp time, insurance benefits, retirement plans, paid holidays, etc.)?

  1 2 3 4 5 6 7 8 9 10

6. With regard to "internal" communication, how would you rate the convenience of obtaining accurate and complete information about technology and resources used within the company/organization (i.e., fax machine use/location, printer and copier use/location, helpful software applications, policy and procedure manuals, etc.)?

  1 2 3 4 5 6 7 8 9 10

7. With regard to "internal" communication, how would you rate the overall level of training procedures within the company/organization (i.e., job training, computer software training, etc.)?

  1 2 3 4 5 6 7 8 9 10

8. With regard to "internal" communication, how would you rate the level of comprehension within the company/organization (i.e., how well do employees understand the company/organization's purpose, processes, policies, procedures, and specific job duties)?

  1 2 3 4 5 6 7 8 9 10

9. How would you rate your company/organization's overall "internal" communication process (i.e., the timeliness in which important information is distributed to staff, and how well pertinent information is explained and comprehended by staff members)?

  1 2 3 4 5 6 7 8 9 10

Additional Comments (Please indicate the question number you are referring to, followed by your suggestion/comment):

External Communications

1. With regard to "external" communication, how would you rate the effectiveness of communicating by telephone (i.e., convenience; using this method as a means of informing others of, or obtaining information for yourself; connecting with others in a reasonable length of time)?

  1 2 3 4 5 6 7 8 9 10

2. With regard to "external" communication, how would you rate the effectiveness of communicating by e-mail (i.e., convenience; using this method as a means of informing others of, or obtaining information for yourself; connecting with others in a reasonable length of time)?

  1 2 3 4 5 6 7 8 9 10

3. With regard to "external" communication, how would you rate the effectiveness of communicating through meetings (i.e., convenience; using this method as a means of informing others of, or obtaining information for yourself; connecting with others in a reasonable length of time)?

  1 2 3 4 5 6 7 8 9 10

4. With regard to "external" communication, how would you rate the effectiveness of your company/organization's Web site (i.e., convenience to site visitors in locating information easily)? Note: If your company does not utilize a Web site, circle "1."

  1 2 3 4 5 6 7 8 9 10

5. With regard to "external" communication, how would you rate your company/organization's level of courtesy (i.e., Are customers greeted by an individual or by a voice recording? Are questions generally handled by the first customer service representative that customers have contact with or are they transferred one or more times before their questions/requests are appropriately responded to, etc.)?

  1 2 3 4 5 6 7 8 9 10

6. With regard to "external" communication, how would you rate the level of customer complaints—"1" being minor, "10" being major? (Consider your average number of customer contacts in any given day and the ratio of complaints or dissatisfied customers with regard to that number. To obtain your answer, simply divide the number of dissatisfied customers by the number of total customers. For example if you are in contact with 10 different customers per day and of that number, 2 customers are dissatisfied, divide 2 by the number 10 — your answer would be .2—you would then circle the number 2 to indicate your answer. If necessary, please round up or down accordingly—for example, if your answer is .25, round the number up to 3.)

   1 2 3 4 5 6 7 8 9 10

7. With regard to "external" communication, how would you rate the availability and accuracy of your company/organization's "published" promotional and/or informational materials (i.e., brochures, newsletters, etc.)?

   1 2 3 4 5 6 7 8 9 10

8. How would you rate your company/organization's level of concern regarding customer satisfaction (i.e., "1"—customer satisfaction is not a major concern, "10" customer satisfaction is of utmost importance)?

   1 2 3 4 5 6 7 8 9 10

9. Overall, rate the level of customer satisfaction, promptness, professionalism, courtesy, quality, etc., of your company/organization in comparison to similar companies/organizations. (Circle "1" if you personally would choose to do business with someone else, "10" if you feel that your company/organization exceeds the services of its competitors, or a number in between.)

   1 2 3 4 5 6 7 8 9 10

Additional Comments (Please indicate the question number you are referring to, followed by your suggestion/comment):

General Questions

1. How long have you been employed with this company/organization?

2. What is your current job position? Please summarize what it entails.

3. What are some concerns (if any) that you currently have about your company/organization's communication-related practices? (Please include both internal and external communication concerns.)

4. If you do have communication-related concerns, do you have any comments or suggestions that might improve your company/organization's current communication-related practices?

5. If we have additional questions how may we contact you? (Please provide your name, e-mail address, and/or telephone number.)

Source: Talon Communications Group. Used with permission.

Notes

Chapter 1

1. Watson Wyatt, *Communication ROI Study,* 2003.

2. Paul A. Argenti, *Corporate Communication* (Boston: Irwin/McGraw-Hill, 1998).

3. American Marketing Association, www.marketingpower.com/mg-dictionary.php.

4. Janelle Barlow and Paul Stewart, *Branded Customer Service: The New Competitive Edge* (San Francisco: Berrett-Koehler, 2004), 144.

5. Argenti, *Corporate Communication,* 89.

6. Charles J. Fombrun, *Reputation: Realizing Value from the Corporate Image* (Boston: Harvard Business School Press, 1996).

7. Argenti, *Corporate Communication,* 32.

8. Kathryn Troy, *Managing Corporate Communication in a Competitive Climate* (New York: Conference Board, 1993).

9. Argenti, *Corporate Communication.*

10. Interviews in this chapter with Karen Horn, Leza Raffel, Shirley Gilbert, Diane Nix, John Clemons, Joyce LaValle, Laura Luke, Francesca Karpel, Norman Crouse, and Kathryn Yates were conducted in March, April, and May 2005.

11. Argenti, *Corporate Communication.*

Chapter 2

1. Charles J. Fombrun, *Reputation: Realizing Value from the Corporate Image* (Boston: Harvard Business School Press, 1996), 37.

2. Interviews in this chapter with Larry Smith, Benjamin Rudolph, Scott Sobel, and Francesca Karpel were conducted in March, April, and May 2005.

3. Janelle Barlow and Paul Stewart, *Branded Customer Service: The New Competitive Edge* (San Francisco: Berrett-Koehler, 2004), 138–140.

Chapter 3

1. Paul A. Argenti, *Corporate Communication* (Boston: Irwin/McGraw-Hill, 1998), 33.

2. Charles J. Fombrun, *Reputation: Realizing Value from the Corporate Image* (Boston: Harvard Business School Press, 1996), 194.

3. Fombrun, *Reputation*.

4. Interviews in this chapter with John Clemons, Benjamin Rudolph, and Karen Horn were conducted in March, April, and May 2005.

5. Louis C. Williams Jr., *Communication Research, Measurement and Evaluation: A Practical Guide for Communicators* (San Francisco: IABC, 2003), 214–215.

Chapter 4

1. Angela D. Sinickas, *How to Measure Your Communication Programs,* 3rd ed. (Irvine, CA: Sinickas Communications Publishing, 2004).

2. Interviews in this chapter with Angela Sinickas, Kathryn Yates, and Karen Horn were conducted in March, April, and May 2005.

3. W. Edwards Deming, http://www.idealhealthnetwork.com/results.html.

4. Louis C. Williams Jr., *Communication Research, Measurement and Evaluation: A Practical Guide for Communicators* (San Francisco: IABC, 2003), 6–7.

Chapter 5

1. Interviews in this chapter with Mary Heimstead and Larry Smith were conducted in March, April, and May 2005.

2. John L. Hines Jr. and Michael H. Cramer, "Protecting Your Organization's Reputation Against Cybersmear," *SHRM Legal Report,* SHRM Online, www.shrm.org/hrresources/lrpt_published/CMS_005107.asp, May–June 2003.

3. National Investor Relations Institute, "New NIRI Survey Shows Overwhelming Number of Companies Are Maintaining Open Communications with Shareholders and Analysts," news release, June 11, 2003.

4. MessageBank, news release, 2003.

5. Mark Utting, "Readable MD&A," IRontheNet.com, March 2003.

6. Louis Thompson Jr., SEC Financial Disclosure and Auditor Oversight Roundtable, 2002.

7. Charles J. Fombrun, *Reputation: Realizing Value from the Corporate Image* (Boston: Harvard Business School Press, 1996), 195.

8. Portland Business Alliance, www.portlandalliance.com.

9. Fombrun, *Reputation,* 195.

10. James H. Quigley, "America's CEOs Reveal Benefits of Volunteer Programs in Points of Light Report," Points of Light Foundation news release, November 2003.

Chapter 6

1. Shel Holtz, *Corporate Conversations: A Guide to Crafting Effective and Appropriate Internal Communications* (New York: AMACOM, 2004), 6–7.

2. Interviews in this chapter with Kathryn Yates, Larry Smith, and Karen Horn were conducted in March, April, and May 2005.

3. Roger D'Aprix, ABC, *The Face-to-Face Communication Toolkit: Creating an Engaged Workforce* (San Francisco: IABC, 2004), 129.

4. Angela Sinickas, *How to Measure Your Communication Programs,* www.sinicom.com.

5. Lin Grensing-Pophal, "What New Employees Really Need to Know," October 2000, www.shrm.org.

Chapter 7

1. Interviews in this chapter with Tim O'Brien, Mary Heimstead, Timothy Brown, Larry Smith, Scott Sobel, and Rick Chambers were conducted in March, April, and May 2005.

2. Sherry Devereaux Ferguson, *Communication Planning: An Integrated Approach* (Thousand Oaks, CA: Sage Publications, 1999), 204–210.

3. Robert Irvine, from interview with Larry Smith, April 3, 2005.

4. Sherri A. Fallin, "The Five Most Common Mistakes in Crisis Planning and How to Avoid Them," PR Tactics, 2005. Reprinted with permission by the Public Relations Society of America (www.prsa.org).

Chapter 8

1. Interviews in this chapter with Kathryn Yates were conducted in March, April, and May 2005.

2. Shel Holtz, *Corporate Conversations: A Guide to Crafting Effective and Appropriate Internal Communications* (New York: AMACOM, 2004), 56.

3. Sherry Devereaux Ferguson, *Communication Planning: An Integrated Approach* (Thousand Oaks, CA: Sage Publications, 1999), 14–16.

4. Lin Grensing-Pophal, "10 Steps to Better Communication," *Communication World,* December 2001–January 2002, 17–19.

Chapter 9

1. Interviews in this chapter with Leonard Lee, Leza Raffel, Jane Shannon, Simma Lieberman, and Kerry Patterson were conducted in March, April, and May 2005.

2. MSN Encarta, www. encarta.msn.com/encyclopedia.

3. Roger D'Aprix, ABC, *The Face-to-Face Communication Toolkit: Creating an Engaged Workforce* (San Francisco: IABC, 2004), 129.

4. MSN Encarta.

5. American Marketing Association, online dictionary of marketing terms, www.marketingpower.com/mg-dictionary.php.

Chapter 10

1. Lawrence Ragan Communications, Inc., *Ragan Survey of CEO Communications,* Ragan Research Report, 2002.

2. Interviews in this chapter with Norman Crouse, Francesca Karpel, Kathryn Yates, Simma Lieberman, Charlie Melichar, and Leza Raffel were conducted in March, April, and May 2005.

3. Lin Grensing-Pophal, "Getting a Seat at the Table: What Does It Really Take?" SHRM white paper, August 2000, reviewed December 2002.

Chapter 11

1. Material in this section is adapted from Lin Grensing-Pophal, "Communication Pays Off," *HR Magazine,* May 2003, p. 77–82.

2. Interviews in this chapter with Angela Sinickas, Kathryn Yates, and Jody Buffington Aud were conducted in March, April, and May 2005.

3. Grensing-Pophal, "Communication Pays Off."

4. Material in this section is adapted from Lin Grensing-Pophal, "Health Education Turns Proactive," *HR Magazine,* April, 2005, online.

5. Jathan W. Janove, "Management by Remote Control," *HR Magazine,* April 2004, online.

6. Material in this section is adapted from Lin Grensing-Pophal, "Moving En Masse," *HR Magazine,* February 2005, 75–80.

7. Towers Perrin, "HR Rises to the Challenge: Unlocking the Value of M&A."

8. Al Himegarner, "Mergers & Acquisitions: HR Transition Model and Issues to Be Considered When Companies Integrate," SHRM white paper, May 1998, reviewed November 2002.

9. Ronald Adler, Donna Bernardi Paul, and Nancy Glube, "Restructuring and Downsizing: Managing Disruption," SHRM white paper, October 2001, reviewed November 2002.

10. Material in this section is adapted from Lin Grensing-Pophal, "Involve Your Employees in Cost Cutting," *HR Magazine,* November 2003, 53–56.

Chapter 12

1. Interviews in this chapter with John Clemons, Don Herrmann, and Kathryn Yates were conducted in March, April, and May, 2005.

2. Jane Shannon, *73 Ways to Improve Your Employee Communication Program* (Glen Rock, NJ: Davis & Company, 2002).

For Further Reading

Argenti, Paul A. *Corporate Communication*. Boston: Irwin/McGraw-Hill, 1998.

Barlow, Janelle, and Paul Stewart. *Branded Customer Service: The New Competitive Edge*. San Francisco: Berrett-Koehler, 2004.

Bazerman, Max H., and Michael D. Watkins. *Predictable Surprises: The Disasters You Should Have Seen Coming and How to Prevent Them*. Boston: Harvard Business School Press, 2004.

Harvard Business Essentials: Guide to Business Communication. Boston: Harvard Business School Press, 2003.

Crisis Management: Master the Skills to Prevent Disasters. Boston: Harvard Business School Press, 2004.

D'Aprix, Roger, ABC. *The Face-to-Face Communication Toolkit: Creating an Engaged Workforce*. San Francisco: IABC, 2004.

Dennis, Lloyd B., ed. *Practical Public Affairs in an Era of Change*. New York: Public Relations Society of America, 1996.

Devereaux Ferguson, Sherry. *Communication Planning: An Integrated Approach*. Thousand Oaks, CA: Sage Publications, 1999.

Dilenschneider, Robert L., ed. *Dartnell's Public Relations Handbook*. 4th ed. Palm Beach Gardens, FL: Dartnell, 1996.

Face-to-Face Communications for Clarity and Impact. Boston: Harvard Business School Press, 2004.

Fombrun, Charles J. *Reputation: Realizing Value from the Corporate Image*. Boston: Harvard Business School Press, 1996.

Goodman, Michael B. *Corporate Communications for Executives*. Albany, NY: State University of New York Press, 1998.

Harvard Business Review on Crisis Management. Boston: Harvard Business School Press, 2000.

Heath, Robert L. *Management of Corporate Communication: From Interpersonal Contacts to External Affairs*. Mahwah, NJ: Lawrence Erlbaum Associates, 1994.

Holtz, Shel. *Corporate Conversations: A Guide to Crafting Effective and Appropriate Internal Communications.* New York: AMACOM, 2004.

Kotter, John P., and James L. Heskett. *Corporate Culture and Performance.* New York: Free Press, 1992.

Marconi, Joe. *Crisis Marketing: When Bad Things Happen to Good Companies.* Chicago: Probus Publishing, 1992.

Saffir, Leonard, with John Tarrant. *Power Public Relations: How to Get PR to Work for You.* Chicago: NTC Business Books, 1996.

Sinickas, Angela D., ABC. *How to Measure Your Communication Programs.* 3rd ed. Irvine, CA: Sinickas Communications Publishing, 2004.

Additional Titles from the Society for Human Resource Management (SHRM)®

Carrig, Ken, and Patrick M. Wright. *Building Profit through Building People: Making Your Workforce the Strongest Link in the Value-Profit Chain*

Collier, T. O., Jr. *Supervisor's Guide to Labor Relations*

Cook, Mary, and Scott Gildner. *Outsourcing Human Resources Functions: How, Why, When, and When Not to Contract for HR Services*

Gardenswartz, Lee, and Anita Rowe. *Diverse Teams at Work*

Grensing-Pophal, Lin, SPHR. *Human Resource Essentials: Your Guide to Starting and Running the HR Function*

Landry, R.J. *The Comprehensive, All-in-One HR Operating Guide.* 539 ready-to-adapt human resources policies, practices, letters, memos, forms . . . and more.

HR Source Book Series

Bliss, Wendy, J.D., SPHR, and Gene Thornton, Esq., PHR. *Employment Termination Source Book*

Deblieux, Mike. *Performance Appraisal Source Book*

Fyock, Cathy, CSP, SPHR. *Hiring Source Book*

Hubbartt, William S., SPHR, CCP. *HIPAA Privacy Source Book*

Lambert, Jonamay, MA, and Selma Myers, MA. *Trainer's Diversity Source Book*

Practical HR Series

Bliss, Wendy, JD, SPHR. *Legal, Effective References: How to Give and Get Them*

Oppenheimer, Amy, JD, and Craig Pratt, MSW, SPHR. *Investigating Workplace Harassment: How to Be Fair, Thorough, and Legal*

Phillips, Jack J., PhD, and Patricia Pulliam Phillips, PhD. *Proving the Value of HR: How and Why to Measure ROI*

Shaw, Seyfarth, LLP. *Understanding the Federal Wage & Hour Laws: What Employers Must Know about FLSA and Its Overtime Regulations*

How to Order from SHRM

SHRM offers a member discount on all books that it publishes or sells. To order this or any other book published by the Society, contact the SHRM-Store.®

Online: www.shrm.org/shrmstore

Phone: 1–800–444–5006 (option #1); or 770–442–8633 (ext. 362); or tdd 703–548–6999

Fax: 770–442–9742

Mail: SHRM Distribution Center, P.O. Box 930132, Atlanta, GA 31193–0132, USA

Index

About the Series Adviser

WENDY BLISS, JD, SPHR, has experience as a human resource executive, attorney, senior editor, and professional speaker. Since 1994, she has provided human resource consulting, corporate training, and coaching services nationally through her Colorado Springs–based consulting firm, Bliss & Associates.

Ms. Bliss is the author of *Legal Effective References: How to Give and Get Them*, the coauthor of *The Employment Termination Source Book: A Collection of Practical Samples*, and a contributor to *Human Resource Essentials*, all published by the Society for Human Resource Management. She has published numerous articles in magazines and periodicals, including *HR Magazine, Employment Management Today, HR Matters*, and the *Denver University Law Review.*

Ms. Bliss received a BA degree with highest distinction from the University of Kansas and a JD degree from the University of Denver College of Law. She is certified as a Senior Professional in Human Resources by the Human Resource Certification Institute. Since 1999, she has conducted human resource certificate programs for the Society for Human Resource Management. Previously, she was an adjunct faculty member at the University of Colorado at Colorado Springs and at the University of Phoenix, where she taught graduate and undergraduate courses in human resource management, employment law, organizational behavior, and business communications. Additionally, Ms. Bliss has served on the board of directors for several professional associations and nonprofit organizations and was a president of the National Board of Governors for the Society for Human Resource Management's Consultants Forum.

National media, including *ABC News, Time* magazine, the *New York Times,* the Associated Press, the *Washington Post,* USAToday .com, and *HR Magazine,* have looked to Ms. Bliss for expert opinions on workplace issues.

About the Writer

LIN GRENSING-POPHAL, MA, SPHR, ABC, is an independent business journalist with an extensive background in marketing, corporate communications, and employee relations. She has worked as a copywriter, creative director, and marketing and corporate communication manager in the fields of continuing education, energy, and health care, and has managed all aspects of corporate and marketing communication, including employee communication, public relations, advertising, and market research. Grensing-Pophal has written hundreds of business and employee management articles for both general and trade publications and is the author of several books, including *Marketing with the End in Mind* (IABC, 2005) and *Human Resource Essentials* (SHRM, 2002).

About the Society for Human Resource Management

The Society for Human Resource Management (SHRM) is the world's largest association devoted to human resource management. Representing more than 170,000 individual members, the Society's mission is to serve the needs of HR professionals by providing the most essential and comprehensive resources available. As an influential voice, the Society's mission is also to advance the human resource profession to ensure that HR is recognized as an essential partner in developing and executing organizational strategy. Visit SHRM Online at www.shrm.org.

Acknowledgments

Lin Grensing-Pophal would like to thank the many professional business communicators and HR professionals who contributed their expertise, insights, and experiences to this book. Thanks also to Wendy Bliss, series adviser; Laura Lawson, Manager of Book Publishing for the Society for Human Resource Management; Melinda Merino, executive editor at Harvard Business School Publishing, along with Julia Ely, assistant editor; Brian Surrette, editorial coordinator; and Jane Gebhart, production editor. These individuals' input and contributions greatly strengthened the book, ensuring valuable guidance and real-world perspectives for readers.

The Results-Driven Manager

The Results-Driven Manager series collects timely articles from Harvard Management Update and Harvard Management Communication Letter to help senior to middle managers sharpen their skills, increase their effectiveness, and gain a competitive edge. Presented in a concise, accessible format to save managers valuable time, these books offer authoritative insights and techniques for improving job performance and achieving immediate results.

These books are priced at $14.95 U.S.
Price subject to change.

To order, call 1-800-668-6780, or go online at www.HBSPress.org